SOURCES OF INEQUALITY IN EARNINGS:

Personal skills, random events, preferences towards risk and other occupational characteristics

CONTRIBUTIONS
TO
ECONOMIC ANALYSIS

96

NORTH-HOLLAND PUBLISHING COMPANY – AMSTERDAM · OXFORD

AMERICAN ELSEVIER PUBLISHING COMPANY, INC. – NEW YORK

SOURCES OF INEQUALITY IN EARNINGS:

Personal skills, random events, preferences towards risk and other occupational characteristics

PAUL J. TAUBMAN

University of Pennsylvania

1975

NORTH-HOLLAND PUBLISHING COMPANY – AMSTERDAM · OXFORD

AMERICAN ELSEVIER PUBLISHING COMPANY, INC. – NEW YORK

Library of Congress Catalog Card Number: 75–23117
North-Holland ISBN for the series: 0 7204 3100 X
North-Holland ISBN for this volume: 0 7204 3201 4
American Elsevier ISBN: 0 444 10965 X

Publishers:

NORTH-HOLLAND PUBLISHING COMPANY – AMSTERDAM
NORTH-HOLLAND PUBLISHING COMPANY, LTD. – OXFORD

Sole distributors for the U.S.A. and Canada:

AMERICAN ELSEVIER PUBLISHING COMPANY, INC.
52 VANDERBILT AVENUE
NEW YORK, N.Y. 10017

Library of Congress Cataloging in Publication Data

Taubman, Paul, 1939-
Sources of inequality in earnings.

"Parts of this study have been given at a Conference on Income and Wealth at Ann Arbor, Michigan in May 1974 and at the Royal Economic Society Conference at Lancaster, U. K. in July 1974."
Bibliography: p.
1. Income distribution--United States. I. Title.
HC110.I5T34 1975 339.2'0973 75-23117
ISBN 0-444-10965-X (American Elsevier)

PRINTED IN THE NETHERLANDS

Introduction to the series

This series consists of a number of hitherto unpublished studies, which are introduced by the editors in the belief that they represent fresh contributions to economic science.

The term *economic analysis* as used in the title of the series has been adopted because it covers both the activities of the theoretical economist and the research worker.

Although the analytical methods used by the various contributors are not the same, they are nevertheless conditioned by the common origin of their studies, namely theoretical problems encountered in practical research. Since for this reason, business cycle research and national accounting, research work on behalf of economic policy, and problems of planning are the main sources of the subjects dealt with, they necessarily determine the manner of approach adopted by the authors. Their methods tend to be 'practical' in the sense of not being too far remote from application to actual economic conditions. In addition they are quantitative rather than qualitative.

It is the hope of the editors that the publication of these studies will help to stimulate the exchange of scientific information and to reinforce international cooperation in the field of economics.

THE EDITORS

Preface

My formal interest in research on the distribution of earnings began with a chance encounter with a trustee of the University of Pennsylvania who was on campus to attend the dedication of a new library. This conversation with Carl Kaysen led to my joining in a research project at the National Bureau of Economic Research. During this project, Terence Wales and myself unearthed the so-called NBER–TH data set which is the primary input for our book, *Higher Education and Earnings*, and for this study.

In *Higher Education and Earnings*, we used the sample to estimate the rate of return to education after adjusting for individual differences in ability and a few aspects of family background. We also examined the extent to which the returns to education arose because education acts as a screening device to find the more able rather than as an augmentor of productivity.

While this book estimates regressions that use the Taubman–Wales results as a starting point, our focus is different. Here we are interested in examining the various theories that have been proposed to explain the distribution of earnings. To accomplish this goal, we have constructed and used a variety of new variables, which we hope serve as adequate proxies for the true theoretical constructs. But for some theories, crucial variables cannot be proxied by any information at hand. We have tried to examine these hypotheses by testing certain implications of the dynamic evolution of earnings.

This study has benefited greatly from the advice and criticism of a number of people. My intellectual debt to Terry Wales is immense and occurs far too often in the book to give proper citation at all times. While Jacob Mincer does not agree with some sections of this book, I acknowledge gratefully that he has patiently led me away from many misinterpretations of his analysis. Sherwin Rosen has made numerous suggestions that have improved the analysis and readability of the manuscript.

Parts of this study have been given at a Conference on Income and Wealth at Ann Arbor, Michigan in May, 1974 and at the Royal Economic Society Conference at Lancaster, U.K. in July, 1974. I wish to thank both the organizers and the participants in these conferences for many helpful suggestions. The first draft of the manuscript was written at the University of California, Berkeley, whose facilities were kindly made available to me.

I wish to thank Dr. Abraham Haspel for his excellent research assistance and his many helpful ideas. This manuscript has benefited greatly from the typing and informal editing of Catherine Grant, Diane Haspel and Margo Richardson.

This research was supported by NSF Grant GS-31334 which was made to the National Bureau of Economic Research and the University of Pennsylvania. This book has not been reviewed by the Directors of the National Bureau of Economic Research and is not an official publication of the National Bureau.

PAUL TAUBMAN

To Joan, Geoffry, and Rena

Contents

CHAPTER 1

The distribution of incomes and earnings

All individuals or families do not receive the same income or earnings. This inequality, the most indisputable fact about the distribution of income, has been found in capitalist and socialist economies, in democratic and dictatorial countries, and in Biblical and modern times. There are other characteristics of the income distribution that are nearly as well documented for modern countries. For example, the distribution is not symmetrical but has a longer right-hand tail, and both average income and its variance generally increase with education and with age[1].

Why inequality occurs and why the distribution has its particular characteristics is a matter of concern to many people. Certainly society and government have expressed a desire to establish a minimum floor for members of society–though the level of the floor and the means of achieving it are matters of debate. Besides a direct interest in the questions of the sources of inequality, how to achieve income redistribution and the efficacy of various policy tools, economists are also concerned with establishing how various labor markets operate, how rational individuals are, and how important are individual effort, chance and predestination[2].

Spurred on by these questions, economists have constructed various theories that purport to explain the income distribution. Some aspects of these theories have been tested against empirical observations[3]. This study will extend the range of such tests. In addition, we will generate some new facts that a complete theory should be able to explain.

[1]For international comparisons see Lydall; for the U.S., see Miller (1966).

[2]These terms will be defined more rigorously below.

[3]See, for example, Mincer (1974).

1. Shares of income

Most of the earliest theories of the income distribution concentrated on the shares of total national income received by factors of production such as labor and capital. This type of analysis dates back at least to Ricardo. It received further stimulus from the development of the theory of marginal productivity and perhaps its most complete statement within the context of neoclassical growth models[4]. Excluding Ricardo's analysis of rent, the basic mode of analysis in these works is that (with perfect competition) the payment that any homogeneous factor receives is equal to the price of a unit of output it produces times the marginal product of the last unit of that factor[5]. Assuming diminishing marginal productivity, such theories imply that an increase in the supply of one factor will lead to a decrease in its own price, but the factor's share of total income, e.g. wage payments/total income, can increase or decrease depending on whether the percentage change in the price is less than or exceeds the percentage change in the quantity sold[6]. The many theoretical and empirical analyses of factor shares have greatly expanded our knowledge of the distribution of income among broad aggregates, but the analysis of such aggregates will do little to explain individual differences in income and earnings which is the subject matter of this study.

We might approach the study of the distribution of personal income by dropping the assumption of a single group of homogeneous labor, etc[7]. Yet while it is interesting to determine the relative earnings of people in each of n groups, it really does not advance us as far as we wish. That is, such models can tell us that skilled workers may make more than unskilled because of their greater marginal productivity and that relative wages for skilled and unskilled workers may vary with shifts in the supply and demand for skilled and unskilled workers. But there still remains the

[4]See Ricardo, Clark, Cobb and Douglas, and Solow and, for a good overall treatment, Bronfenbrenner.

[5]The marginal product is defined as the change in output resulting from the addition of one more unit of a factor while holding all other factors of production constant.

[6]Even the own price conclusion need not hold when the price of two or more factors contain some common elements. See, for example, Taubman–Wilkinson.

[7]While there are technical difficulties in examining models in which there are many types of labor, the problems are surmountable. For many of the subtleties and questions connected with factor share analysis, see Bronfenbrenner.

fundamental questions of why some workers are skilled and others are not and how the unskilled can become skilled[8].

2. The personal distribution of earnings

Personal income is equal to the sum of labor earnings, returns to capital, and transfer payments. Transfer payments are determined by political and societal forces and will not concern us in this study. While the distribution of income from capital is partly determined by economic forces, it will not be the primary focus of this study – partly because of the paucity of data in our sample. Earnings from work, to which the introductory statements on inequality also apply and which will be the primary focus of our study, currently constitute about two-thirds to three-fourths of national income.

Most theoretical and related empirical work on the distribution of earnings fall into the 'human capital' or 'stochastic' theory categories or a blend thereof. The human capital model assumes that people are paid a wage equal to their (real) marginal product which varies over individuals because of differences in inherited or acquired skill levels. The stochastic theories assume that an individual's earnings over time depend on the cumulative history of random events. Before describing various features of prototypes of these models, it is useful to examine a very simple supply and demand model as a building block to more complex models.

3. Supply and demand for labor

Suppose for the moment that all people are homogeneous with respect to skills that determine earnings, and that there are no nonmonetary rewards or costs associated with any and all occupations. Assume that with a given quantity of capital and other factors of production, the marginal product of labor decreases as the number of employees increases[9]. In a

[8]The terms 'skilled' and 'unskilled' may be poor choices since they tend to conjure up images of, say, carpenters and ditchdiggers. Yet skill levels or at least earnings also vary among carpenters and ditchdiggers.

[9]The marginal product is the extra output obtained from employing one more worker.

competitive labor market (with no on-the-job training) employers will hire that number of workers at which the marginal product is equal to the real wage rate, W/P (for convenience we will set P at 1 and henceforth speak of wages only). This demand curve is given at DD in fig. 1.

In fig. 1 the supply curve for the population is SS which is assumed to slope upwards because it takes higher wage rates to induce people to forego leisure[10]. The equilibrium wage rate of W_0 will clear the market and everyone who works the same hours will earn the same amount.

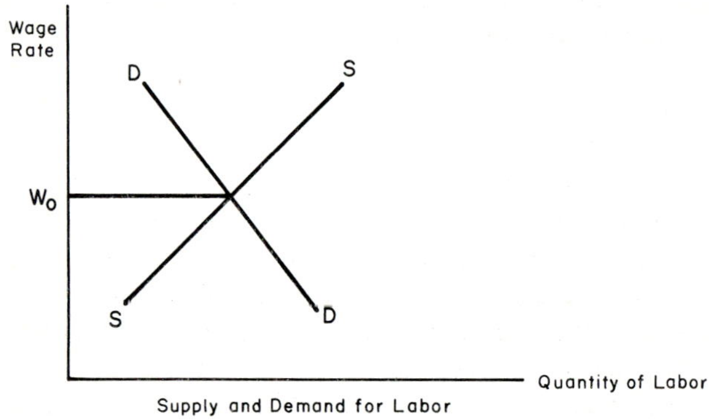

Fig. 1.

This conclusion which is, of course, contrary to fact depends crucially on the assumption that each person has the same skills. This study is to a large extent based on the proposition that many different skills – inherited and acquired – help determine earnings. It is fairly easy, however, to incorporate many types and levels of skills into the above analysis *if what is known as an 'efficiency units' model is valid.* Suppose individual one, who has a particular complex of skills, is designated the 'standard' person. Let capacity be designated as C. As long as C_j/C_1 *always* equals b_j, we can state that the jth person is equivalent to b_j standard workers.

Since the employer would be indifferent to hiring person 1 at a wage of

[10]In this chapter, we will be concerned with the hourly wage rate.

say W_0 or person j at wage of b_jW_0, the demand curve in fig. 1 can be redrawn in standard worker units[11]. The supply curve can also be drawn in efficiency units as $\Sigma_j b_j Q_j$ where Q_j is the quantity of labor the jth person would offer at a particular standardized wage rate. In this efficiency model a person who is 110% of standard capacity will always receive a wage 110% of the standard wage, but the equilibrium level of the standard wage will vary with the supply and demand curves.

An important set of questions that arise with this model are: what particular skills determine capacity; are these skills inherited or acquired; and, is the quantity of acquired skills consistent with the amount economists would define as optimum? Before considering these questions, however, we will examine briefly a model in which relative capacity, C_j/C_1 is not fixed but varies.

The world of work is subdivided into many different occupations which are associated with different tasks and levels of responsibility. For example, the *Dictionary of Occupational Titles* differentiates thousands of occupations. Some occupations and tasks require physical strength, some mental ability, etc., and some require combinations of particular skills. A person's relative capacity may remain constant within an occupation but vary over occupations[12]. Thus a person's observed or effective relative capacity would depend on his occupation choice which in turn depends in part on the occupational wage structure that varies over time. Although this model is complicated, in principle it is still possible to formulate and solve it as a general equilibrium model, in which individuals choose that occupation which yields them the highest income or utility[13,14].

One particularly important feature of this occupation–skill model is that some skills may not be at all useful in some occupations. Suppose, for example, the only two occupations are manager and manual worker and

[11]If it requires more room to house the extra workers, the extra plant cost at an annual rate would have to be included in the analysis.

[12]Even this need not be true. For example, different types of skills may be more or less important depending on the types of machinery used.

[13]Tinbergen has formulated this type of model and Reder has examined some features of such a model though he uses somewhat different terminology.

[14]Indeed the usual general equilibrium models admit of the interpretation that each individual is a separate factor of production with his own bundle of skills.

that intelligence received such a high wage in managerial work that all people with an I.Q. above 110 are managers. Assume also that physical strength is of no importance as a manager but that among manual workers strength increases capacity while I.Q. doesn't. Finally assume all those with I.Q. greater than 110 have above average strength (although the correlation is not perfect). Then for people with I.Q. above 110, variations in strength would not affect earnings while for those with lower I.Q.'s, and less strength, only variations in strength would affect earnings. Thus in this example each skill is redundant in one occupation and only a portion of the distribution of each skill determines earnings. This analysis, of course, suggests that it may be necessary to examine earnings functions within occupations and that in the whole sample the effect of a skill may have upper and lower limits. In ch. 5 we will return to this question but for now let us return to the simpler efficiency units model.

4. *Types of skills*

At the end of our previous discussion of this model, we raised certain questions about what skills determine earnings or capacity. At a general level we can classify these skills as cognitive, affective, physical, and psychological. Cognitive skills include learned facts and information, as well as recall and decision-making abilities. Affective skills include leadership and social behavior. Physical skills include strength, coordination, and dexterity while psychological skills include extroversion, reaction to stress, and degree of neuroticism, etc.

At this stage of our knowledge, we hardly know which particular skills determine earnings or capacity since no sample contains reliable measures of all feasible skills and few samples contain direct measures of even a representative skill from each of the categories mentioned[15,16]. How-

[15]Indeed, for some possible skills, appropriate measures have not yet been designed.

[16]Perhaps the Terman sample contains the most information, but it is small and limited to people with I.Q.'s (as children) of 140 and over. The Project Talent and, to a lesser extent, the Little–Sewell sample have more skill information for the period when their respondents were in elementary and high school, but currently little in the way of earnings data since the people graduated high school no earlier than 1958.

ever, several studies have shown that certain aspects of intelligence and of leadership are valid. See Taubman–Wales, Griliches and Mason, Wise, and Featherman.

Suppose, however, that we had measurements on an exhaustive list of skills for each individual. We could then estimate on earnings equation such as

$$Y = aX_1 + bX_2 \ldots cX_n + u, \tag{1.1}$$

where Y is earnings, $X_1 \ldots X_n$ are the N measures of skill, and u is a random error representing 'luck' or institutional phenomena[17].

Each coefficient in the equation indicates the effect on earnings of increasing the associated X by one unit, i.e. the implicit wage rate of the X. It is worth noting that such wage rates may not be stable over time. For example, suppose there is a big increase in the supply of any X. In the efficiency units model, this will lead to shifts in the supply curve (in efficiency units) and a decrease in the standard wage rate which in turn would decrease all coefficients proportionately. In more complex models, the effect on the coefficients of an increased supply in any one skill level depends upon the individual supply and demand elasticities for each skill as well as cross elasticities of demand. But in general the coefficients will not change proportionately[18].

While estimation of eqn (1.1) with many skills would represent a major achievement, our task would not be over since we would then want to know what determines the level of each X or what policies could affect the distribution of earnings. We will return to this topic shortly.

[17]As eq. (1.1) is written, all skills have an independent, linear effect. This representation was chosen for simplicity. Interactions between skills should not be assumed away in empirical work especially because Roy has demonstrated that if skills affect earnings multiplicatively, symmetric skill distributions yield asymmetric earnings distributions – an important feature of the observed distribution. See also Mandelbrot. In later chapters we will generally not try to test for interactions, but only because we are trying to establish the role of a large number of hitherto unexamined variables and forces.

[18]There is one other special case to note. It is possible that only skill differences relative to the average matter, e.g. the brightest lawyer may receive twice as much per case as the average lawyer. If all lawyers received more training and increased their legal skills $X\%$, none may receive more earnings. However, the effect on earnings on legal brightness between lawyers should be given by the coefficients in (1.1).

4.1. Inherited and acquired skills

The level of any skill or attribute a person possesses at any point of time is determined by or 'produced' by his genetic endowments and by his environment[19]. Our use of the term 'environment' includes all post-conception events that influence the individual. Thus it encompasses formal and informal training for all the skills discussed earlier, pre-natal diet, expenditures on health which determine whether skills can be used, and random events. A huge literature has been devoted to assessing the relative importance of nature and nurture for particular skills and attributes[20]. As we come closer to estimating eqn (1.1), this literature will become more important in economics; but at the current time, it does not seem necessary to summarize it[21].

Since we have not measured all the possible skills nor know their nature–nurture combination, we will not estimate eqn (1.1). We will, however, make use of a modified procedure. Suppose each of the X_j's is produced by a function of genetics and environment. If, for example,

$$X_{ji} = c_j G_i + d_j N_i, \tag{1.2}$$

where G is genetic endowments and N is environment, and i is the individual, we can then rewrite eqn. (1.1) as

$$Y_i = \Sigma_j a_j c_j G_i + \Sigma_j a_j d_j N_j + u = e_i G_i + f_i N_i + u. \tag{1.3}$$

Equation (1.3) represents progress primarily because we do have measures of several aspects of environment (as well as a few G's as approximated by I.Q.)[22].

[19]The genetic effect can be both direct and indirect. For example, a person's knowledge level can depend on innate ability and on educational attainment which is partly determined by innate ability.

[20]See for example Jinks and Fulker, Burt, Cavalli–Sforza, or Mittler.

[21]The relative importance of nature and nurture can vary over time as the distribution of genetic endowments and of environment changes. In particular, new environments such as better schooling, day care centers, and pre-natal diet could have large effects even if nurture was not important for older cohorts.

[22]Of course, if any unmeasured variable is omitted, we can not obtain unbiased estimates of other coefficients of variables correlated with the unmeasured variable.

4.2. Training

People produce or increase their skill levels in many ways with some methods better for some skills than others. However, some of the most important 'training' institutions are the family, peer group, school, military, and work.

The family can affect the child's cognitive, affective, physiological, and psychological development by a variety of subtle and obvious means including: the behavior and attitudes of parents and siblings; material and nonmaterial goods and services provided to the child; love and affection; and degree of permissiveness in rearing. It would be most useful and convincing if we could incorporate measures of parental love, behavior, material goods, etc. in our equations. We do not have such information and are reduced to using proxies which are more or less crudely related to the true variables we wish to include[23].

We will use proxy variables such as family income and wealth, religion, urban or rural residence, parent's education and occupation, which are all often available and made use of. We will supplement this list with other proxies that we think are related to child rearing techniques and family atmosphere[24].

The peer group can also affect the amount of schooling a person acquires and can directly affect all broad skill categories through its attitudes and reward structure, but we have little or no data on the peer group, except as it influences the level of certain of our variables.

Schooling can affect cognitive, affective, physiological, and psychological skills. Changes in each of these skills could affect earnings although

[23]There are several difficulties in interpreting the coefficients of a proxy. A proxy, by definition, is assumed to be correlated with the true but unobserved variable. But the proxy may be insignificant, although the phenomena it tried to represent is important, because the proxy is too crude a measure, i.e. has too low a correlation with the true variable. Alternatively, the proxy used may be correlated with several true variables whose separate effects we may be interested in. For example, father's education may be related to his earnings, his methods of child rearing and certain genetic (and thus partially inheritable) abilities. Fortunately, if several proxies are used, it can be shown that each proxy will tend to reflect the underlying variables to which it is most highly correlated. (See Crockett.)

[24]Family status coefficients in an earnings equation only represent the direct effect of such status. Generally, there is also an indirect effect since family background helps determine the level of educational attainment (and other parts of 'environment') a person acquires.

there is little reliable information on which determine earnings[25]. By asserting that schools can produce marketable skills, we do not intend to imply that this is all schools do or intend to do. Clearly college and pre-college education can affect such nonmarket activities as types of leisure enjoyed and how much time is spent in civic work. But it is just as important to emphasize that many courses can affect marketable skills almost as a byproduct. For example, ability to think logically can be developed in many different types of courses. Education can also affect earnings if employers use level of schooling as a credential.

The most common though obviously very crude measure of education is years of schooling which we will represent by a set of dummy variables. Recent work has also emphasized that 'quality' of schooling can affect productivity and earnings[26]. Following the lead of Solmon and Wachtel, who used the same sample, we will also incorporate certain measures of college quality[27].

The amount and type of work and of learning on the job can affect earnings. Indeed a major innovation in the earnings distribution literature is Mincer's theory of investment in on-the-job training, which is described below in more detail and subject to empirical verification in ch. 7. We will not study the question in this book of whether the Army makes men since all the people were in the military.

Thus far we have indicated that several types of training might produce marketable skills. In principle, we can examine the importance (as defined in ch. 4) of each of these types of training by obtaining adequate proxies. We have not indicated, however, why people have the skill levels they do. Also we have not adequately explored what other training mechanisms might be important. Finally, we have not considered what inferences may be drawn about unmeasured variables. To be able to accomplish these

[25]For evidence on some noncognitive effects as well as the mechanism by which education causes these changes, see Simon and Ellison.

[26]See Solmon, Wales, Wachtel, and Welch. There is also an extensive literature on what school inputs produce more cognitive development. See Mostellar and Moynahan. Noncognitive developments are studied in Astain.

[27]A problem with many of these measures is that they seem more related to cognitive development than the other skills. However, certain information on type and size of college may be related to noncognitive changes.

ends, it is necessary to reconsider the problem we have just examined within several different frameworks.

5. *Human capital theory*

By definition, investment in human capital occurs when people spend resources (including time) to increase their *future* earnings or nonmonetary rewards. Of course, a person can also inherit skills such as 'intelligence'; but the economic literature on human capital has relegated this 'conceived stock' of human capital to a secondary role and concentrated on schooling, health expenditures and other means by which a person can acquire or maintain skills. In part, this emphasis occurs because if a person must invest to acquire a set of skills, it is possible to ask both what factors determine how much investment a person will acquire and what is the optimal amount of investment a rational person should make in any time period[28].

Some people who believe in and use the human capital concept do not subscribe to the idea that individuals have invested optimally e.g. to the point where the cost of capital equals the rate of return. Others would agree that individuals try to make such optimal decisions but earnings observed after the investments have been made do not provide (even on average) information on the rate of return on investments or the level of investments because the necessary data are not available to the investor when he must make his decisions. However, since anything that these two groups define as investment in human capital would also be so defined by those who believe in the rational investor model, we will turn to that class of models.

Becker, for example, examines a model in which the (derived) demand curve for education is a function of its rate of return (r_j), innate ability, and tastes. Becker's schooling model assumes that each dollar spent on education – through tuition, government subsidy, or earnings foregone from not working – will increase skills, attributes, etc. These new skills and attributes will yield both a new, constant level of earnings and

[28]An additional reason for this emphasis is that it is difficult to obtain measures of the elements of the conceived stock (with the partial exception of intelligence).

nonpecuniary returns to the individual. Becker then asks what the distribution of earnings would be if each person were a rational investor who is certain of his yield from education[29]. Becker shows that the equilibrium condition is that $r_j = m_j$ where r_j is the marginal rate of return on and m_j the financial cost of schooling for the jth person. Becker assumes equal inputs of schooling or dollar investments yield successively smaller increases in human capital; hence r as a function of these costs is subject to diminishing returns while m is assumed to increase with education and depend on family resources[30]. Assuming that nonpecuniary returns or their net value are zero, he then derives the earnings distribution under alternative assumptions and shows, for example, that this distribution can be skewed to the right. The particular answer, however, depends on the distribution of (the functions of) m and r and their covariance[31]. The hallmark of this model is that people have invested rationally, but it is difficult to test this assumption because the assumption that the value of nonpecuniary returns net out to zero is almost surely incorrect. Of course, if the weaker assumption is made this value is nonnegative, it would be possible to test the weak hypothesis that r_j is less than m_j. Since the financial costs of capital also is seldom known, it may be necessary to test a still weaker hypothesis that if the average m_j varies systematically over certain groups, the average r_j should vary in the same way. We will not pursue this argument in this book[32].

This schooling model assumes that the extra earnings from education would be constant over time; but, in fact, extra earnings increase with age[33]. Mincer, however, has demonstrated that the human capital analysis can account for rising age–earnings profiles, which vary by education

[29]Or, is risk neutral if there is uncertainty?

[30]This may not be as true in our sample since the G.I. Bill provided for tuition up to $500 a year and a stipend of $100 a month. These payments in effect reduce m to zero and sharply reduce tuition and foregone earnings.

[31]For example he concludes that the distribution depends on the correlation of r_j and m_j (over individuals).

[32]Similar models can be constructed for the quality of education, health expenditures, etc. as in Welch and Grossman.

[33]These changes could be due to maturity (with an interaction with education) but available evidence would suggest that from age 20 to 50, maturity *per se* is not important for changing the level of most cognitive and affective skills.

level, if people invest rationally in 'general' on-the-job training (OJT)[34,35]. By definition, general training is that which is as useful to other employers as the one giving the training. But since training is embedded in the worker, after being trained he can offer his services to any employer (in the absence of enforceable long-term employment contracts). Therefore, in a competitive labor market, the employee would receive wages equal to his new, higher marginal product, or in other words, all the benefits of the training.

The model, at this point, is indistinguishable from a learning by doing model. Mincer, however, takes the analysis one very important step further. Specifically, Mincer argues that a person will choose that occupation which offers him the largest amount of lifetime earnings, discounted to the present. Suppose, therefore, that occupation *A* involved training and occupation *B* did not. Also assume that initial wages were the same in both occupations; hence, occupation *B* would offer the larger discounted stream[36]. In this case, workers would leave *B* for *A* and new entrants would choose *A*. As the supply of workers for *A* increased and *B* decreased, the starting wages in *A* would drop and those in *B* rise. This adjustment would continue until the discounted value of both lifetime earnings streams would be exactly the same. Note that as a result of the adjustment process, wages in *A* initially will be below those in *B* and later above. The (unobserved) drop in wages in the first year of work is the *investment* in on-the-job training in that year[37].

As shown more fully in ch. 7, Mincer derives a human capital earnings function such as:

$$\ln Y_t = \ln \bar{Y} + eS + ft,$$

where S is years of schooling, e is the rate of return on S, f is the rate of return on OJT and $\bar{Y}$ is the level of earnings determined by genetic

[34]His model can also explain a changing age profile of the variance of earnings. With some modifications, his model applies to the specific training paid for by the worker.

[35]Other people such as Rosen, Johnson, Lillard, and Chiswick have constructed similar models but Mincer has drawn out more fully the implications for the distribution of earnings throughout a person's lifetime.

[36]The occupation definition in this case is broader than in our normal use since it encompasses a whole occupational career moving from stock boy to president.

[37]In calculating the investment costs in other years, an adjustment would have to be made for returns on prior investments.

endowments and the other elements of the environment that affect skills and earnings.

Another way to view Mincer's model is that earnings only change over time because of continued investment in the on-the-job training[38]. His earnings model, therefore, can be rewritten as:

$$Y_t = \bar{Y} + r\Sigma\lambda_{t-n}Y_{t-n} - \lambda_t Y_t,$$

where λ is the percent of current gross earnings invested in OJT. As long as λ decreases over time, earnings will increase with age. Mincer, moreover, demonstrates that in this model the variance of Y_t and of log Y_t need not be constant over time but may increase or decrease monotonically or even follow nonmonotonic paths[39].

Mincer's theory is in the tradition of much of economic analysis of competitive markets and has the attractive feature of being consistent with such observed regularities as rising age earnings profile and with nearly any age profile of the variance of earnings. Moreover, as Mincer has noted, it is possible to obtain estimates of e and f, the two rates of return, within a decade of individuals entering the labor market.

While the model has all these advantages, it has several particular disadvantages. First of all, the model assumes that because of individual actions the market always generates the type of equilibrium he makes use of. But consider for a moment the informational requirements necessary for this market to function. On the schooling side the individual must estimate the expected increase in his earnings for each year of his working life[40]. The worker also has to be able to calculate the increase in skills or the general learning-by-doing contained in any occupation[41]. These severe informational requirements may result in labor market failure, i.e. the market may not act as predicted.

[38]This is not quite true in the sense that Mincer allows for transitory events in any year and for maturation and senescence. But these can be ignored at this point.

[39]See Mincer (1974), p. 98.

[40]If the person is not risk neutral, he will also have to examine the variance (or other measures of dispersion) of the extra earnings. If Mincer's model is correct, only the constant earnings difference, $\Delta\bar{Y}$, need to estimated but the worker would need to read Mincer to know how to calculate this figure from available data.

[41]In addition, in both instances the worker will have to estimate if the current information that he can obtain, say from Census data, is applicable to the future or if an equilibrium situation is about to become disequilibrium or vice versa.

Even if the information requirements are met, the above equations may not hold nor be interpreted as above because of nonpecuniary returns to education. Evidence at least as reliable as that on earnings indicates that education has nonpecuniary rewards. Similarly, the OJT model should incorporate such nonmonetary returns as pride and status as, e.g. in the professional labor market. Since the rational investor model requires these nonpecuniary returns be included in the r that is to be equalized to m, the coefficients on S or t in an earnings need not equal the rate of return on investment unless the nonpecuniary rewards are held constant.

Finally the models assume that since a unit of schooling or OJT always emits the same capacity as a person ages, and that variations in a person's earnings as he ages (with hours and wage rates fixed) must reflect additional changes in human capital. As explained below, such an assumption seems invalid for some labor market situations.

While it is difficult to construct a definitive test of the schooling model, it is possible to test some aspects of Mincer's OJT theory because of its predictions of wage changes. We will expound on this in greater detail and perform the indicated tests in ch. 7.

5.1. Family environment and the human capital model

Earlier we suggested that family environment, broadly defined to include love and affection, child rearing techniques, and amount and composition of material goods, can affect a child's earnings skills and we shall find family background to be very important in our empirical section. That a family's activities can help mold the personality and psychology of a child is hardly a startling idea. Of course, some economists have wondered how such effects can be fitted into an economist's framework and particularly the rational investor model. In a formal sense this is not difficult to do. For example, the work begun by Becker on the allocation of time in market and nonmarket activities could be amended to include in a parent's utility function the children's future earnings, mental health, personality, etc. which are produced by a variety of inputs. This type of model has recently been examined by Stafford and Hill, Leibowitz, and Parsons. It seems to yield the usual type of results and indicates that in principle one could calculate the outcomes.

Undoubtedly, parents do make choices in the rearing of their children and such choices clearly can affect the child. But once again I find it difficult to believe that the type of model just described mimics reality. The choices are more likely determined by habit, parents' personality, subjective estimates of consequences which probably give little weight to future earnings, and perhaps the latest fad in child rearing techniques. But even if people do not behave as if they were economists, it is still possible to study the consequences of parents' actions on the offspring's earnings.

5.2. Sorting and signalling models

The human capital model assumes that both workers and firms know or can identify costlessly each worker's marginal product. There are indeed some occupations, such as fruit picker and commissioned salesman, in which it is possible to determine quickly and cheaply the marginal product of an individual worker. In these occupations, a firm should be willing to set a piece rate and hire anyone who applies for a job. There are other jobs such as a position on an assembly line in which it may be possible to determine the number of bolts tightened and not tightened by a worker but where the failure of any one worker on the line will reduce or destroy the output of other workers. In this interdependent situation, the firm would be able to measure a person's marginal product once he begins to work, but as long as it cannot collect for the destroyed units, the firm may find it profitable to try to minimize the number of people with less than the necessary skill level needed for the job. Finally, there are some jobs such as manager in which it is difficult to measure both the actual and potential productivity of any worker and in which there are interdependencies. Here again the firm may want to sort people into groups which have more or less of the skills associated with success on the job. Based on such considerations, Spence has formulated models in which firms use education as a signal to a person's true ability. Taubman and Wales have derived a means to test the extent to which education increases earnings because of increases in productivity and because of screening.

Within most firms there are a number of 'career ladders' within the semi-skilled, skilled, and managerial-professional categories with some possibility of going from one ladder to another. When the firm does not know a person's productivity and when a complex and difficult to measure set of skills are needed for success, it is possible for firms to use various 'signals' to assign a person to a particular job and then monitor his performance to determine whether to retain, promote or fire the person[42].

Recently Ross has demonstrated that *profit maximizing* firms will use such sampling techniques and move people up ladders as they determine a person's capacity. Thus, persons with a given skill level will, on average, have more income as time on the job increases. The sorting model suggests that the extra earnings from education need not be constant over time although his *potential capacity* is. This is especially true if Mayer and Lydall's observations on span of control, capacity and hierarchial organizations are valid. While the firm learns of the individual's talents, the individual can also receive training and knowledge which is specific to the firm. As shown in Becker, part of specific training shows up in higher wages of the trainee. Specific training can occur in a world without signalling. But the chance to acquire or the capacity to benefit from specific training may be related to position in the firm, which is dependent on signalling.

The sorting and signalling models, which can be based on profit maximizing behavior, would still imply that earnings depend on inherited and acquired skills but the coefficients would have different interpretations than in the Becker–Mincer model. The models also have different implications for the relationship between annual and lifetime earnings since those who are more skilled will always have above average earnings.

5.3. Tastes for risk and nonpecuniary rewards

The models we have been examining explain earnings by differences in skills. It is possible, however, to explain some features of the distribution by differences in tastes towards work or nonpecuniary returns from

[42]Several people including Arrow and Spence have examined signalling models. Taubman and Wales have constructed a test for the use of education as a signal and have concluded that perhaps one-half of the educational earnings differences are due to increased productivity produced by education, and the remainder is due to signalling on in their terminology screening. In a sense the sorting model is implicit in some Markov schemes, but Wise has explicitly made use of such a sorting model to explain how earnings may vary with education. Reder has also suggested that the amounts and types of firms specific training may vary by type of job while signals are used to allocate people to initial jobs.

work. Friedman, for example, has suggested that skewness arises because while most persons are risk averse, some people are risk lovers[43]. Those in the latter group may initially choose an occupation in which there is a small chance of a very high income. Since success is not won overnight, eventually we observe some of these who succeed; and over time, the average earnings of the winners grows more than those who were risk averse. There is no corresponding group of people with large losses because, as Lebergett points out, the inept (risk lover) generally can't raise enough financial capital as the successful one. Lebergett, in fact, presents some evidence that for the nonself-employed the earnings distribution is nearly symmetric – although of course this need not follow from the above model since there are some risky salaried occupations such as stock broker.

Friedman's model is closely aligned with that of von Neumann–Morgenstern in which a person bases his decisions on the expected value of the utility of a set of outcomes, defined as $\Sigma P_j U(A_j)$ where P_j is the probability of the A_j event occurring and $U(A_j)$ is its utility. Consider two alternatives A and B, where A has only one possible outcome, A_1, and B a whole set but an average outcome, $\bar{B}$. Suppose A_1 equals $\bar{B}$. Then it can be shown that if a person has diminishing marginal utility, he will attach more utility to and choose A. In other words, he is averse to risk. Alternatively, if his marginal utility exhibited increasing returns, he would be a risk lover and choose B in the above example.

The variability of earnings, which is related to the degree of risk, varies by jobs. Thus differences in risk preferences can affect job choice and eventually the observed differences in earnings[44]. Indeed, we would also expect riskier occupations to pay, on average, higher earnings to compensate for the added risk – if the marginal person is risk averse.

In a recent very interesting paper, Rosen has in fact analyzed, in a supply demand model, the effects of differential occupational death and

[43]Alternatively he has also suggested that people are risk averse to small changes but are willing to gamble to achieve major gains.

[44]Weiss has tried to estimate the parameters in the utility function that characterize the risk and average return trade off. However, as he is aware, he treats all within class dispersion as arising from random events while some unknown portion is due to differences in skills.

injury rates on wages. He shows (in the absence of employer purchased insurance) that wages will adjust to compensate for the (expected) value of the nonpecuniary loss attached to the job.

There can be many other positive and negative nonpecuniary rewards attached to jobs. Those rewards are important in our study of the determinants of the earnings distribution because nonpecuniary rewards can induce offsetting changes in monetary rewards[45]. The choice between pecuniary and nonpecuniary rewards can be treated in the general framework of utility maximization. It is possible, however, that tastes or the parameters of the utility function are partly determined by family background or by education, in which case the extra earnings attributed to, say, education are inadequate as a measure of the total returns to education unless measures for tastes are also included in the equation[46].

5.4. *Luck*

With the partial exception of Friedman, the above theories assume that earnings reflect individual differences in skills or tastes. Some economists have suggested that the earnings distribution at a point of time reflects the cumulative history of luck starting from an initial distribution based on skills. For example, one version of these theories can be expressed as:

$$Y_t = Y_{t-1} + e_t = Y_0 + \sum_{k=0}^{t} e_{t-k} \tag{1.6}$$

where e_t is random error that is uncorrelated with Y_{t-1} and all other e_{t-k}'s. In these models Y_0 can be determined by skill levels, but over time these skills should become less important determinants of earnings and the distribution should approach that of e_{t-k}. Depending on certain assumptions, the stochastic theories can generate (asymptomatically) lognormal, Pareto or other skewed to the right earnings distributions[47]. In ch. 7 we will see if the implied assumptions on the distribution of the growth in

[45]For example, reasoning from personal introspection, some economists have explained thusly the low earnings (and the rate of return on educational investment) for Ph.D.'s and theologians.

[46]See, for example, Clark et. al.

[47]See Champernowne, Aitchison, and Brown, or the excellent survey of Mincer (1970).

earnings are correct. Also in ch. 4 we will test the proposition that systematic determinants become less important as people age.

In summary, we will try to measure variables suggested by the various theories. If a variable is significant, there is a presumption that the theory has some validity. If a variable is not significant but is an accurate representation of the construct suggested by a theory, we can reject the theory. However, some variables suggested by theory do not have good measurable approximations. To examine the theories, it will be necessary to examine predictions generated by the theories.

CHAPTER 2

The distribution of earnings in NBER–TH – an overview

It is not easy to find a sample that has measures of all the variables discussed in the previous chapter. In this study, our empirical work will be based primarily on the 5100 men in the NBER–TH sample. In this chapter and associated appendices, we will discuss the main features of the sample and give an overview of the distribution of earnings in its several years[1].

The sample was drawn from a group of some 75000 men who during 1943 volunteered to enter the army air force's pilot, bombadier and navigator training program. The people in this group obviously had to meet the health and physical requirements to be in the Army. Also according to Thorndike and Hagen (TH) to enter this program, 'a man first had to be single, be between the ages of 18 and 26, pass a fairly rigorous physical examination, and pass a screening aptitude test, the Aviation Cadet Qualifying Examination. This examination was primarily a scholastic aptitude test, though perhaps with a slightly technical and mechanical slant. The qualifying score on the screening test was set at a level that could be reached by approximately half of the high school graduates, the country over'[2]. The men who qualified and volunteered for the program were then given a battery of some seventeen tests which measured various types of mental and physical skills. These test scores as well as certain biographical information on hobbies and family background determined which of the men were accepted for the Air Cadet program.

Thorndike and Hagen decided in 1955 to undertake a study of the usefulness of the seventeen tests in predicting vocational success with the hope of being able to aid the vocational counseling and choice of high school students. They drew a sample of 17000 men who had taken a given

[1]Much of the descriptive material is drawn from Taubman and Wales, ch. 4 and from B. Wolfe's unpublished dissertation.

[2]Thorndike and Hagen, pp. 8 and 9.

battery of tests between July and December, 1943. Beginning in late 1955 and throughout 1956, TH received responses from some 10000 civilians and 2000 men still in the military. The questionnaire they used, which is reproduced in Appendix A, contains among other things an earnings occupation history from World War II to the date of the questionnaire. It is important to note that because of their vocational emphasis, much care and attention was paid to assigning occupation codes[3].

In 1968 Taubman and Wales (TW) contacted Professor Thorndike and learned that he had retained a printout of the test scores, earnings and a few other items for 9700 people who were civilians in 1955 and the completed questionnaires for about 8600 of these men. With the concurrence of the Air Force, Professor Thorndike kindly agreed to make available all this information as well as the address list as of 1956.

It was recognized almost immediately that it was possible to update addresses via army serial numbers and the VA's life insurance and claims file[4]. Thus, John Meyer and Thomas Juster of the NBER quickly agreed to conduct another interview using National Bureau funds. This questionnaire, which is also reproduced in Appendix A, was eventually answered in 1969 and early 1970 by some 5100 out of about 7500 people for whom good addresses were available. TW initially used the detailed information on education, ability, family background and personal characteristics from the two surveys (for about 80% of the men) to examine the rate of return to education and the use of education as a screening (signalling) device.

The respondents had been promised summaries of the results of the questionnaire. When mailing these summaries in 1971, the NBER included a short questionnaire to try to resolve some of the puzzles raised by TW and others. Some 3000 people responded to this one mailing. When funding was received from the NSF for this project, another large questionnaire dealing with more aspects of family background and other matters was sent out and returned by 4474 people[5]. These last two questionnaires are also given in Appendix A.

[3]See their description on pp. 15–17.

[4]The VA graciously provided new addresses at no charge. Additional updated addresses were obtained by checking phone books of the city of the last known address.

[5]The NSF funds also enabled the NBER to extract more information from the TH questionnaire including the details on the job and earnings history.

In a moment the sample will be compared to the U.S. population of the same cohort. But first we wish to note that TH found little in the way of response bias in 1955 – perhaps because they employed expensive means such as the Retail Credit Corporation – to locate men. Taubman and Wales have shown that in 1969 the mentally more able and educated were more likely to respond. However, TW also showed that there was no significant difference in the 1955 earnings equations between those who did and did not respond in 1969; thus, the data can be used for structural analysis[6].

1. *Sample characteristics*

The qualifications needed to be a potential member of this sample guarantee that the NBER–TH sample will not be representative of the U.S. male population of the same age. As shown in Appendix B, table 4, about one-quarter of the men fall into each of the categories of high school graduate, some college, bachelor's degree, and at least some graduate work[7]. Also, a person had to be in the top one-half of the I.Q. distribution to enter this program and the average ability level has been heightened by the aforementioned response bias.

The average age in 1943 was 21 with three-quarters of the men aged 19–22. At least in 1943, the program's qualifications assure us these men were, on average, in better mental and physical health than the U.S. male population aged 18–26. Given that these men volunteered to train for flight duty, it seems likely that they are less risk averse than the population as a whole, which may be a partial explanation of the high percentage of people who are self-employed in 1969[8]. We do not know how many nonwhites, if any, are in the sample although the education and

[6]For the post-1969 questionnaires, we have adopted the practice of including a 'no response' dummy variable. Since this tends to be significant, over time the more successful are continuing to respond more.

[7]This is a much higher level of education than among World War II veterans – even if we restrict ourselves to high school graduates. See Miller (1960).

[8]The high percentage may also be due to the availability of VA guaranteed loans, better financial position of parents and in-laws, or business competence.

test aptitude qualifications suggest to us that whites probably make up 99% of the group[9].

In her dissertation, B. Wolfe has compared this sample and the corresponding U.S. age cohort of white males on a number of characteristics. Several of her tables are reproduced in Appendix B. She finds a higher percentage of Jews and smaller percentage of Catholics in this sample. The men in this sample have fathers with above average education (and occupational status) and father-in-law's with even higher educational attainment. Also, the people in this sample have above average earnings in each year studied, even if the comparison is made with white males of the same education and age. These differentials are greater at later ages and at lower levels of education where the sample is less representative of the population. (See below, or TW, ch. 4.)

It is of some interest to compare the earnings inequality in this sample with that of the random sample of white males aged 45–59 (in 1966) studied by Kohen, Parnes and Shea. They find, for example, that the share of total family income received in 1968 by the bottom 25, 50, and 75 and 95% of families is 14, 35, 62, and 89% respectively. In the NBER–TH sample, each of the corresponding figures are smaller by 5 to 6 percentage points. Thus, despite having a more restricted range in mental ability, education, and risk aversion, the NBER–TH sample has more inequality in family income than a nationwide cohort of about the same age. This result may be due to the heavier concentration of self-employed in NBER–TH or to the heavier concentration of people in the NBER–TH in the right hand tail of the earnings distribution.

Clearly, the sample is not representative of the U.S. population, and in the case of education and I.Q. does not have any members of a large portion of the population. Moreover, some of the dimensions in which it is nonrandom will be shown to be related to earnings. The nonrepresentativeness and truncation of some variables will mean that the distribution of earnings should not correspond to that for the U.S. population. Still the sample can be thought of as a random stratified sample in which the weights for various strata do not correspond to the population weights[10]. *It is well known that such unequal weighting will not affect the unbiased-*

[9]However, several of the highest ranking black Air Force generals in 1972 were in the Air Cadet program during World War II.

[10]The reader is reminded that TW rejected the hypothesis of a success bias even though there is a response bias by education and ability level.

ness of coefficients estimated from the data[11]. Thus we can use this sample to study the epects of education, ability, etc. on various aspects of inequality. We cannot, however, extrapolate the results to those levels of education and ability not included in our sample. And as noted above, measures of inequality, such as variance, need not be the same as in the population. However, such inequality measures calculated *within* education and ability groups or the changes in the measures over time can apply to the population. (This is argued in more detail in ch. 4.)

2. The distribution of earnings

Keeping in mind all these problems, let us examine briefly the distribution of earnings in 1955 and 1969 – the two years when the people were surveyed[12]. In 1955 when the mean age was 33, the average earnings (in thousands of 1958 dollars) was \$7.3 with a standard error of \$3.8[13]. By 1969, the average constant dollars earnings had doubled to \$14.5, while the standard error jumped to \$9.5. In both years the earnings distribution was skewed to the right, but (as demonstrated in ch. 4) the distribution is not log normal.

3. Inequality in earnings

The inequality in earnings can be measured in several ways[14]. The various moments of the distribution – such as the mean, variance, skewness, and

[11]If the equation is: $Y = X\beta + u$, the least squares estimate of β will be $b = (x'x)^{-1}x'Y$. The $E(b) = \beta$ if $E(x'x)^{-1}x'u = 0$. This last condition requires X and u to have zero linear correlation but does not depend on the relative weights in the various strata.

[12]The sampling actually took place over two years in both instances, i.e. in 1955 and in 1956, and in 1969, 1970.

[13]Since the people in the sample are all in the top half of the I.Q. distribution and have better than average backgrounds, we would expect the average earnings in this sample to exceed that of the U.S. population of the same age level. In addition, the I.Q. cutoff should mean that the difference by I.Q. between the sample and the U.S. population should decrease with education. Since we show mental ability affects earnings, average earnings in the sample should exceed those in the population more at lower levels of education. As shown in TW, these hypotheses are borne out.

[14]See Atkinson, Mincer (1974) and Kravis (1962).

kurtosis – can be calculated and analyzed. Another approach which has some appeal is based on the Lorenz curve. Formally the Lorenz curve is defined as:

$$\int_{-\infty}^{A} Y_i \Big/ \int_{-\infty}^{\infty} Y_i F(Y_i)\,\mathrm{d}Y_i = \frac{1}{N\bar{Y}} \int_{-\infty}^{A} Y_i\,\mathrm{d}Y_i,$$

where A varies from $-\infty$ to ∞. In simpler language, the Lorenz curve indicates the percentage of total earnings accruing to the bottom 5, 10...100% of the people.

The Lorenz curves for 1955 and 1969 are presented in fig. 1. Also drawn in that figure is a diagonal which is the Lorenz curve that would be observed if each person had the same earnings, i.e. the 'bottom' 10% would have 10% of the earnings, etc. In all years studied, earnings are not distributed equally; hence, each year's Lorenz curve lies below the diagonal.

How unequal a distribution is, or whether one curve is more unequal than another, depends on how 'far' the observed curve lies from the diagonal. Since the observed Lorenz curves cannot be everywhere parallel to the diagonal, the distance is not constant at all income levels and some weighted average must be taken. A number of summary measures of inequality with different implied weighting schemes have been proposed in the literature[15].

As the weights change from one measure to another, we generally would expect differences in the degree of and rankings of inequality. Atkinson, however, has demonstrated that all summary measures of relative inequality of two Lorenz curves will yield the same ranking, *provided* the two curves do not intersect. Conversely, if the curves intersect, there always are some weighting schemes that would disagree on whether curve 1 or 2 is more unequal.

The Lorenz curves never intersect in fig. 1. But it is still necessary to establish that the Lorenz curves are significantly different from one

[15]Some of the more common ones, which Atkinson describes and compares on the basis of various criteria, are (1) variance, (2) coefficient of variation, (3) the Gini coefficient which is a simple transformation of the area between the diagonal and the Lorenz curves, and (4) the standard deviation of the log of earnings. A cruder measure is the share of earnings of say, the top 10%.

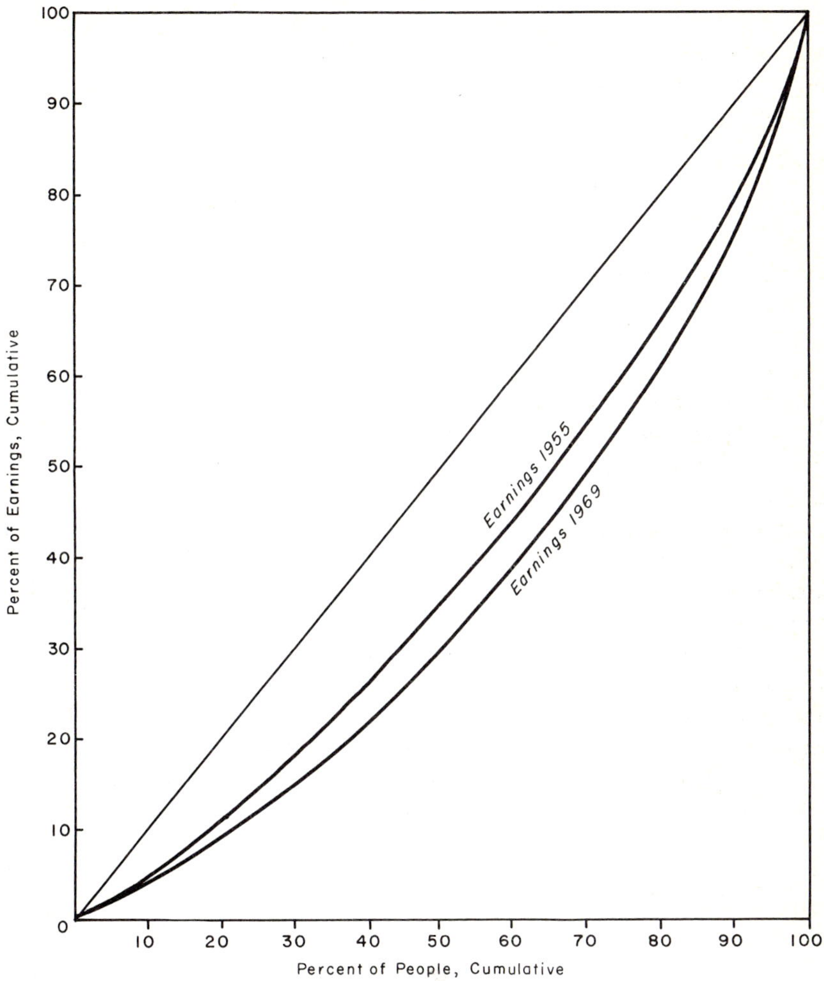

Fig. 1. Lorenz curves 1955 and 1969.

another before we can conclude that inequality increased with age. In this sample, earnings do not follow the log normal, normal, Pareto distributions, or any other well-known distribution as far as we can tell. Thus, to test the null hypothesis that the two curves are the same, we use the nonparametric Kolmogorov–Smirnov (KS) test which is based on the maximum difference between two cumulative functions and which is more powerful for any finite sample size than the Chi-square test[16,17]. In fig. 1 the maximum vertical difference between the 1955 and 1969 Lorenz curves is .056 which far exceeds the 5% level of significance of .027. Thus the 1969 curve is statistically different from the 1955 curve. In subsequent chapters, we will try to explain why inequality is greater in 1969.

From previous research, it is known that inequality in earnings in any year is partly due to differences in education and in intelligence. In 1969, for example, there is about a 40% difference in average earnings between high school and college graduates or people in the top and bottom one-fifth of the sample's mental ability distribution[18]. There is, however, substantial inequality within education or ability groups. In either 1955 or 1969, the Lorenz curve for any education or ability level is like one another and the overall curve for that year. Using pairwise comparisons, we cannot reject (at the 5% confidence level) the null hypothesis that the Lorenz curves are the same at each education or ability level. However, for any ability or educational level between 1955 and 1969, inequality increases.

In subsequent chapters we will try to isolate some of the sources of inequality and to determine how the 1955 Lorenz curve was converted into the 1969 curve. Since those chapters indicate the differences due to education, etc., with all other variables held constant, it seems unnecessary at this time to present earnings tables cross-classified by one or two variables.

[16]See Kendall and Stuart for a derivation of this test and a comparison with the Chi-square.

[17]Strictly speaking, the KS test can only be used when the distribution is completely specified, i.e. no parameter is estimated from sample data. Thus we will adopt the convention that $Y_i/\Sigma Y_i$ is the variable whose distribution we are concerned with. If a parameter is estimated, some people believe that the test becomes conservative, making rejection of the null hypotheses more difficult; however, Darling also indicates the test is no longer distribution free.

[18]The 40% does not represent the effect of education or of ability since other earnings determinants differ between the groups.

CHAPTER 3

Determinants of earnings in 1955 and 1969

A primary purpose of this study is to identify variables which determine the distribution of annual and lifetime earnings and to use these empirical findings to answer such questions as the relative importance of inherited and acquired skills, and of systematic and random elements. Much of the analysis in this study is based on regressions for earnings in various years which are presented in tables 6 and 7 at the end of this chapter. These regressions contain many variables which are supposed to be direct or proxy measures of various personal traits, attributes, skills, as well as attitudes towards risk and nonpecuniary rewards. The particular variables used and their relationship to the skills, etc. in question are discussed in the text.

It is very easy, however, to become so bogged down in the swamp of regression coefficients that one loses sight of the general topography of results. Thus, rather than discussing each variable in the 1969 and 1955 equations, we will compare the relative importance of successive groups of variables both at a point of time and over time. The tables in the text are drawn from the regressions presented in tables 6 and 7 at the end of the chapter. Generally, we concentrate on the results from eqn (3.2) in these tables. Similar equations for log Y are given and discussed in Appendix C.

While the sample contains earnings from a number of years, we are concentrating on 1955 and 1969 because the earnings were collected in those two years rather than being recalled as are the estimates for the other years[1]. Preliminary analysis of several of the other years has lead the author to conclude that there are substantial measurement errors in the recalled data. The 1969 earnings were requested (on an annual basis) from main job only but recalled estimates of total earnings in 1968 suggest that the omission of the second job earnings does not affect greatly the

[1]In both instances part of the sample answered in the next calendar year.

coefficients of the independent variables. The 1955 figure is based on 'last monthly salary' on a particular job and probably refers to main job. Earnings variables are measured on an annual basis in thousands of 1958 dollars. We excluded an individual if he did not report earnings in either year.

In examining these results the reader is reminded that our underlying theoretical model is that pecuniary and nonpecuniary rewards depend on a person's marginal productivity. The various skills and talents that determine productivity as well as tastes towards risk and nonpecuniary rewards are partly inherited and partly acquired from schools, friends, family, etc.

1. Importance

An obvious measure of importance is the R^2 or the amount of the variance explained by a set of variables[2]. But the R^2 in our sample may not generalize to the U.S. population because our sample is truncated in education and ability and is drawn more heavily from some strata than others. Since we do not know all respects in which this sample differs from the U.S. population and how to extrapolate the results to the truncated portion of the population, we will not try to calculate a weighted R^2. Many of these problems are less severe when we compare total or partial R^2's for the same people but in different years.

The variance explained by a set of independent variables combines two elements – the predicted value of the dependent variables, Y_i, as compared to the mean of $\bar{Y}$, and the number of times each Y_i occurs. An alternative measure of importance is the difference in the average level of earnings, $Y_1 - Y_2$, caused by a set of variables. This range measure is related to the $Y_1 - \bar{Y}$ portion of the variance but does not indicate how many people are at each Y_i.

In our equations we usually use a set of zero–one dummy variables to represent each possible response (a reference category is omitted to keep the matrix from being singular). The coefficients on these dummy

[2]It is well known that it is difficult to measure the contribution of one variable versus another to the total R^2 when the independent variables are not orthogonal.

variables indicate the net difference or range in average earnings between the reference group and the particular category, e.g. high school graduate and college graduate, with all other characteristics in the equation in the appendix held constant[3]. The variables in the equation, which will be described more fully below, that are held constant include: education, mathematical ability, various measures of socioeconomic background of the respondent and of his wife; information on self employment and on teaching; a crude measure of risk preference, age, and work experience, health, hours worked, marital status, and attitudes towards nonpecuniary rewards. While we have included many variables, we never explain more than 45% of the variance in earnings. The coefficients of any included variables will be biased if correlated with any omitted variable which determines earnings.

Because of computer capacity limitations, we were forced to drop some variables which were consistently nonsignificant in preliminary runs. Table 4 in Appendix C lists all the variables we tried but which were not significant in our earnings equation. In the equations presented, therefore, all the variables are either significant in one or more years or were significant in either the next to last runs or in the Taubman–Wales (TW) equations from which this analysis commenced. When we cite coefficients for variables not in the last equation, the numbers are taken from the most complete version of the final equation in which the variable appeared.

One final prefatory note is that the equations are based on the information in the 1955, 1969, and 1972 questionnaires. For the some 700 people who had answered the earlier two surveys but did not respond to the 1972 questionnaire, we included a nonresponse dummy variable which is one if the 1972 questionnaire was not returned. (For the other variables, we replaced the no response with modal values which is the most likely group the person would be found in.)

Equation 1 in tables 6 and 7 is very similar to the final Taubman–Wales equation, based on 80% of the sample[4]. Adjusting for the difference in the units in which earnings are measured in the two studies, their and our coefficients (and R^2) are essentially unchanged in magnitude, relative

[3]However, these coefficients only indicate the direct effect of a variable. There can also be indirect effects; for example, parental income can determine educational attainment.

[4]See their eqn 5, table 7, ch. 5.

importance, and statistical significance. There is no need at this time to discuss the individual coefficients since we have greatly improved the TW equation.

2. Formal education

Formal schooling can affect physical, cognitive, psychological, and affective skills[5]. It would greatly increase our understanding of how and what schooling does if we could identify the particular skills that affect earnings and measure the change in all skills produced by schooling. But since we do not have such measures nor even know what the appropriate skills are, we will have to be satisfied with crude measures of quantity and quality of schooling.

We represent quantity by level of education obtained. We use dummy variables for various responses. Earnings in 1969 generally increase with education. But despite our having included variables to hold constant nonpecuniary rewards, including those associated with pre-college teaching, risk preference and self employment, those with just a bachelor's degree earn more than those with some graduate work. As shown in table 1, the *increase* in earnings from education for the average high school graduate ranges from 8% for some college to 82% for nonself-employed M.D.'s with bachelor's degree holders receiving 20% more[6]. (We have standardized by the average nonself-employed high school graduate's earnings of $10300.)

[5]See, e.g. Simon and Ellison, or Clark et al. for some evidence on the noncognitive developments.

[6]These calculations assume that all post-high school graduates attend a college of the average quality of people who had only had some college. The quantity effects are slightly larger when quality is omitted, but never by more than $200. If self-employment variables were not included, the increase would be: 14% for some college; 28% for bachelor's; 80% for L.L.B.; and 110% for M.D. These increases are less than those given in TW primarily because of the introduction of self-employment variables although the graduate level coefficients were much smaller before we introduced some variables related to nonpecuniary returns. Essentially, the same percentage increases are obtained from equations using the log of earnings. If we adopt Mincer's model, these percentage changes divided by the associated number of years of education beyond high school are an estimate of the rate of return from education which is less than 6% at all education levels.

Table 1.
The increase in earnings from education in 1955 and 1969.

	Time period			
Percentage increase from education[b]	1955 average age 33 (%)	1969 average age 47 (%)	# of observations as of 1955	# of observations as of 1969[c]
Some college	05	08	1145	1162
Bachelor's degree	11	20	1415	1332
Some graduate	08	18	220	250
Master's degree	06	29	336	419
Ph.D.	13	43	238	298
L.L.B.[a]	06	53	140	140
M.D.[a]	71	82	48	48

Source: eqn 2 in tables 6 and 7.

[a]In this equation this variable was also included in Ph.D. group. Moreover, these are salaried people only.

[b]Calculated for the average high school graduate, not self-employed, who attended the quality of college of the average person with just some college.

[c]In the high school category, there were 1246 observations in 1955 and 1139 in 1969.

In 1955 the same general pattern emerges except that the effects of education are uniformly smaller and not always statistically significant. For example, obtaining a bachelor's degree or some college would add 11 and 5% more to the $6000 (1958 prices) received by the person who had the average characteristics of a nonself-employed high school graduate. *However, our self-employment variables are only measured in 1969. The resulting measurement error has probably caused us to overstate the relative returns to education of the nonself-employed in 1955*[7].

The total effect of education may be understated if one of the mechanisms by which education alters earnings is measured after the completion of education and is also included in our equations. One such route would be the occupation the person was in. The variables on

[7]When the self-employment information is omitted, the 1955 differentials are: some college 11%; bachelor's degree 14%; L.L.B. 14% and M.D. 82%, which are very close to those given in TW.

occupation we have used in these equations are teacher, self-employed businessman and professional, and business assets. The teacher variable is included because we felt that teachers receive more nonpecuniary rewards as a substitute for earnings than are received in other occupations[8]. The various self-employment measures are designed to eliminate all of the return on financial capital included in the earnings estimate; rewards for bearing the extra risk of entrepreneurship; and perhaps unmeasured attributes that lead to being a successful businessman. However, it is possible that these measures have incorporated some of the influences of education. For example, education's affect on prior earnings could conceivably explain much of the difference in the accumulation in business assets; however, crude analysis suggests that such effects of education would be small. Moreover, if the self-employment variables were not included, the bachelor's, some college and master's degree coefficients would all be *smaller* because the self-employed are more concentrated at the lower education levels.

It is also possible that a person's tastes for nonpecuniary rewards or risk bearing are partially formed by education. The inclusion of the so-called nonpecuniary variables caused the some college and bachelor's level coefficients to increase in both years.

3. *College quality*

College quality can mean many things and can be measured in various ways. Because the effects of quality in this sample are being studied extensively by Solmon and others, we restrict ourselves to the use of an index of academic quality constructed annually since 1955 by Gourman. We use the 1955 index for last undergraduate school attended and assume that quality ratings had not changed much during the previous decade when most college attendance occurred. (For the schools with no Gourman rating, the Educational Testing Service provided estimates.) In his calculations Gourman includes such things as the average college board scores of attendees, library facilities, information on faculty, etc. The index is scaled to correspond to college board scores and in the

[8]However, the variable could mean that on some unmeasured aspect of the ability, teachers are less able.

population has a mean of 500, standard error of 100, and ranges from 200 to 800. The people in our sample attended a fairly representative sample of schools, the range is from under 300 to over 750 and the mean and standard error are almost those of the population.

Since the index is scaled arbitrarily, there is no need for its effects to be linear, and both Wales and Solmon have found nonlinearities. However, when we include both the index and its square we do not obtain a better representation than using the index by itself. Because of space limitations, the final equation contains only the index which was not broken up into dummy variables.

In 1969 we find that attendance at a school that ranked 100 points (the standard deviation) higher in the index is associated with a \$450 increase in earnings. After our usual standardizing, the effect of the 100 point difference in college quality of 4½% is about half the size of the effect of obtaining some college. In 1955 a 100 point increase in undergraduate school quality leads to a \$140 increase in earnings of 2½% after standardization. Once again this is about half the size of the coefficient on the some college variable.

The introduction of the quality variable caused a 5 to 10% reduction in the coefficients of the Jewish, year of first job, attendance at private high school and attendance at private elementary school variables as well as a 10% increase in the pre-college teacher dummy in 1969 and smaller changes in 1955. The quality index may still be acting as a proxy for unmeasured attributes, but we would hope that it in part measures the extra value added by better schools[9].

4. Mental ability

In TW, it was shown that while the seventeen tests taken by the people in 1943 contained at least four factors, only the first factor which was denoted mathematical ability but which probably correlates well with a standard I.Q. measure, was a significant determinant of earnings[10]. Since we convert the test score data into dummy variables for the different

[9] Recently Wachtel has found that various dimensions of high school quality also affect earnings.

[10] No attempt was made here to reinvestigate the usefulness of the other factors.

fifths of the factor score distribution, we are assuming that post test taking events (not otherwise measured) do not change the fifths of the ability distribution a person would belong to in each of the particular years studied. Since the test score information provides us with an ordinal index, we can not distinguish between nonlinear effects of a cardinal measure of intelligence and a nonlinear scaling of an ordinal index.

In both 1969 and 1955, we tested for an interaction between mental ability and all other variables by computing separate equations within each ability fifth. Using analysis of covariance, we could not reject the hypothesis that the effects of all variables, including education, were independent of the level of ability in each year.

In both 1955 and 1969 as shown in table 2, the coefficients on each of the top four-fifths are significantly different from the bottom fifth[11]. These coefficients are not sensitive to the inclusion of the self-employment related variables.

The effects of each fifth increase in ability adds a greater percentage to earnings in 1969 than in 1955, with the differences more pronounced in the top two ability fifths. Since the ability index is ordinal, we cannot distinguish between nonlinear effects along a given measure or scale of ability and a nonlinear transformation of the ordinal index.

The numbers in table 2 can be compared directly between those in the top and bottom fifths of ability (14 and 19% in the two years) exceeds the effect of obtaining a bachelor's degree in 1955 and is nearly as large in 1969.

A person's test scores generally depend on his innate ability, the quality and quantity of pre-test schooling, and differences in other aspects of 'environment'. Often we would like to know what portion of test scores (and associated earnings) are due to genetics and to environment. Suppose that the measure of religion, parent's and own educational attainment, occupation, and income, etc. included in our earnings are the only environmental differences that determine test scores, then ability coefficients in the earnings equations would be net of the environmental influences[12]. Of course, if other aspects of environment affect test scores,

[11]Since people had to be in the top one-half of the ACGT to be able to volunteer for the program, these fifths are more like tenths.

[12]If the true equation is $Y = a(\text{innate ability}) + bX$ but we estimate $Y = a^*(\text{innate ability} + cX) + b^*X$, then our least squares estimate of a^* and b^* are identical with those for a and $b - ac$.

Table 2.
Increase in earnings in 1955 and 1969 from ability differences.

	Time period		
Percentage change in earnings from ability (bottom fifth to the fifth shown)[b]	1955 average age 33 (%)	1969 average age 47 (%)	# of observations[a]
2nd fifth	05*	05	848
3rd fifth	05	07	925
4th fifth	09	14	972
top fifth	14	19	1047

*Not significant at the 5% level.

The variables in the equation which have been held constant include: education, mathematical ability, various measures of socioeconomic background of the respondent and of his wife; information on self employment and on teaching; a crude measure of risk preference, age and work experience, health, hours worked, marital status, and attitudes towards nonpecuniary rewards.

[a]In the bottom fifth, there were 808 observations.

[b]The dollar difference is divided by the nonself-employed high school graduates' average earnings.

the ability coefficient will still be a mixture. TW examined the question of whether pre-test differentials in schooling affected observed scores. They conclude that in the *tests we are using*, this is not a problem. This conclusion is reinforced by our findings in ch. 8. This finding in no way tells us innate ability is more important than learned knowledge since we have not examined the effects of various types of learned knowledge on earnings.

5. Family environment

Socioeconomic standing (SES) can influence earnings indirectly, through, say, educational attainment. But family differences in child rearing techniques can lead to differences in skills or in tastes towards nonpecuniary rewards and risks. Also, family wealth can be used to purchase items which increase skills or can lead to good jobs through nepotism.

Finally, certain measures of family background can be proxies for genetically inherited abilities. While ideally we would want to identify the unmeasured skills, or the types of child rearing techniques that form the skills, at our current state of knowledge we will have to rely on various proxies. Since child rearing techniques vary widely between families, and since many different types of skills may be produced by various environments, there is no reason to restrict ourselves to only one of two SES variables. Indeed by examining many variables which are related differently to family wealth atmosphere and attitudes, we may obtain a better understanding of the underlying causes. In this regard, we have examined many potential proxies for the various aspects of SES. We are, of course, open to the charges that ex post we can probably concoct a story to justify any such variable, and that when an open-ended list of variables are tried without a strong theoretical basis, we will always find some chance correlations. We will return to this issue at the end of this section where we will argue that our results are probably not due to chance. However, we are perfectly willing to agree that our results need to stand the test of replication in other samples before being accepted as valid.

The measures of family background we have analyzed include: father's education and occupation; mother's education and labor force participation; wife's education and her parent's education and occupation; various data related to family income, wealth, and size while the respondent was growing up; how the respondent spent his time while growing up, age at entering school, and religious preference[13].

In TW the two measures of SES used were father's education and the so called biography variable. This biography variable is based on the respondent's parental income and education, his hobbies, sports and interests, and his pre-test education and grades as reported in 1943[14].

It was, of course, a bit frustrating that a variable made up of so many disparate items which could represent so many different things deter-

[13]This is a wider list than that used in most previous studies, and some of the variables require justification as SES measures but almost all of these variables are significant in both 1969 and 1955. Several of the variables have been used at one time or another by others; see, for example, Blau and Duncan, and Sewall et al.

[14]The weights of this index are based on how well the items predicted success in pilot and navigator school. The original items, which were collected by the military, are not extant although much information has been recollected in 1969 and 1972.

Table 3.
Increase in 1955 and 1969 earnings associated with various socioeconomic measures.

Percentage increase in earnings from differences in various SES characteristics[b]	1955 average age 33 (%)	1969 average age 47 (%)	# of observations in category
Father's education			
Attended high school	6*	7*	1409
Attended college	4*	5*	770
Father's occupation			
Business owner	2*	5*	1699
Teacher	1*	−8*	360
Mother's education			
Attended high school	3*	3*	1671
Attended college	2*	4*	685
Family never moved before H.S. grad.	−1*	−5*	1452
Jewish	33	40	239
Protestant	−3*	−9	2910
Religious school several times/week	−9	−11	236
Never went to religious school	−.1*	−3*	1509
Biog.[a] 2nd fifth and biog. 3rd fifth	4	5	1795
Biog. 4th fifth and biog. top fifth	11	8*	1893
Father-in-law education (per year)	1	1	[d]
Mother-in-law high school or college	−1*	6	2294
Private elementary school	4*	27*	21
Private high school	25	29	99
Time spent on sports[c]	4*	10	[d]
Time spent on chores[c]	−3*	−10	[d]
Time spent on hobbies[c]	3*	−6*	[d]
Time spent on part-time job[c]	5	11	[d]

*Not significant at the 5% level.

[a]Biog. is a weighted average of information on activities, education, preferences and family background which was formed by Thorndike and Hagen from data collected by the military in 1943. See p. 26.

[b]The dollar difference is divided by earnings of the average, nonself-employed high school graduate.

[c]Difference between spent most time and hardly any time.

[d]Continuous variables.

The omitted categories can be found by subtracting the included ones from 4600.

The variables equation which have been held constant include: education, mathematical ability, various measures of socioeconomic background of the respondent and of his wife; information on self employment and on teaching; a crude measure of risk preference, age and work experience, health, hours worked, marital status, and attitudes towards non-pecuniary rewards.

mined earnings. Thus, we are happy to report that inclusion of information collected in 1969 and 1972 similar to some of that collected in 1943 has substantially reduced the size of the biography coefficient, but the top two-fifths are still significant and the coefficients are monotonic. The differences between the top two- and bottom-fifths are 11 and 8% in 1955 and 1969. This is one of the few variables that has a smaller percentage effect in 1969. It is interesting to note that the big shift in the 1969 and 1955 coefficients occurred only after we included information on tastes towards nonpecuniary rewards and a proxy for family wealth, implying that these were components in the biography variable that had influenced earnings in the TW sample.

In this study, father's education is reduced to insignificant in both 1969 and 1955. Part of the reduction of significance of this variable occurs when the *father is an owner* variable is introduced. But the reduction in size and significance of the coefficient is primarily associated with the introduction of the respondent's business assets variables. Since this variable is not often used in other studies, there is a suggestion that father's education is a proxy for family wealth and business ownership[15].

There are other SES variables which are significant. Perhaps the most interesting of the new measures are the Jewish and Protestant variables[16]. Compared to Catholics, (as well as atheists, agnostics, and others who all earn about the same amount in the various years), Jews received from 33 to 40% more earnings than the average high school graduate and Protestants from 3 to 9% less[17]. The reader is reminded that these differences are net of the influence of education (including M.D.) mental

[15]This also suggests that the business asset variable reflects inheritances or nepotism rather than the cumulative affect of education etc. arising out of extra earnings.

[16]In 1969 the respondents were asked to indicate their religious preference by checking one of Protestant, Catholic, Jewish, None, Other. It is possible that different answers would have been obtained if 'the religion you were raised in' was asked. Compared to the U.S. white population the NBER–TH had 1.7% more of both Jews and others and 5% fewer Catholics. However, the differences from white males in the particular cohorts who were at least high school graduates would probably be smaller.

[17]If self employment and M.D. are not held constant, Jews earn even more. The asset variable is measured imperfectly, but it is difficult to attribute a difference of $4000 a year to this.

ability, self employment, and various other personal attributes and family SES dimensions[18].

At least for the generation being discussed, it seems likely that those who are Jewish had more of a taste for acquiring knowledge and, as shown in ch. 9, achieve more education and go to better schools, given ability and other SES measures[19]. Hence, for given levels of schooling and mental ability in 1943, Jews may have acquired more knowledge useful in earning a living. Given the evidence in ch. 9 and in Featherman, I would suggest that religious upbringing affects motivation and other psychological skills. We cannot, however, rule out the possibility that some unmeasured genetically determined characteristics are related to religion. Unfortunately, since we do not know what unmeasured attributes are important determinants of earnings, we cannot usefully examine the genetics literature to see what, if any, differences exist by religion[20].

That the extent of religious commitment or the different environment in families of various religions can mold the individual receives some further support in the sample. That is, we find that those who remembered attending religious classes (not parochial school) several times a week earn 9 to 11% less than those who attended once or twice while those who did not attend earn 1 to 4% less. Since the latter group would not have

[18]In a study of college graduates of the first half of the century, Hunt also found similar qualitative results. Also using the same basic data source as Hunt, Haveman and West found that being Jewish was the most important determinant of earnings of people who graduate college in the first half of this century. Featherman also found Jews to earn more and some Catholics, such as French, to earn more than the average Protestants. Both the Hunt and Featherman studies hold constant education and mental ability as well as other variables.

[19]For example, Bruce Eckland finds that for given test scores and social class, Jews go to higher quality institutions of learning. This would indicate either higher tastes for education, more motivation and drive, or lower costs relative to returns. He also finds certain ethnic groups of Catholics do better than the average Protestants. Given the education cut off to be in the Air Force program, it seems likely that our Catholics come largely from these successful ethnic groups.

[20]We also cannot rule out the possibility that the Jews and other nonProtestants are a more select group of their respective populations. However, given the nature of the Air Force work they volunteered for, it might be argued that those who volunteered could include more people who wanted to gain revenge on Germany or inflict destruction in large doses quickly. But the revenge motive would seem to suggest that Jews and, to a lesser extent, Catholics would be a more random (less select) group of their religious compatriots.

come from 'typical' families of the 1920s and 1930s, it seems possible that the variable represents attitudes towards material success.

Another set of variables which reflects both the type of family and affective, physical and cognitive, and psychological attitudes that can be formed by the family and peer group is contained in the question (asked in 1972) of 'indicate how you spent your time while growing up'[21]. The categories examined were sports, hobbies, chores, part-time job, reading, and other. The last two groups were never significant and will not be discussed here except to note that reading is related to the ability measure and educational attainment. The remaining categories were significant in 1969 but only part-time job was significant in 1955.

The difference in earnings of those who spent practically no time and the most time on part-time jobs is 5 and 11% in 1955 and 1969. It seems likely that these men came from poor families and needed money for themselves and/or valued financial success greatly. These men would be willing to work hard and apparently have succeeded, with success being cumulative over time[22]. In 1955 and 1969, those who spent much time on sports while growing up earn 4 and 10% more than those who spent practically no time. Several explanations of this result are available. First, activity in sports may show up in later life as better physical fitness; and, as shown below, healthiness is related to earnings. (In this explanation, 1955 has a smaller impact because of less health deterioration at that age.) Second, most sports involve both a competitive and cooperative structure which are also found in many work situations. That is, a boy's play is training for a man's work. Third, activity in sports may be indicative of energy and aggressiveness that pays off in the business world[23]. Finally, there is some indication in Thorndike and Hagen that in 1955, sports

[21] 1 is for practically no time spent and 5 is for the most time spent.

[22] If we are right about the type of families these men came from, we would expect them to have a high rate of time preference, and less access to capital early in their lives; thus, I would find it hard to interpret the growth in earning over time as an investment theory as in Mincer.

[23] Related to this last viewpoint is the idea that people who play sports may be more able to make decisions quickly. If intellectualism is taken as evidence of the opposite personality, it is interesting that the Phi Beta Kappas among top management earn substantially less than other people. See the Taubman–Wales appendix using the Llewellen data.

distinguishes company presidents and vice presidents from treasurers. This suggests that sports in the 1920s and 1930s was an indicator of family wealth and availability of leisure time, or an indicator of attitudes such as risk taking.

The hobby variable has practically no effect in 1955 but in 1969 those who spent the most time on hobbies received 6% less which is significant at the 10% level in the final equation. The most obvious explanation for this finding is that many, although not all, hobbies represented the opposite of sports and that the effects should be reversed.

The last and perhaps most difficult of these results to explain is the chore result. Those who spent much time on chores earn 3 and 10% less in 1955 and 1969 with the former not significant. Initially, I had expected chores to be a proxy for 'willingness to take on responsibility' and to have a positive effect. Merton, however, argues that families who insist on their children doing chores are lower middle class and are very interested in conformity. He further argues that these families will produce 'tame' individuals who make the ideal bureaucrat and who receive less earnings that people in riskier jobs (see below). We should add that Merton only refers to one piece of empirical evidence, which, he acknowledges, is not very compelling.

As might be expected, time spent on chores and on part-time job are positively correlated ($R^2 = .13$) but the differences in emphasis of paid and family work apparently reflect different types of environment and different types of men[24].

Thus far we have included SES measures which are strongly related to family upbringing and taste formation. Parental income or wealth can also influence a child's earnings by being used to purchase goods that produce marketable skills, by being a proxy for nepotism, or by being a proxy for genetically determined skills.

One possible proxy for family income is father's education, which we have already indicated is not significant once business assets are included in the equation. Another possible proxy is father's occupation; but this

[24]The difference in environment is also suggested by the finding in ch. 9 that these variables have different effects on educational attainment.

also does not explain directly much of the differences in earnings, with the other variables held constant[25].

Two extremely important determinants of earnings are type of elementary and high school attended. The coefficient on private elementary school is positive but not significant, probably because 22 of the 29 people who went to private elementary school went to private high school. Those who attended both private elementary and high school in 1955 earn 29% more than those who always went to public schools. In 1969, those who went to private elementary and private high school earn 56% more than those who did not go to private school.

Our explanation for this result is that those who went to private schools in the 1920s came from very wealthy families who provided a good home environment and/or genes or who used pull to aid their sons. The pull argument seems to be the most likely since the variable is primarily a proxy for large amounts of wealth[26,27].

We are still left with explaining the change in the coefficient between 1955 and 1969. (The coefficient is significant in the growth rate equations of ch. 6.) I would argue that even if nepotism is involved, you want to see how good the person is before you give him an important job, although of course a person can probably become vice president quicker if his father owns the company. This explanation will be imbedded in a sorting model explained more fully in ch. 7.

[25]There are, however, several caveats that must be attached to this conclusion. First, father's occupation, (and resulting income) has an indirect effect on earnings through the amount of schooling the respondent receives. Second and more importantly, father being an owner is significant when the self-employment variables are not included. Third, in 1968 the father's occupation and education have a much greater impact on the range in family *income* than on earnings of the *head*. This suggests that income inequality is perpetuated through generations directly through financial inheritance (including business assets) and indirectly through educational attainment. The biography variable also includes some parental wealth indicators although it is not clear what aspects of the variable determine earnings.

[26]Indeed, when we include a crude measure of net worth in our equations, the private school variables become insignificant and much smaller.

[27]Since private schooling is both different from and more costly to the respondent's parents than public schooling, it might be argued that these results are due to quality differentials. But if this argument is accepted, it is difficult to explain why in ch. 9 neither type of private school is significantly related to our ability measure, which contains some learned knowledge.

Another interesting finding in our equations that suggests nepotism is that *father-in-law's education*, measured continuously in years, is a significant determinant of the respondent's *earnings* in both 1955 and 1969[28]. A primary explanation of these results is that business and social contacts provided by the father-in-law are important. But there can be other explanations. For example, daughters from good social backgrounds may have the necessary graces – not learned in school – which help to promote their husbands. Alternatively, women with successful fathers may be able to spot and marry men with those characteristics that made for their father's success, or push their husbands into achieving success.

Interestingly, mother-in-law's education also is positively related to earnings in 1969, with the high school variable somewhat greater than the college variable, although the two are combined in the final equation. This finding makes it less likely that women are marrying men who are like their fathers and suggests nepotism.

Thus far, we have been concerned with the effects of individual aspects of SES on earnings. Except for religion none of these has an impact as large as ability or education on the range of earnings in 1955 and 1969. But it is possible for a person to fall into the top or the bottom category of all SES measures. Using the significant coefficients only, the average difference in earnings for such 'extremists' would total about \$14000 or 140% of our average earnings in 1969 and \$5500 or 90% in 1955 and far exceed the direct effect of ability or education on earnings[29].

The other dimensions of SES we have tried but found to be insignificant include: whether the respondent was the youngest or oldest sibling, additional crude proxies for family wealth based on type of house, the labor force status of the respondent's mother when the respondent was less than 5 and less than 14 years old; being reared on a farm; size of city or town he grew up in; the region of the country in which raised; and age at time of entry into school.

To conclude this section, we would like to discuss several objections that have been raised about the SES variables and also might apply to

[28]Dummy variables for father-in-law's occupation and spouse's education are not significant.

[29]This only includes items in table 3. Business assets and some other variables may be partly determined by SES.

some of the taste and other variables still to be discussed. One set of objections is that the variables used have multiple interpretations and have not been validated as measures of the phenomena we ascribe to them. Our defenses against this set of objections are: that when many proxies are used, each one tends to represent the one or several forces it correlates with most closely; that since we do not yet know what dimensions of SES affect earnings nor have a theory to guide us, it is important to use the empirical information at hand to suggest variables which should be validated; that a form of validation is replication which has been performed successfully in the 1955 and 1969 earnings equations and in ch. 9 for education, ability, and variables.

Another set of objections is that, perhaps because of the absence of a well specified theory, I have tried many variables and may only be observing chance correlations. This argument suggests that 5% of my SES variable might be significant due to chance but I have found more like 40% significant. More importantly, none of the variables not significant in 1969 are significant in 1955 and nearly all the variables significant in 1969 are also significant in 1955[30]. The R^2 between earnings in the two years does not exceed .2; thus, the probability of finding coefficients significant at the 5% level and with the same sign in both years does not exceed $\frac{1}{3}$ of 1%. In other words, the 'replicated' results strongly reduce the probability of chance findings. I, of course, would urge further replication and refinement; and I am following this advice in a large survey I am currently supervising.

6. *Maturation and work experience*

A well-known and documented result is that (real) earnings increase with age until at least age 40. While we do not have data for all ages, the results for 1955 and 1969 certainly are in accord with this finding. The general explanations for the upward sloping age earnings profiles are: (1) as

[30]The ones not significant had small coefficients in both years (although smaller in 1955), but we explain more of the earnings variance in 1969. Since $(X'X)$ is nearly the same in the two years, the variance of the coefficients relative to the size of the coefficients is smaller in 1969. Presumably, a similar explanation explains why some of the education coefficients are not significant in 1955.

people age, mental and physical maturation increases those skills that determine earnings; (2) work experience and learning by doing increase earnings related skills; (3) people are promoted on the basis of performance on the job and/or seniority; and (4) beyond a certain age, senescence sets in or skills depreciate[31].

For the moment, without distinguishing type of work experience, time on the job can be represented as $TJ = (\text{Age} - \text{Year of First Job} - H)$ where H represents such things as time not working because of illness, unemployment and departures from the normal period of time to complete a given level of schooling. If maturation is important, then age should have a separate effect from TJ.

Both age and year of first job (at the 6% level) are significant in 1969 though apparently senescence or depreciation has set in since age in table 4 is negative. In 1955, the separate age effect is nearly zero. The year of first job coefficient can be treated as the negative of the experience coefficient. Thus, contrary to most findings, the absolute value of the

Table 4.
Age, experience, and hours worked.

Coefficients on	1955	1969
Age	.08	−.11
Year of first full time job	−.11	−.15
Hours worked, first job, 1969	−.01*	.07
Hours worked, second job, 1969	−.03	−.12
Weeks lost illness, 1969	−.03*	−.18

*Not significant at the 5% level.

The variables in this equation which have been held constant include: education, mathematical ability, various measures of socioeconomic background of the respondent and of his wife; information on self employment and on teaching; a crude measure of risk preference, age and work experience, health, hours worked, marital status, and attitudes towards nonpecuniary rewards.

[31]It is also possible that age is a proxy for particular cohorts or vintages. While most people are within seven years of one another, the youngest people did not begin work until after serving in the military while many of the older people began work before World War II.

experience coefficient is greater later in life, even though we have deflated by the CPI. However, between 1955 and 1969 the effect of years of experience has only risen about 50% which is less than the percentage increase in average earnings of nonself-employed high school graduates or people with any other education level. That experience is more important that maturity in 1955 is not surprising given the evidence in Mincer. It is somewhat surprising to find large senescence effects in 1969 since the discussion in Bloom suggests little changes in intelligence and certain other skills before age 50 and since weeks lost through illness have been held constant[32]. However, the results may also be due to discrimination on account of age for those who were fired in 1968 or 1969.

To try to refine the work experience measure, we included both dummy variables for a length of military service after initial discharge. We find these variables insignificant which implies that the additional military experience is a good substitute for civilian experience or (contrary to the above) experience on the job is not important[33].

Earnings depend on hourly wage rates and hours worked. Unless there is a backward bending supply curve of labor, higher wage rates will lead to greater hours worked and more earnings[34]. In 1969 each additional hour per week on the first job adds \$70 to annual earnings[35]. If we use an average hourly wage rate per week of \$350, we would estimate σ in the footnote as about -1.2. Each additional hour on the second job is associated with a \$120 decrease in earnings apparently because some of

[32]Also, we have not included those with zero earnings which would include those (if any) retired or unemployed for mental or physical health reasons.

[33]In ch. 5, we find that the earlier people enter into high paying occupations, the more they earn in 1969 and that some 1955 jobs are better preparations than others, depending on one's 1969 occupation. These results suggest that some training is not general and that some people were in wrong jobs in 1955 if they wanted to maximize their lifetime earnings since the ranking of occupations is about the same in all years.

[34]Earnings $= WH$. $\partial \text{Earnings}/\partial W = H(1+\sigma)$, where $\sigma = W\partial H/H\partial W$. While this is the usual way of viewing the problem, our equations relate earnings to H. $\partial \text{Earnings}/\partial H = W(1+1/\sigma)$. With backward bending supply curves, σ might be negative.

[35]Part of this earnings increase represents the substitution of material goods for leisure. Unfortunately, the hours data which were only collected in 1969, do not mesh perfectly with the earnings data since the earnings in 1969 are those on main job only while we have separate estimates for hours on first and second job. However, the 1968 earnings data, which includes second job, gives similar results so that this caveat need not be important.

those people with low wage rates want higher material standards[36].

Despite the fact that the hours data refer to 1969, we included them in 1955. The hours on second job are still significantly negative while the hours on first job have become negative and insignificant. The two results for hours on second job suggest that the variable distinguishes between those with strong and weak tastes for material goods. Those with strong tastes have lower hourly wage rates. Not only do moonlighters work hard over long periods of time, but their wives are also more likely to be working.

Weeks lost through illness in 1969 has a negative impact on 1969 and 1955 earnings but only the 1969 coefficient is significant. The \$180 a week lost would indicate a \$9000 a year job if the figures exclude paid sick leave, but we have no way of knowing if this is how the question was interpreted. Incidentally, this variable caused the self-assessed healthiness variable used by TW to become insignificant.

7. *Nonpecuniary rewards*

There are monetary and nonmonetary rewards from a job. Suppose the nonmonetary returns are denoted by P_jN_j where j indicates an occupation. Further, suppose that occupation 0 has no nonpecuniary rewards. We would expect that, in a competitive labor market, $W_1 + PN_1 = W_0$, assuming that the two occupations require equal wages for supply and demand to be equilibrated in both markets. In some instances, we have crude measures of various N. In other cases, we cannot measure N_j directly; but if the labor market is in equilibrium, then those who prefer nonmonetary to monetary rewards will be more likely to choose occupation 1 and to have lower earnings *ceteris paribus*. This section reports the results for some variables that are thought to be measures of N or to be related to the preference of individuals for specific nonmonetary aspects of a job. For example, the respondents were asked, 'assuming that you thought that the financial possibilities were about the same, would you

[36]Also, hours on second job are negatively related to recalled estimates of initial earnings and to the probability of the wife's working in 1968.

prefer to work for yourself or for somebody else or no preference?[37,38]

In this chapter we will *assume* that answers to this and other questions indicate (large) differences in various latent traits. By traits, we mean personality and attitude characteristics. Latent traits are those that help determine behavior in many different areas, e.g. a person who is risk averse in earnings would be risk averse in all areas of decision-making under uncertainty. In fact, the answers need not represent pure differences in traits; the traits need not be latent, and the labels we use for each variable need not be appropriate. These and related issues are discussed below, especially in ch. 8.

In 1955, those who preferred to be salaried earn 6% less than the average (nonself-employed) high school graduate. See table 5. In 1969 the people who preferred to be salaried earn 11% less. It is important to realize that these results are from equations which hold constant being self-employed and amount of business assets.

We are interpreting the answer to this question as indicating risk preference; and that following the expected utility approach, risk averters in choosing their occupation give up some average expected earnings to reduce expected dispersion[39]. We further assume that these expectations are, on average, realized. Is this a reasonable interpretation? We discuss in detail in ch. 8 how this variable could correspond to an economist's definition of risk aversion. We conclude there that, in a formal sense, if respondents thought like economists, the question would distinguish between risk averters and risk lovers. In a less formal sense, people may simply be responding to their belief that this occupation is risky.

It is possible that people who failed in their original occupation chose the salaried answer because of their failure. But in ch. 8, we show that this variable is not related to a (self-reported) measure of the difference

[37] An additional question was asked in which 'about the same' was replaced with 'slightly favorable if you worked for yourself'. This second question was never significant given the first, but the first question always yielded significant coefficients in the earnings equations of various years.

[38] Recently, several other economists have tried to incorporate information on non-pecuniary returns in earnings equations. See Morgan et al., ch. 5, Antos and Rosen, or Thaler and Rosen.

[39] See Haspel for an examination of occupational choice in this sample. As shown in ch. 5, this variable has the same sign in within occupation earnings equations.

Table 5.
Nonpecuniary trade offs with earnings, relative to salary of average high school graduate.

Percentage change in earnings for several variables[b]	1955 (%)	1969 (%)	# of observations in group with designated response
Prefer to be salaried	−6	−10	962
Teacher	−10	−18	256
Reasons for taking 1972 occup. field when started[a]			
Prospects of future fin. success	−9	−17	1200
Chance for indep. work	5*	11	1519
Person-to-person contact	−2*	1*	
Chance to help others	8	8	2090
Represented a challenge	−13	−17	784
Job security	8	13	1415
Free time	−1*	−2*	

*Not significant at the 5% level.
[a]Each coefficient refers to a 'no' for an answer; hence, yes and the no responses are the omitted group.
[b]The dollar differences are divided by the earnings of the average nonself-employed high school graduate.
The variables in this equation which have been held constant include: education, mathematical ability, various measures of socioeconomic background of the respondent and of his wife; information on self employment and on teaching; a crude measure of risk preference, age and work experience, health, hours worked, marital status, and attitudes towards nonpecuniary rewards.

between actual and expected financial success[40]. In that same chapter, we indicate that the variable has effects consistent with risk aversion in other equations.

Another set of questions asked in 1972 was 'as best as you can remember, what factors influenced your decision to enter the occupational field you are in at the present time? Check yes or no to each of the

[40]An alternative explanation of the question might be that those who value being their own boss would earn less, especially since those who prefer independence in working do earn less (see below). While the results do not support the being-your-own-boss explanation, this may mean that this explanation does not dominate the risk interpretation in this sample.

following and indicate factors that were of special importance'[41]. Since we felt that the first three and last item in the footnote did not represent nonpecuniary job aspects, we did not use them, nor any of the special importance categories. In our equations, the dummy variable for each factor used was set at one if the respondent answered 'no'.

In 1969, the salary, person-to-person contact, and free time variables were not significant in preliminary runs although salary nearly was – the other variables indicate that those who were not worried about future financial success received 17% less than those who were worried (or didn't answer);[42] those not interested in independent work earn 10% more; those who wanted to help others earn 8% less; those who wanted to have a challenge earn 17% more; and those interested in job security received 13% less earnings[43]. In 1955, when many of the people were in different jobs and even occupations, nearly all the same variables are significant; and all the signs on the variables significant in 1969 are the same although the magnitude is always less than in 1969. The introduction of these variables has a big impact primarily on the various graduate education variables, which seems quite reasonable since we often think that Ph.D.'s etc. choose nonpecuniary rewards such as independence in work or helping others[44].

Intuitively, all these results seem quite plausible, and each one is internally consistent with the others. But there still is the question of whether these variables are related to nonpecuniary preferences. This

[41]'The factors were: type of training in school, type of training in military, personal contacts, salary offered, prospects of eventual financial success, chance to do interesting work, chance for independent work, chance for a lot of person to person contact, chance to help others, represented a challenge, job security, provided a lot of free time, and always liked that kind of work.

[42]The denominator as usual is the earnings of the average nonself-employed high school graduate. If the current salary variable answer is included, the coefficient is 10%.

[43]For those who want to try to replicate these findings in other studies, it is important to note that several of the variables, e.g. independence, and helping others, were not significant by themselves but became significant after the financial prospects variable was added to the equation.

[44]For a few of these variables, the answers may represent an individual's recognition of his own limitations. For example, those who like to help others may not have the aggressiveness to be a successful manager. But then the variable represents skills that determine earnings.

issue is discussed in more detail in ch. 8, where it is concluded that the variables were probably related to preferences.

The basic threads running through these findings are that people who are willing to work hard on difficult or risky projects will end up with substantially more earnings, while those who are more interested in the intrinsic rewards of the job will receive less. While this is hardly a startling conclusion, I know of no other study which has been able to obtain significant impacts after holding constant such things as education and ability[45]. Moreover, the consistency of findings between 1955 and 1969 both suggest that the 1972 survey responses are not ex post rationalizations and that the results are not due to chance correlations. These conclusions are buttressed by the finding in ch. 8 that responses to these variables are not a function of ex ante/ex post differences in monetary success.

The trade offs of earnings with nonpecuniary returns is quite large. Excluding the teacher dummy which is discussed below, but including all the other significant coefficients in table 5, we find that the differences in earnings due to various nonpecuniary preferences could be as high as 55% or \$5500 in 1969 and 40% or \$2500 in 1955 which are greater than all education differences except M.D.

The last nonpecuniary-related variable we have used is being a pre-college teacher. We find that these people earn 10 and 18% less in 1955 and 1969. The premium paid to be a teacher is even larger before the nonpecuniary variables are introduced, which seems reasonable. We cannot, however, rule out the possibility that teachers earn less because they are less able.

8. *Geographic variables*

Geographic mobility after 1955 is significant, although as shown in Appendix C, mobility between high school and 1969 does not affect earnings. Since this same post-1955 mobility variable is also significant in 1955, it seems likely that it is a proxy for other personal characteristics

[45]Thaler and Rosen have found that probability of death on a job increases earnings.

such as aggressiveness. In Appendix C, we indicate that our earnings equations differ by region.

Another piece of geographic information is very important. As is found in Parnes et al., size of area of residence (or work) is a determinant of earnings. Compared to people who live in areas with less than 10000 people, these people who live in small or large cities and towns (10000–1 million) earn \$1100 and \$500 more than those who live in rural areas in 1969 and 1955; and those who live in areas with populations in excess of 1 million earn \$2900 more and \$900 more, *ceteris paribus*. (More detailed breakdowns were used in preliminary work.) Such locational premiums can arise because of differences in costs of living or taxes, because of the advantages to the worker of a better and more varied labor market, or because certain well-paying jobs are mostly located in New York and other major cities. (If the latter explanation is true, the size variable is a proxy for other skills or contacts.)

9. *Healthiness*

Each week of employment lost through illness reduces earnings by \$180 and 1969. If people are paid on a weekly basis and if for some reason they excluded from their answer the number of weeks of paid sick leave, the implied annual earnings would be about \$9000 or about half the average earnings in this sample. This may suggest that lower paid people are less healthy or that earnings determine healthiness, i.e. the causation in the equation is wholly or partially wrong. But the assumption on paid sick leave may be wrong or certain diseases are occupation specific. More interestingly the weeks–ill variable reduces the self-assessment of health variables, used by TW, to insignificance. This variable is not quite significant at the 5% level in 1955 although still negative.

Another variable which may be related to health is the respondent's 1969 weight and its square of which the latter is negative and both are significant. The equation implies that for these men at this age, the maximum earnings in both years are received by 200 pounders. Once again, there is the possibility that earnings determine weight although research on twins has indicated that adult weight has a large genetic component, and interestingly, a slightly smaller heritability component than adult height, which has a positive but insignificant effect in this sample[46].

10. Business assets

The respondents were asked for their 'earnings' without the concept being defined. But we would expect the self-employed to report their net income from their business since most people would find it difficult to separate earnings derived from labor from those derived from capital. Of course, the returns from financial capital do indicate the marginal product of various skills, but the quantity of such capital may be correlated with a number of the other variables. Thus, to help purify our estimates of the effect on earnings, we must hold constant the returns to financial capital. To try to hold constant the returns from capital, we have included a dummy variable for self-employed businessmen, another dummy for self-employed professionals and most importantly, a continuous variable on amount of business assets[47]. We shall interpret the coefficients on the business asset variable as the rate of return on financial capital invested in business[48]. All of these variables were only measured in 1969. The extra measurement error involved in using these variables in 1955 undoubtedly affects the comparability of our answers and our R^2, although comparisons of 1955 and 1969 equations which only use data available in both years indicate that general conclusions on R^2 are not affected.

In 1969, the coefficient on the business asset variable, which is an estimate of the before tax rate of return, is .12. Such a figure is not unlike

[46]See Mittler on heritability of weight and height.

[47]It also includes nonresidential real estate and other nonspecified items. The variable is crude since people were only asked to check one of 8 categories including 'don't have' and over $80000.

[48]This interpretation, however, may be wrong for several reasons. Consider the results obtained from regressing a person's earnings which equal wage income plus returns from capital (assuming that education, etc. is held constant by sample design). That is, we regress $W + rk = cK$. The expected value of c would be equal to $E\Sigma(w + rK)(K)/\Sigma K^2 = r + \Sigma(wK/K^2)$. If wage income and business assets are not correlated (linearly) the coefficient on K will be an unbiased estimate of the returns from capital but if people with more capital also have higher wage rates (education, etc. constant) then c is biased upwards as an estimate of r.

the 7 to 10 estimates usually found in studies such as Kravis (1959)[49,50]. The dummy variable for self-employed businessman is still significant although assets and hours worked are included in the 1969 equations, and equals 10% of the standardized base. The self-employed professionals, who may not have much in the way of financial investments, receive 31% more than the nonself-employed professionals (although the denominator is too low since for comparability we have divided by the average earnings of high school graduates).

In 1955, the coefficient on 1969 business assets is still highly significant (a 't' of 11) at .03 even though the growth of assets must not have been uniform during the period; and some people must have changed their self-employment/salaried status. Probably because of the increased measurement error involved in using the 1969 asset and hours variables in 1955, the 1969 self-employment businessman dummy is as important in 1955 as in 1969. On the other hand, the 1969 self-employed professional dummy is not significant presumably because many of these people were salaried in 1955 and had not had a chance to display their true worth to their employers.

11. Unobserved variables and luck

The variables included in our 1955 and 1969 equations do not explain all the variance in earnings and do not encompass all the possible personal characteristics that could determine earnings. The remaining variables can be expressed as $\Sigma Z_j b_j + u$ where the Z_j are systematic determinants of earnings and u is 'luck'. It does not seem unreasonable to assume that luck is uncorrelated with the other variables included in our equations. It is less likely that all the Z_j's are uncorrelated, but clearly we make this assumption when we treat our estimated coefficients as being unbiased.

Suppose, therefore, that we maintain this assumption about the Z's and

[49]Also the asset variable must be measured with error since people only checked categories into which their assets fell and because the data was taken from an item in which real estate holdings could be included with the business assets.

[50]Christenson has argued that because unincorporated businesses do not have to pay the corporate income tax, a 7 to 10% return is consistent with the 15% before-tax return made by corporations.

the other variables. Then the observed residuals in 1955 and in 1969 are an estimate of $W_t = \Sigma Z_{jt} b_t + u_t + v_t$ where the t subscripts indicate that the systematic variables, their coefficients, and luck can all change over time, and v represents 'measurement error', that arises because the observed residuals are based on estimated rather than true coefficients of the included variables. Now consider the regression of

$$W_{69j} = {}^{d}W_{55j} + e_j \tag{3.1}$$

$$\hat{d} = \frac{(\Sigma Z_{55j} b_{55j} + u_{55j} + v_{55j})(\Sigma Z_{69j} b_{69} + u_{69j} + v_{69j})}{(\Sigma Z_{55j} b_{55j} + u_{55j} + v_{55j})^2}. \tag{3.2}$$

Suppose that u and v are independent over time and u and v are not correlated with each other or with the Z. Then the expected value of $\hat{d}$ is

$$E(\hat{d}) = E\left(\frac{d\sigma^2_{Z_{55}b_{55}}}{\sigma^2_{Z_{55}b_{55}} + \sigma^2_u + \sigma^2_v}\right) = d\left(\frac{1}{(1 + \sigma^2_u + \sigma^2_v)/\sigma^2_{Z_{55}b_{55}}}\right). \tag{3.3}$$

Thus, $\hat{d}$ is biased towards zero, as is the estimate of the contribution of Z to the explanation of the variance of earnings; and the correlation of the two residuals will understate the importance of the unmeasured systematic variables. This understatement is reinforced if Z's vary randomly over time. Still, such correlations give us a lower bound to the contribution of σ^2_Z and an upper bound to the contribution of σ^2_u to the variance of earnings.

The residuals, of course, can be calculated as $Y_t - X_t b_t = W_t$. By construction, ordinary least squares estimates of W_t are independent of X_t. But, in our equations, X is the same in 1969 as in 1955 (except for age which varies by a constant, and education which increased for about 8% of the sample). Suppose we ignore the change in education. Since Y_{55} is equal to $W_{55} + Xb_{55}$, we know that

$$Y_{69} = Xb_{69} + Y_{55}\gamma_{69} + W_{69} = X(b_{69} + \gamma b_{55}) + W_{55}\gamma + W_{69}.$$

That is, the coefficient on Y_{55} is also the coefficient on W_{55}. The results are shown in the 1969 table at the end of the chapter. In comparison with eqn. (3.2), the R^2 has increased from .32 to .42. Thus, systematic variables could explain at least 43% of the variance in earnings. In addition, the Y_{55} 'variable', with a t value of 29, is highly significant.

12. Conclusion

The many and varied comparisons made in this chapter lead to several important conclusions. First, the effects of nearly all variables change during a person's life cycle and in general display a profile that increases with age. Second, the profiles are steeper for the education variables than most other variables, although as shown in more detail below, the steepest profile is for those who attended private school. Third, even after holding constant a wide variety of variables, we still find that education leads to a large and statistically significant difference in earnings. These differences, however, are relatively small in comparison with those arising from the conglomeration of family background, attitudes and nonpecuniary preferences and are no larger than the differences which are the result of, or are due to, ability.

In addition, it appears that simple, crude questions can yield extremely useful information on preferences. Finally, it appears that different measures of family background than normally used are the more appropriate ones. These new measures may relate more closely to the structure of family environment than parental education and occupation.

Table 6.
1955 earnings equations.

Independent variables	Eqn 1 coef.	*t* value	Eqn 2 coef.	*t* value
Education:				
Some college	.63	4.1	−.21	−1.0*
Bachelor's	1.04	6.8	.13	.6*
Some grad.	.79	2.9	−.05	−.2*
Master's	.45	1.8*	−.15	−.5*
Ph.D. + L.L.B. + M.D.	.93	2.1	.22	.5*
L.L.B.	.07	.14*	−.38	−.8*
M.D.	4.25	6.5	3.49	5.3
Ability:				
2nd fifth	.39	2.2	.28	1.6*
3rd fifth	.41	2.4	.31	1.9*
4th fifth	.62	3.5	.56	3.3
top 5th fifth	1.00	5.7	.82	4.8

Table 6 (*contd*).

Independent variables	Eqn 1 coef.	*t* value	Eqn 2 coef.	*t* value
Biography:				
2nd fifth / 3rd fifth	.29	1.9*	.21	1.5*
4th fifth / 5th fifth	.94	6.1	.66	4.5
Father education	.03	1.9*		
Mother education	.10	2.9		
Religion:				
Jewish	2.68	10.6	2.00	7.7
Protestant	−.15	−1.3*	−.15	1.3*
Attended religious school often			−.51	−2.0
Attended religious school never			−.01	−.1*
Father-in-law education			.05	3.0
Mother-in-law high school+			−.01	−.1*
Time spent on sports			.06	1.7*
Time spent on chores			−.05	−1.3*
Time spent on hobbies			.04	1.0*
Time spent on part-time job			.07	2.1
Never moved before high school			−.06	−.5*
Attended private high school			1.49	3.9
Attended private elementary school			.23	.3*
Factors influenced entering occupation				
Future financial prospects, no = 1			−.54	−4.2
Independence, no = 1			.27	2.1
Challenging work, no = 1			−.76	−5.0
Help others, no = 1			.48	3.8
Job security, no = 1			.48	4.0
Prefers to be salaried			−.37	−2.9
Other assets (own business, real estate), 1969			.03	11.5
Self-employed businessman, 1969			.72	4.4
Self-employed professional, 1969			.45	1.7*
Teacher, pre-college	−1.45	−5.6	−.61	−2.4
Hours on main job, 1969				
Hours on second job, 1969			−.03	−3.3
Weeks lost from illness, 1969	−.03	−1.6*	−.03	−1.6*
Mobility 1955 to 1969			.08	2.7
Age	.07	2.9	.08	3.3
Year of first job	−.10	4.4	−.11	−5.1
Current residence in town of 50, to 1000000			.46	3.6

Table 6 (*contd*).

Independent variables	Eqn 1 coef.	t value	Eqn 2 coef.	t value
Current resident in excess of 1000000			.92	5.1
College quality (Gourman rating)			.0014	3.5
Weight, 1969			6.68	2.7
Weight squared, 1969			−1.69	−2.5
Dummy for nonresponse in 1972	.76	3.4	1.23	3.9
Constant	6.00	3.5	−.97	−.3*
R^2	.10		.19	
Standard error	3.61		3.43	
Degrees of freedom	4573		4548	

13. Definition of variables

The variables used in this and subsequent tables are defined in terms of the 1955, 1969, 1971, 1972 surveys – I, II, III, IV – and military records, MR. The variables are listed in order of use.

Earnings in 1955 – source I, Q5; multiplied by 12 to put on an annual basis, in thousands of dollars.

Education in 1969 – source II, Education Section, Q1. Broken up into dummy variables which do not overlap except for Ph.D. + L.L.B. + M.D. with L.L.B. and M.D. Ph.D. includes other earned doctorates. High school graduates are the omitted group. (Education in 1955 is taken from same source except adjusted for education taken after 1955 as indicated in II, Education Section Q1.)[51]

Ability – source MR. Factor analysis was performed by A. Beaton to reduce 17 test scores to 4 abilities which are described in TW and are reproduced in Appendix A. The factor used loads heavily on mathematical and some verbal tests. The factor analysis and break points for the fifths were based on the 9700 people in the TH sample. Dummy variables for being in a fifth are used. Bottom fifth is omitted.

Biography – source MR. Factor analysis was performed by TH on some 120 biographical items dealing with parental income and respondent's

[51]TW used a different method which yielded slightly inferior R^2's.

Table 7.
1969 earnings equations.

Independent variables	Coef.	t value	Coef.	t value	Coef.	t value
Education:						
Some college	1.88	5.0	−1.10	−2.0	−.82	−1.6*
Bachelor's	3.68	9.4	.16	.3*	.11	.2*
Some grad.	3.05	4.7	−.01	.0*	.11	.2*
Master's	3.81	6.5	1.15	1.6*	1.48	2.3
Ph.D. + L.L.B. + M.D.	5.47	5.8	2.52	2.6	2.62	2.9
L.L.B.	3.89	3.4	1.12	1.1*	1.28	1.3*
M.D.	9.14	5.9	4.13	2.9	.77	.6*
Ability:						
2nd fifth	.94	2.2	.54	1.4*	.29	.8*
3rd fifth	1.00	2.4	.71	1.9*	.43	1.2*
4th fifth	1.55	3.7	1.40	3.7	.89	2.6
(top) 5th fifth	2.54	5.9	1.98	5.1	1.22	3.4
Biography:						
2nd fifth	.84	2.3	.56	1.7*	.36	1.2*
3rd fifth						
4th fifth	1.76	4.7	.80	2.4	.21	.7*
5th fifth						
Father education	.07	1.8*				
Mother education	.28	3.5				
Religion:						
Jewish	6.79	11.0	4.13	7.0	2.32	4.3
Protestant	−.83	−2.9	−.93	−3.6	−.79	−3.3
Attended religious school often			−1.14	−2.0	−.69	−1.3*
Attended religious school never			−.33	−1.2*	−.31	−1.3*
Father-in-law education			.10	2.7	.05	1.7*
Mother-in law high school +			.57	2.1	.58	2.3
Time spent on sports			.26	2.9	.20	2.5

Table 7 (*contd*).

Independent variables	Coef.	*t* value	Coef.	*t* value	Coef.	*t* value
Time spent on chores			−.27	−2.8	−.22	−2.6
Time spent on hobbies			−.15	−1.7*	−.18	−2.3
Time spent on part-time job			.29	3.8	.23	3.2
Never moved before high school			−.43	−1.7*	−.37	−1.6*
Attended private high school			2.80	3.3	1.46	1.8*
Attended private elementary school			2.98	1.6*	2.79	1.7*
Factors influenced entering occupation						
Future financial prospects, No = 1			−1.77	−6.0	−1.28	−4.7
Independence, no = 1			1.19	4.1	.95	3.6
Challenging work, no = 1			−1.70	−4.9	−1.00	−3.1
Help others, no = 1			.86	3.0	.43	1.6*
Job security, no = 1			1.41	5.2	.96	3.8
Prefers to be salaried			−1.00	−3.4	−.66	−2.4
Other assets (own business, real estate), 1969			.12	20.4	.09	17.0
Self-employed businessman, 1969			1.09	2.9	.40	1.2*
If employed professional, 1969			3.30	5.5	2.87	5.2
Teacher, pre-college	−4.41	−6.7	−1.86	−3.1	−1.40	−2.5
Hours on main job, 1969			.07	4.7	.08	5.9
Hours on second job, 1969			−.12	−5.2	−.09	−4.2

Weeks lost from illness, 1969	−.18	−3.6	−.18	−3.8	−.15	−3.4
Mobility 1955 to 1969			.33	5.1	.26	4.4
Age	−.13	−2.1	−.11	−1.9*	−.18	−3.5
Year of first job	−.17	−3.2	−.15	−3.1	−.05	−1.2*
Current residence in town of 50, to 1000000			1.09	3.7	.67	2.5
Current resident in excess of 1000000			2.89	7.0	2.06	5.4
College quality (Gourman rating)			.0044	4.3	.0031	3.2
Weight, 1969 (100's lbs.)			24.73	4.4	18.57	3.6
Weight squared, 1969			−6.45	−4.2	−4.90	−3.5
Dummy for nonresponse in 1972	1.67	3.1	2.54	3.6	1.42	2.2
Y/55					.90	29.2
Constant	21.91	5.2	−7.74	−1.2*	−7.10	−1.2*
B^2	.14		.32		.42	
Stand error	8.75		7.80		7.16	
Degrees of freedom	4573		4547		4546	

hobbies and tastes. See TH. Bottom fifth omitted and dummy variables for being in middle and top 40% used.

Religion – source II, Activities Section, Q2. Catholics, atheists, agnostics, and no answers are the omitted category.

Attended religious school – source IV, Family Background section, Q8.

In-law education – source II, Education Section, Q2. If no answers, the mode is used. Father-in-law is a continuous variable in years, mother-in-law is a dummy variable for high school graduate or more.

Time spent variables – source IV, Family Background Section, Q10.

Never moved before high school – source IV, Family Background Section, Q3.

Private schools – source IV, Family Background Section, Q6. Omitted category includes public and parochial schools and no answers.

Factors influenced entering occupation – source IV, Occupational History Section, Q3. No. = 1, all others = 0.

Prefers to be salaried – source II, Social Economic and Political Attitudes Section, Q4. Indifferent, prefer to be self-employed and no answer are zero.

Other assets – source II, Assets, Debts, Savings and Purchases, Q1. Thousands of dollars. Mid-points of ranges used, no answer or don't have are set at zero. Open-ended class set at $99000.

Self-employed in 1969 – source II, Job Description Section, Q1.

Pre-college Teacher in 1969 – source II, Work Experience Section, Q1.

Pre-college teacher in 1955 – source I, Q4.

Hours in 1969 – source II, Work Experience Section, Q1. No answer set at 39.

Weeks lost illness 1969 – source II, Work Experience Section, Q2.

Mobility 1955 to 1969 – Addresses used in making surveys I and II. Dummy variable = 1 if change in state.

Year of first job – source II, Work Experience Section, Q1.

Current residence – source IV, General Information Section, Q6. Omitted category is less than 50000 and no answer.

College quality – source II, Education Section, Q1.

Gourman ratings. When no rating in Gourman, estimates were made by Educational Testing Service.

Weight – source II, General Information Q6; 0's replaced by mean in hundreds of pounds. When no answer, mean is used.

CHAPTER 4

Inequality: extent and causes

In this, and indeed, most other samples, the distribution of earnings is skewed to the right[1]. Since most people *assume* that something called 'ability' or capacity is normally distributed, much attention has been paid to the question of why earnings exhibit a skewed distribution[2]. Becker and Mincer have demonstrated that such distributions can be generated by 'acquired' human capital models which can also explain changes in the shape of the distribution as people age. Mandelbrot explains skewness solely in terms of many different inherited skills. Champernowne, Aitchison and Brown, and others have shown that stochastic processes that operate continuously can generate skewed distributions[3]. In Friedman's model, skewness arises from behavior towards risk rather than differences in abilities.

Most of these theories are not mutually exclusive. In addition all of the theories make various assumptions about the functioning of the labor market and/or the distribution of skills, events, etc. Therefore, it is appropriate for us both to test various hypotheses generated by each theory to determine if the theory is correct, and to estimate the contribution of each theory or (more realistically) a set of variables to earnings inequality. This chapter will be concerned primarily with the effects of various sets of variables on inequality. In ch. 7, we will examine in more detail the validity of the different hypotheses.

[1]See Lydall or Kravis (1962) for surveys of other samples. Lebergett suggests that among full-time males who are not self-employed, the earnings distribution (in 1959) approaches normality. For some purposes, however, the self-employed and unemployed should be included in the earnings distribution.

[2]There is little direct evidence on the distribution of capacity. I.Q. scores, for example, are generally *scored* so as to be normally distributed.

[3]For an excellent summary of all these models, see Mincer (1970).

1. Inequality in earnings

The inequality in earnings can be measured in several ways[4]. For example, in ch. 2, we used the Lorenz curve as an overall summary. For the reader's convenience, the Lorenz curves for 1955 and 1969 are presented once again in fig. 1[5]. Also drawn in that figure is a diagonal, which is the Lorenz curve that would be observed if each person had the same earnings. In all years studied, earnings are not distributed equally and are below the diagonal.

As explained in ch. 2, all summary measures of relative inequality of two Lorenz curves will yield the same ranking *provided* the two curves do not intersect[6]. Conversely, if the curves intersect, there are always some measures that would disagree on whether curve 1 or 2 is more unequal. Results of the Kolmogorov–Smirnov Test in ch. 2 indicate that the 1969 curve is statistically different from (more unequal than) the 1955 curve. The cause of this increase in inequality will be examined below; but a mechanical explanation is that when individuals are grouped by their position in the earnings distribution, the growth rate in average earnings was higher for each successive tenth. For example, the average level of earnings in the bottom tenth increased from \$3.5 to \$7.2 thousand or 106%, while in the top tenth the growth rate was 220%. (See table 2 below.)

In ch. 2, we also examined the Lorenz curves for various education and mental ability groups[7]. In either 1955 or 1969, the Lorenz curves for any two mutually exclusive groups, such as high school and some college, were never significantly different at the 5% level although many were at the 10% level. For any particular group, the 1969 curve always was beneath the corresponding 1955 curve; and the maximum differences which range from 6 to 10 points were always significant at the 5% level. Thus, there is little difference in inequality in earnings between various education and ability groups in any year, but more inequality in each case in 1969 than in 1955.

[4]See Atkinson, Mincer (1974), and Kravis (1962).

[5]The initial year data have been adjusted to a common starting year. See ch. 3.

[6]See Atkinson.

[7]The education and ability groups are those defined in ch. 3.

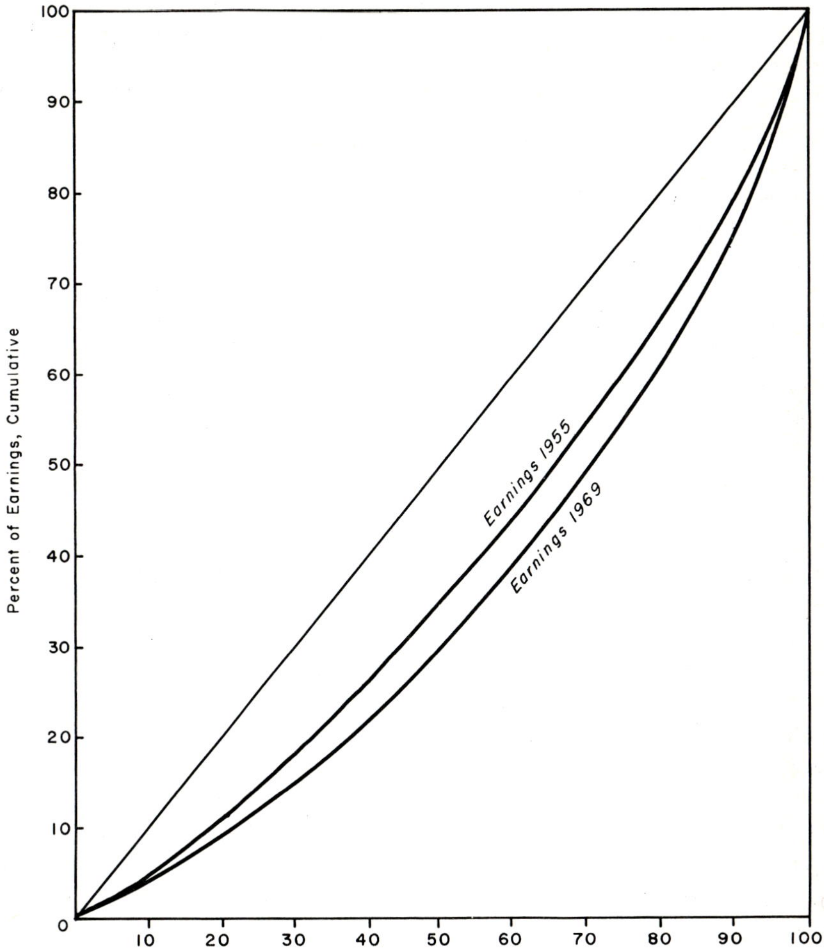

Fig. 1. Percent of people, cumulative.

2. *From variance to kurtosis*

Thus far, we have indicated that earnings inequality has varied from year to year. For many purposes, however, it is necessary to ask how particular features of the distribution have changed over time and to what extent these features and their change are the consequence of the distribution of education, mental ability, etc. A quantifiable and, at times, decomposable description of a distribution can be obtained from various 'moments' of the distribution[8]. The first four moments measure the mean, variance, skewness and kurtosis of the distribution.

As shown in table 1, 1969 average earnings (in 1958 prices), were \$14500. As indicated in ch. 2, this average far exceeds the average earnings for men in the same cohort with the same education – reflecting the restricted and particular nature of the sample. In 1969 our standard deviation, σ, is \$9.4[9]. In some types of labor markets we would expect σ to increase when average earnings did. For these cases, a standardized measure is provided by the coefficient of variation, σ/mean, which is about $\frac{2}{3}$ in 1969.

Several measures of symmetry have been proposed in the literature. To avoid reranking the observations as we hold constant education and other sets of variables, we will use the third moment standardized (to eliminate scale effects) by the second moment[10]. A distribution is skewed to the right when this measure is positive, as is our 1969 estimate of 3.0. At the 5% level we can reject the null hypothesis that the population is normally distributed (which is symmetric), using a test developed by Fisher.

[8]We will assume that the expected values of the first four moments can be estimated from the actual value. This need not be true. For example, if the distribution were Pareto, the expected value of the variance would be infinite although a number could be obtained from the data.

[9]To insure comparability with the regression results and to save on costs, the 1955 and 1969 statistics are based on the approximately 4600 people who reported earnings in both years.

[10]The formula for skewness is

$$\frac{\Sigma(X_i - \bar{X})^3}{N} \Big/ \left(\frac{\Sigma(X_i - \bar{X})^2}{N}\right)^{3/2}.$$

Scheffé, ch. 10, recommends using the standardized variable for decomposition of the 3rd and 4th moments.

Table 1.
Moments of earnings and LN earnings in 1955 and 1969.

Year	Mean	Standard deviation[a]	Skewness[b]	Kurtosis[c]
Earnings				
1955 (58$)	7.3	3.8	5.4	62.0
1969 (58$)	14.5	9.4	3.0	13.9
Percentage change 55–69	100	147	−44	−78
LN earnings				
1955 (58$)	1.9	.38	.73	2.67
1969 (58$)	2.5	.50	.67	.92

[a] $\Sigma(Y_i - \bar{Y})^2/(N-1)$.
[b] $\Sigma(Y_i - \bar{Y})^3/[\Sigma(Y_i - \bar{Y})^2]^{3/2} n^{1/2}$.
[c] $(\Sigma(Y_i - \bar{Y})^4/\sigma^4)n - 3.0$.

Kurtosis measures the frequency of observations in the tails or near the mean of the distribution. We use the fourth moment divided (standardized) by the second[11]. From this ratio, we subtract 3 which is the expected value of the kurtosis in a normal distribution. Larger values such as our 12, indicate that there are too many observations in the tails or too few near the mean as compared with the normal curve.

Next, let us examine the 1955 results. Mean earnings are $7300 (in 1958 prices). The standard deviation is $3.8 and the coefficient of variation is about $\frac{1}{2}$. Our skewness and kurtosis estimates are 5.4 and 62.0 respectively, neither of which would be in accord with the null hypothesis that the distribution is normal. Thus, in both 1955 and 1969, the distribution of earnings is skewed to the right and has larger numbers of people in the tails.

Given the oft-mentioned differences between our sample and the U.S. population, the results on the various inequality measures in any one year have restricted interest at least until we control for education, ability, etc. But the changes during the 14 years are of substantial interest – especially

[11]The formula for kurtosis is:

$$\left[\frac{\Sigma(X_i - \bar{X})^4}{N} \Big/ \left(\frac{\Sigma(X_i - \bar{X})^2}{N}\right)^2\right] - 3.0.$$

since such data are not generally available over such a time span and so late in the life cycle.

Between 1955 and 1969, mean earnings in constant dollars grew by about 100%. Since the standard deviation increased by a greater amount than the mean, the coefficients of variation in table 1 increased by 27%[12]. The changes in the skewness and kurtosis measures are both negative. Thus, contrary to the usual interpretation of stochastic theories, the distribution is becoming *less* asymmetric and less deviant from a normal curve as the people age (although the 1969 curve is far from a normal curve).

The skewness and kurtosis estimates are divided by the standard deviation (raised to the third or fourth power). (The unstandardized third and fourth moments grew less than the rescaled standard deviation.) Since the Lorenz curves analysis indicated that the bottom (top) tenth of people held a smaller (larger share of total earnings in 1969 than 1955 and since the third and fourth moments give more weight than the second moment to extreme observations, the above results imply that the earnings of people in the middle portion of the distribution must be further from the mean in 1969 than 1955. Table 2, which contains the average earnings for people who fall into a particular tenth in a given year, confirms this[13]. That is, the lowest average increase in earnings is in the bottom tenth; and the average increase is larger the higher the tenth. (This is generally true within education groups but there are a few exceptions.)

One skewed distribution that has been used to describe the earnings distribution is the log normal. In table 1, we also present the moments for the log of earnings. The skewness and kurtosis results in this table are not consistent with the null hypothesis that earnings in 1955 or 1969 are distributed log normally. Careful analysis of nationwide random samples has generally concluded that earnings do not follow the log normal distribution for high levels of income, but probably because of the

[12]Given our earlier results on (nonintersecting) Lorenz curves and Atkinson's theorems, the coefficients of variation and the standard error are measures of inequality which must increase.

[13]Later, when we examine the growth rates for people who were in a particular tenth in 1955, we find the highest growth rate for those at the bottom in 1955. This is not a contradiction, since in the present discussion, we are comparing people in particular tenths in each year, rather than the same people in both years.

Table 2.
Average earnings in various tenths in the earnings distribution and their percentage change in 1955 and 1969 (thous. $).

	Total			High school			Some college			Bachelors			Graduate		
%	1955 $	1969 $	%Δ 55 to 69	1955 $	1969 $	%Δ	1955 $	1969 $	%Δ	1955 $	1969 $	%Δ	1955 $	1969 $	%Δ
Bottom 10	3.5	7.2	106	2.8	5.9	111	3.1	6.4	106	3.4	7.5	121	3.1	7.5	142
10 ≤ 20	4.4	9.6	118	4.0	8.3	108	4.4	9.4	114	4.8	11.4	138	4.5	11.5	156
20 ≤ 30	4.9	11.0	129	4.6	9.3	102	4.8	10.3	115	5.3	12.8	141	5.0	13.2	164
30 ≤ 40	5.3	12.4	134	4.8	10.1	110	5.3	11.7	121	5.7	14.6	156	5.4	14.9	176
40 ≤ 50	5.8	14.1	143	5.2	11.2	115	5.8	13.1	126	6.1	15.9	161	6.0	16.4	173
50 ≤ 60	6.1	15.5	154	5.5	12.2	122	6.1	14.9	144	6.6	17.9	171	6.4	18.3	186
60 ≤ 70	6.9	17.8	157	6.0	13.6	127	6.8	16.6	144	7.2	19.9	176	7.1	20.7	192
70 ≤ 80	7.6	20.7	172	6.5	15.6	140	7.4	19.4	162	8.3	23.0	177	8.8	30.8	300
80 ≤ 90	8.9	26.6	200	7.6	20.1	164	8.6	25.7	199	9.8	28.7	193	9.8	33.7	283
90 ≤ 100	14.2	46.0	224	10.1	35.3	250	14.0	45.8	227	11.2	48.6	334	12.8	49.9	290

restricted distribution of education, mental ability and age in our sample, the deviations from log normalcy (on a chart not shown) are greater and occur over a wider range of earnings in this sample.

3. Sources of variance, skewness, and inequality

Our sample is, of course, better educated, mentally more able, probably less risk averse, and more limited in age than the population. Since all these characteristics affect earnings in our equations in ch. 3, and since their distribution is different than in the population, there is no reason to expect to find that the distribution of earnings is the same as that in the population. Despite this, we can still use the sample to study some problems of interest. For example, suppose the true equation *in the population* is

$$Y_i = X_i a + u_i \tag{4.1}$$

where X_i is a vector of (measured) independent variables, a the associated vector of coefficients and u_i are errors arising from random events and unmeasured variables. Because our distribution of the X's differs from the population, we have an unequally weighted stratified sample. It is well known that such samples yield unbiased estimates of the a's. Thus, we can use the equations we have developed to examine the effect of the various X's on earnings, for the range of each X in the sample. Moreover, as long as the u's are distributed the same as in the population, we can study the distribution of $Y - Xa = u$ to determine what the population distribution would be if everyone had the same education, ability, etc[14].

In examining the sources of various aspects of inequality, several things must be noted. First, since the equation's coefficients are selected so as to minimize the variance of the residuals with no attention given to the skewness or kurtosis, the results (on sources) are less reliable for

[14]We are interpreting each a as an estimate of the wage paid to a particular x. If the supply of any x changed, we would expect its wage, as well as wages of other x's to change. Thus, we are only studying the partial adjustment of inequality to changes in education, etc.

these latter two measures than for the variance[15]. Second, despite, this caveat, the effects of the X's on skewness or kurtosis might be larger than those on variance. For example, suppose the variable being considered is a zero one dummy variable, Z. The ones in the Z variable could all be located just so that eliminating the effect of Z would eliminate completely any (not normal) kurtosis or skewness in the earnings distribution. Finally, since most of our variables have been transformed into dummy variables, the effects of, say, schooling depend on the distribution of people by education level and their coefficients[16].

Table 3 contains estimates for 1969 of the standard error, skewness, and kurtosis with the latter two standardized by the standard error raised to the appropriate power[17].

We present the estimates for earnings (Y) and residual earnings, ($Y - X^*a$) where X^*a refers to a subset or all of the variables used in the equations in tables 6 and 7 of ch. 3. It is worth noting that if we had estimated an equation with just a subset of the X's, we would have obtained different estimates of these coefficients (unless the omitted parts of X were orthogonal to the included ones). But since such coefficients would be biased estimates of the true parameters, it was felt that it was better to use the estimates from the comprehensive equation[18,19].

As discussed earlier, the standard error of earnings in 1969 is \$9.4. Using the most comprehensive equation available, the standard error of the residual earnings is reduced by about 18% to \$7.8 in row 2 of table 3.

[15]Since most of our variables are (zero, one) dummies, our coefficients are estimates of the mean in various cells. Provided our model specifications, including interactions and homoskedasticity, are correct the residuals represent the distribution within various cells and can be used to study skewness and kurtosis.

[16]Some models relate earnings to b (years of schooling). We can convert our dummy variables into this form by changing the b's to b^* such that b^* (years) equals the average difference in earnings between two education levels.

[17]See Scheffé, ch. 10. This standardization is appropriate since we are primarily interested in the question of whether the distribution would be normal or would be much less skewed if ability, etc., were the same for everyone. But variables which reduced the residuals will also reduce u^3 or u^4; thus, the resulting series could be as skewed although $\Sigma(Y_i - \bar{Y})^3$ would be smaller.

[18]However, part of the effects of, say, education may be appearing in other coefficients whose variables are partially determined by education.

[19]Some calculations based on earlier equations with different coefficients are presented in Appendix E.

Table 3.
Sources of inequality in 1969 and 1955.

	Standard error	Skewness	Kurtosis
1969			
Y	9.42	3.05	13.90
$Y - Y_1$	7.75	2.76	14.75
$Y - Y_2$	9.11	3.22	15.27
$Y - Y_3$	9.33	3.11	14.31
$Y - Y_4$	8.63	2.82	13.39
$Y - Y_5$	9.20	3.12	14.61
$Y - Y_6$	9.33	3.05	13.91
$Y - Y_7$	9.06	3.11	14.78
$Y - Y_8$	9.37	3.01	13.71
1955			
Y	3.81	5.35	61.99
$Y - Y_1$	3.41	5.56	78.24
$Y - Y_2$	3.74	5.47	65.09
$Y - Y_3$	3.78	5.41	62.88
$Y - Y_4$	3.65	5.40	68.50
$Y - Y_5$	3.74	5.46	64.29
$Y - Y_6$	3.80	5.32	62.34
$Y - Y_7$	3.69	5.42	65.12
$Y - Y_8$	3.80	5.33	61.99

The Y_1 through Y_8 series are based on eqn 2 in tables 6 and 7 of ch. 3.

Y_1 = all variables.

Y_2 = education coefficients, including M.D. and L.L.B., and the Gourman rating.

Y_3 = mental ability variables.

Y_4 = business assets, and the self-employed businessmen and professional dummies.

Y_5 = prefer to be salaried and the 4 other non-pecuniary variables.

Y_6 = age, year of first job, hours worked, hours on second job.

Y_7 = time spent, private schools, in law, biography, religion, size of current town, never move variables.

Y_8 = teacher, no response in '72, weeks lost from illness, age entered school, religious school attendance, and weight variables.

The remaining rows in the table indicate the effects of various sets of variables, which are identified at the bottom of the table. For purposes of reference, Y_2 will be called education, Y_3 mental ability, Y_4 self employment, Y_5 nonpecuniary trade offs, Y_6 work-related experiences, Y_7 socioeconomic standing (although size of current residence is included), and Y_8 is miscellany.

The self-employment data, which, for the most part, indicate differences in financial investment rather than in skills, reduce the standard error by 8% with business assets being the most important single variable. The SES variables reduce σ by 5%. The quantity and quality of education variables (including M.D. and L.L.B.) reduce σ by less than 4% and all other sets of variables have even smaller impacts on σ. The reductions in σ are, incidentally, the partial R's for each set of variables but because reductions in variance depend upon the covariance of the independent variable, the effects of the individual rows are not additive[20]. Other than presenting the partial R's, these results mostly restate those presented in the discussion of the regression analysis although education is more important than in the discussion of the range.

In the sample, the standardized skewness measure is 3.05. As shown in the $Y - Y_1$ row, the full set of variables reduces the skewness, standardized by the second moment of the $Y - Y_1$ series, by 10% to 2.76[21]. Thus, even if education, ability, SES, business assets, etc., were equal for all individuals, the earnings distribution would be about 90% as skewed as originally, or in other words, our variables explain more of the standard error than of skewness.

Which of the variables held constant contribute to this reduction in skewness? Interestingly when education, ability, and the nonpecuniary trade offs are held constant individually, the *standardized* skewness measure *increases* between 1 and 5%. On the other hand, the self-employment variables *reduce* the relative skewness by 7%; and the miscellaneous variables in Y_8 reduce skewness 1%.

Thus, we can conclude that if everyone in the sample had the same education, ability, and nonpecuniary preferences, the earnings distribu-

[20]All the moments in table 3 are calculated about the mean that applies to each row.
[21]The reduction in $\Sigma(u_i^3)$ is about 50%.

tion would have been slightly more skewed[22]. We can also conclude that differences in self employment (size of business assets and being self-employed) have contributed greatly to the existing skewness in the distribution in this sample.

Now let us examine kurtosis. In the sample the standardized kurtosis measure has a value of 13.9 which is far from and significantly different from the zero expected in the normal distribution[23,24]. The standardized kurtosis measure of the residuals in eqn 2 is increased by 6%. Looking at the other rows, we find that only holding constant self employment and the miscellany in Y_8 has led to a reduction in relative kurtosis. Even with self employment held constant, the distribution of earnings would exhibit kurtosis. On the other hand, the elimination of education differences leads to a big increase in kurtosis. This suggests that education pushes more people away from the mean and makes for a smoother transition to the tails whose existence is not related to education.

One striking aspect of table 3 is the substantial role played by self employment. Lebergett has suggested that among full-time employees (plus the institutionalized population), the earnings distribution is approximately normal with skewness etc. in the population arising from self employment and unemployment. We have recalculated our results for 1969 separately for the nonself-employed and self-employed nonfarm businessman and professionals. Since below we will discuss inequality within various occupations with adjustments based on each of the within occupation equations, we only discuss these results briefly.

We find (in tables not shown) that for the nonself-employed, the standard error is somewhat less than in the sample as a whole but that the 1969 earnings are as skewed and depart from the normal and log normal distributions at least as much as the total sample does. The standard error of earnings for the self-employed is substantially greater. However, their skewness and kurtosis are smaller than for the nonself-employed. Indeed, the self-employed 1969 earnings are distributed log normally. Using the coefficients from the overall equation, we find a reduction of a bit more

[22]This increase is partly due to the distribution of people in each category, e.g. nearly rectangular over the education groups, and partly to the pattern of the coefficients.

[23]We have already subtracted 3 which is the value if the distribution is normal.

[24]The unstandardized measure of kurtosis, Σu_i^4, would decline substantially, but even with the initial variance, the distribution would not be normal.

than 10% in the standard error for both groups. Skewness in the residuals is decreased slightly for the nonself-employed but unchanged for the self-employed. Kurtosis is increased in both groups.

4. 1955

Our analysis of the source of inequality in 1955 earnings distributions is handicapped by the fact that several of our most important variables – including the self-employment ones – are measured only in 1969 and must have changed between 1955 and 1969. Nevertheless, let us examine the same statistics on inequality. As shown in table 3, the standard error of earnings in 1955 in \$3.8 (in thousands of 1958 dollars). Since the 1955 equation has a smaller R^2, the standard error of $Y - Y_1$ has only been reduced by 10%. The standard error of earnings is reduced by about $1\frac{1}{2}$ to 3% by each of education, ability, risk of preference and nonpecuniary variables, work experience, SES and the miscellany in Y_8 but the self-employment variables reduce the standard deviation by 4%.

The 1955 skewness measure is 5.3, which is much greater than in 1969. Examining the various rows, we find that holding constant any subset (except work experience and the miscellany) of the whole set of the characteristics in eqn 2 *increases* relative skewness. The major difference between the 1969 and 1955 results for the self-employment variables may well be due to the measurement problems; i.e. some in the right hand tail in 1955 are no longer self-employed in 1969 while some with large business holdings in 1969 were not yet self-employed.

Much the same pattern appears on kurtosis. The residuals from the full or any partial set of variables (except the miscellany) have greater standardized kurtosis than in the original earnings data, and this kurtosis is greater in 1955 than in 1969. In subsequent sections, we will try to explain why 1955 exhibits more skewness and kurtosis than 1969; but first we will examine the results at a more disaggregated level.

5. Pattern by education level

Since we have eliminated the average difference in earnings for people with different amounts of education, ability, etc., the above analysis essentially analyzes the *between cell* contribution of education, ability, etc. to inequality. For several purposes, it is important to study inequality within various education and ability cells. As shown in table 4, in 1955 the standard error is lowest for those with just a high school education, at the peak for those who started or completed college, and intermediate for

Table 4.
1955 and 1969 earnings distributions (in 1958 dollars) by education level.

	Earnings					
	1955			1969		
	σ	Skewness	Kurtosis	σ	Skewness	Kurtosis
High school	2.81	2.87	13.68	7.12	3.59	21.36
Some college	4.30	5.37	51.00	9.79	3.29	15.20
Bachelor's degree	4.25	6.30	77.92	9.64	2.81	11.50
At least some grad.	3.33	2.53	10.29	10.02	2.96	12.73
	LN earnings					
High school	.36	.52	1.84	.46	.92	1.73
Some college	.40	.84	3.07	.51	.91	1.11
Bachelor's degree	.38	.92	3.59	.47	.64	1.02
At least some grad.	.37	.48	1.52	.48	.54	1.31

those with more formal education than a bachelor's degree[25]. (As shown in the section below on heteroskedasticity, the differences are significant.) The relative skewness and kurtosis measures increase sharply from high school through a bachelor's degree and then fall to their lowest level for those with at least some graduate work. In each education group, neither earnings nor the log of earnings are distributed normally.

In 1969, it is still true that the earnings distribution is neither normal nor log normal. In other respects, the pattern is much different than in 1955. While high school graduates still have the lowest standard error, graduate students, (including M.D.'s and L.L.B.'s) have the highest. The skewness

[25]There are from 950 to 1330 people in each cell.

and kurtosis measures are greatest for high school graduates and then decrease through the bachelor's level followed by a slight increase at the graduate level. The major change in the high school category between 1955 and 1969 requires comment. We suggest that the above average growth in the standard error and the large absolute and comparative increases in the skewness and kurtosis measures occur because even the talented or lucky individual among high school graduates finds that it takes longer to get to the top[26]. Thus, in 1955, these people would not be so far out in the right hand tail as they are in 1969. Perhaps because of a different distribution of talent among the more educated, because of credentialism based on education or because of nepotism, this same phenomenon does not occur in other education classes.

More light can be shed on these and other issues by examining the distribution of the residuals in each education class. Since in ch. 4 we were not able to find significant differences in the coefficients by ability or education level, we can use the same sets of coefficients as previously in making these calculations[27].

The major question we want to ask is: will inequality be equalized within different education groups after holding constant the other variables? Consider first the 1955 results in table 5. The effect of holding constant all the variables can be judged by comparing the Y and $Y - Y_1$ rows. Such comparisons reveal that at each education level the standard error declines by about 10%, with the self-employment variables ($Y - Y_4$) generally responsible for the largest reduction in the standard error and the SES ($Y - Y_4$) and nonpecuniary trade offs ($Y - Y_5$) variables nearly as important.

In all but the bachelor's group, holding the self-employment variable constant causes a reduction in the relative skewness measure. The opposite is true in table 4 for the total sample. It seems likely that this difference is due to the use of a separate standardization factor in each education level or, in other words, the total sample combines within education distributions which have different parameters. In the high

[26]The private education variables, which we think are a proxy for nepotism, have bigger range effects and partial R^2's in 1969 than in 1955.

[27]That the coefficients do not differ significantly, of course, tells us nothing about the pattern of inequality in the residuals as education varies.

Table 5.
Effects of various sets of variables on inequality by four levels of education, in 1955 and 1969.

	1955			1969		
	Standard error	Skewness	Kurtosis	Standard error	Skewness	Kurtosis
High school						
Y	2.81	2.87	13.68	7.12	3.59	21.36
$Y - Y_1$	2.50	1.97	9.79	5.74	2.68	17.50
$Y - Y_2$	2.82	2.84	13.50	7.12	3.61	21.50
$Y - Y_3$	2.80	2.89	13.97	7.07	3.61	21.62
$Y - Y_4$[a]	2.64	2.34	10.74	6.28	3.18	19.41
$Y - Y_5$	2.73	2.79	13.26	6.84	3.56	21.64
$Y - Y_6$	2.80	2.79	13.10	7.07	3.60	21.68
$Y - Y_7$	2.75	2.82	14.04	6.84	3.47	20.39
$Y - Y_8$	2.82	2.80	13.48	7.13	3.52	21.37
Some college						
Y	4.30	5.37	51.00	9.79	3.29	15.20
$Y - Y_1$	3.87	5.25	53.81	8.32	2.87	15.45
$Y - Y_2$	4.29	5.30	51.17	9.72	3.30	15.32
$Y - Y_3$	4.30	5.38	50.98	9.75	3.29	15.30
$Y - Y_4$	4.14	5.33	52.67	9.02	3.09	15.58
$Y - Y_5$	4.25	5.45	52.48	9.58	3.36	15.96
$Y - Y_6$	4.29	5.39	51.45	9.72	3.28	15.12
$Y - Y_7$	4.13	5.30	51.18	9.37	3.23	15.36
$Y - Y_8$	4.30	5.30	50.21	9.76	3.23	14.84
Bachelor's degree						
Y	4.25	6.30	77.92	9.64	2.81	11.50
$Y - Y_1$	3.93	6.94	99.70	8.38	2.57	11.35
$Y - Y_2$	4.23	6.36	79.06	9.58	2.85	11.80
$Y - Y_3$	4.22	6.34	78.52	9.60	2.85	11.76
$Y - Y_4$	4.13	6.41	85.69	9.02	2.48	9.69
$Y - Y_5$	4.19	6.40	79.79	9.50	2.85	11.85
$Y - Y_6$	4.22	6.40	80.63	9.50	2.84	12.76
$Y - Y_7$	4.15	6.53	83.65	9.35	2.90	12.60
$Y - Y_8$	4.26	6.32	78.25	9.58	2.78	11.28
Graduate work						
Y	3.33	2.53	10.29	10.02	2.96	12.73
$Y - Y_1$	2.89	1.56	8.08	8.19	2.65	13.63
$Y - Y_2$	3.12	2.21	9.35	9.55	3.16	14.54
$Y - Y_3$	3.29	2.60	10.84	9.93	3.00	13.02

Table 5 (*contd*).

	1955			1969		
	Standard error	Skewness	Kurtosis	Standard error	Skewness	Kurtosis
$Y - Y_4$	3.14	2.33	9.55	9.08	2.79	12.74
$Y - Y_5$	3.27	2.62	11.03	9.79	3.05	13.53
$Y - Y_6$	3.32	2.53	10.30	9.85	2.97	12.85
$Y - Y_7$	3.32	2.50	10.77	9.80	3.01	13.49
$Y - Y_8$	3.27	2.47	10.01	9.83	2.97	13.04

For definitions, see table 3 of this chapter.
[a]While this row should repeat the row for Y, there is a small recorded change because a few people whom we treat as not having attended college went for less than a semester and have a Gourman rating.

school and graduate level, kurtosis decreases when self employment is held constant while the opposite is true at the other two education levels. No other set of characteristics has a large impact on skewness or kurtosis in 1955 at more than one education level.

In 1969 the picture is more varied. The standard error of $Y - Y_1$ is nearly identical for all but the high school category which remains the lowest; and much of the difference in skewness, and to a lesser extent, kurtosis disappears. At each education level holding constant, the self-employment variable substantially reduces the standard error, the relative skewness and the estimates of relative kurtosis of the high school and bachelor's degree groups. Once again, SES and nonpecuniary variables play an important secondary role in determining the standard error but have little effect on skewness and kurtosis.

6. *Mental ability*

Since very little information has ever been presented about the distribution of earnings by mental ability, it is appropriate to repeat the above analysis by the five ability levels. Table 6 contains the distribution

Table 6.
1955 and 1969 earnings distribution by ability level.

	1955			1969		
	Standard deviation	Skewness	Kurtosis	Standard deviation	Skewness	Kurtosis
Earnings						
Bottom fifth	2.91	2.92	14.79	7.81	3.39	17.89
2nd fifth	3.90	5.39	49.39	9.14	3.50	17.95
3rd fifth	3.32	3.02	13.73	9.06	3.36	16.44
4th fifth	3.82	3.80	23.84	9.66	2.77	11.42
top fifth	4.50	7.27	95.12	10.26	2.77	11.29
LN earnings						
Bottom fifth	.36	.73	1.60	.47	.84	1.36
2nd fifth	.38	.86	3.58	.49	.87	1.20
3rd fifth	.37	.68	2.30	.47	.89	1.56
4th fifth	.39	.63	2.67	.50	.59	.61
top fifth	.38	.82	3.61	.49	.40	1.12

statistics for earnings and the log earnings for each ability fifth[28]. In 1955, the standard error is lowest for the bottom fifth and highest for the top. The middle fifth, however, has a lower standard error and coefficient of variation than the group on either side. Since the standard error of the log of earnings does not vary with ability, the above results may be due to a few extreme observations as is also suggested by the skewness and kurtosis measure. Both skewness and kurtosis follow the same pattern, with highest values in the top fifth; however, none of the earnings distributions within an ability cell are normal or log normal.

In 1969, the standard deviation follows the same pattern as in 1955 (although the largest fifth has the lowest coefficient of variation). Skewness and kurtosis are substantially lower in the top two fifths than in the lowest three; however, none of the distributions are normal or log normal.

[28]It is important to remember that the ability measure is more mathematical than a standard I.Q. measure and that to be in the sample a person had to score in the top half of the Air Cadet Qualifying Test. The fifths, therefore, are more like tenths for the U.S. population.

Table 7 presents the inequality pattern by ability level once other variables have been held constant. As we have consistently found in 1955, the self-employment variables cause the biggest reduction in the standard error in most ability fifths, with the SES and nonpecuniary trade off contributions almost as large. In 1969, holding self employment constant substantially reduces the standard error and skewness.

At first glance, the inequality pattern seems confusing. For example, when comparing the education results, we find high school to be (about) the lowest on skewness and kurtosis in 1955, but the highest in 1969[29]. A similar reversal occurs in the ability results. But as will be indicated in ch. 7, several different models can explain these patterns.

7. *Heteroskedasticity*

We can use a Chi-square test developed by Bartlett to determine if the variances within the various education and ability groups are the same, i.e. whether the variances are homo- or heteroskedastic. The test statistic for the education groups are 270 and 156 in 1955 and 1969, while the test statistics for the five ability groups are 171 and 65 for the two years. Since for three and four degrees of freedom, the critical values at the 5% level are 7.8 and 9.5, we can reject in each instance the null hypothesis that the errors are homoskedastic.

In one sense, the above paragraph says that the discussion in the previous section is based on 'real' differences and not just 'noise'. But the findings raise another issue since heteroskedasticity applies to the residuals as well as to the original Y series. Our use of the 't' statistics in the equations in previous chapters are based on various assumptions including homoskedastic errors which, e.g. Ramsey indicates is an important assumption. Taubman–Wales, using a truncated version of our model, report in an appendix to their ch. 5 that reestimation by generalized least squares had very little effect on the size of their coefficients or the t values. We have not reestimated our equations using generalized least squares because of their results and because such estimation is costly.

[29]Since the adjustments for the other variables never change the rank order on any inequality measure, we will base our statements on the inequality in Y.

Table 7.
Effects of various sets of variables on inequality by five ability levels.

	1955			1969		
Ability fifth	Standard error	Skewness	Kurtosis	Standard error	Skewness	Kurtosis
Bottom fifth						
Y	2.91	2.92	14.79	7.81	3.39	17.89
$Y - Y_1$	2.67	1.90	9.54	6.71	2.98	20.23
$Y - Y_2$	2.88	2.89	14.96	7.60	3.55	19.83
$Y - Y_4$	2.83	2.45	12.36	7.24	3.29	20.36
$Y - Y_5$	2.85	2.94	15.27	7.61	3.45	18.49
$Y - Y_6$	2.91	2.81	13.84	7.76	3.40	17.96
$Y - Y_7$	2.83	2.64	12.60	7.68	3.25	17.48
$Y - Y_8$	2.91	2.86	14.67	7.75	3.26	17.02
2nd fifth						
Y	3.90	5.39	49.39	9.14	3.50	17.95
$Y - Y_1$	3.53	5.41	56.95	7.52	2.98	17.57
$Y - Y_2$	3.86	5.41	50.26	8.89	3.55	18.28
$Y - Y_4$	3.78	5.37	52.09	8.38	3.16	17.11
$Y - Y_5$	3.83	5.47	50.96	8.89	3.55	18.66
$Y - Y_6$	3.88	5.44	50.47	9.07	3.47	17.83
$Y - Y_7$	3.76	5.31	49.88	8.86	3.56	19.15
$Y - Y_8$	3.89	5.36	49.29	9.04	3.44	17.61
3rd fifth						
Y	3.32	3.02	13.73	9.06	3.36	16.44
$Y - Y_1$	2.86	2.20	9.98	7.52	2.95	16.64
$Y - Y_2$	3.22	2.89	13.11	8.81	3.50	17.87
$Y - Y_4$	3.07	2.67	11.89	8.16	3.05	15.37
$Y - Y_5$	3.25	3.07	14.28	8.84	3.44	17.32
$Y - Y_6$	3.32	2.94	13.32	8.97	3.37	16.65
$Y - Y_7$	3.27	2.99	13.93	8.79	3.44	17.48
$Y - Y_8$	3.30	2.98	13.46	9.05	3.31	16.16
4th fifth						
Y	3.82	3.80	23.84	9.66	2.77	11.42
$Y - Y_1$	3.40	3.66	25.99	7.76	2.66	13.56
$Y - Y_2$	3.75	3.89	25.00	9.39	2.95	12.73
$Y - Y_4$	3.63	2.65	23.43	8.75	2.66	11.86
$Y - Y_5$	3.74	3.87	24.71	9.42	2.81	11.93
$Y - Y_6$	3.81	3.76	23.74	9.53	2.77	11.61
$Y - Y_7$	3.70	3.87	25.24	9.19	2.84	12.18
$Y - Y_8$	3.83	3.78	23.83	9.59	2.71	11.12

Table 7 (*contd*).

	1955			1969		
Ability fifth	Standard error	Skewness	Kurtosis	Standard error	Skewness	Kurtosis
5th fifth						
Y	4.50	7.27	95.12	10.26	2.77	11.29
$Y - Y_1$	4.17	7.77	114.43	8.81	2.45	10.41
$Y - Y_2$	4.47	7.33	96.74	10.00	2.89	12.16
$Y - Y_4$	4.36	7.51	104.38	9.55	2.49	9.69
$Y - Y_5$	4.45	7.33	96.34	10.12	2.83	11.85
$Y - Y_6$	4.48	7.31	96.70	10.15	2.75	11.15
$Y - Y_7$	4.39	7.41	99.69	9.85	2.82	11.93
$Y - Y_8$	4.49	7.26	95.45	10.21	2.78	11.46

See table 2 for definitions. $Y - Y_3$ omitted since Y_3 only contains the ability variables.

8. *Inequality within occupations*

Several people have argued that certain prominent features of the earnings distribution are connected with or arise because of occupational differences. Lebergett, for example, argues that the earnings distribution is normal for all but the self-employed[30]. Others have argued that within occupation distributions are normally distributed, but that the mean and variance in each occupation varies in such a way as to produce a skewed distribution overall. Moreover, Weiss suggests that since occupations vary in riskiness, people can make choices on occupation based on their preferences and opportunities. It is useful in this regard to determine differential riskiness by occupation after eliminating both personal characteristics which were not measured by Weiss.

The mean standard error and our standardized skewness and kurtosis measures by occupation are given in table 8, *A* through *H*. The mean earnings in (1958 dollars) in 1969 range from \$18.5 for owners to \$8.0 for service workers. Ranked from top to bottom in order of average earnings,

[30]The self-employed are not distributed normally because of limitations on borrowing and thus on losses.

Table 8.
Standard error, skewness, and kurtosis by occupation and year.

	Standard error	Skewness	Kurtosis
1969 owner: number = 798, mean earnings = 18.52			
Y	13.36	2.32	7.07
$Y - Y_1$	11.27	1.89	6.57
$Y - Y_2$	13.14	2.34	7.26
$Y - Y_3$	13.33	2.27	6.94
$Y - Y_4$	12.37	2.22	7.11
$Y - Y_5$	13.10	2.30	7.09
$Y - Y_6$	13.35	2.30	7.04
$Y - Y_7$	12.70	2.15	6.82
$Y - Y_8$	13.36	2.27	6.85
1969 manager: number = 1482, mean earnings = 15.89			
Y	8.69	2.87	12.69
$Y - Y_1$	7.42	2.59	12.35
$Y - Y_2$	8.49	2.97	13.65
$Y - Y_3$	8.62	2.91	13.07
$Y - Y_4$	8.42	2.75	12.10
$Y - Y_5$	8.50	2.90	13.17
$Y - Y_6$	8.47	2.80	12.26
$Y - Y_7$	8.35	2.95	14.17
$Y - Y_8$	8.70	2.59	10.94
1969 service: number = 138, mean earnings = 8.04			
Y	2.27	1.08	2.46
$Y - Y_1$	2.31	0.19	−0.09
$Y - Y_2$	2.12	0.81	1.28
$Y - Y_3$	2.38	0.78	1.04
$Y - Y_4$	2.39	0.91	2.17
$Y - Y_5$	2.35	0.80	2.59
$Y - Y_6$	2.33	0.98	2.18
$Y - Y_7$	2.18	0.98	1.91
$Y - Y_8$	2.21	0.95	1.94
1969 salesman: number = 308, mean earnings = 12.78			
Y	6.80	2.45	9.17
$Y - Y_1$	6.50	2.47	9.57
$Y - Y_2$	6.70	2.48	9.22
$Y - Y_3$	6.81	2.45	9.17

Table 8 (*contd*).

	Standard error	Skewness	Kurtosis
$Y - Y_4$	6.81	2.45	9.24
$Y - Y_5$	6.69	2.47	9.37
$Y - Y_6$	6.81	2.43	8.98
$Y - Y_7$	6.68	2.45	9.22
$Y - Y_8$	6.79	2.50	9.65
1969 office worker: number = 84, mean earnings = 8.17			
Y	5.12	7.38	60.03
$Y - Y_1$	5.20	7.17	57.97
$Y - Y_2$	5.04	7.14	57.67
$Y - Y_3$	5.26	7.37	59.90
$Y - Y_4$	5.16	7.23	58.54
$Y - Y_5$	5.09	7.50	61.30
$Y - Y_6$	5.14	7.38	60.10
$Y - Y_7$	5.28	7.17	57.96
$Y - Y_8$	5.00	7.39	60.25
1969 technical: number = 282, mean earnings = 12.40			
Y	6.69	1.68	1.99
$Y - Y_1$	6.04	1.56	2.20
$Y - Y_2$	6.68	1.68	1.99
$Y - Y_3$	6.64	1.69	2.06
$Y - Y_4$	6.55	1.69	2.25
$Y - Y_5$	6.53	1.66	2.06
$Y - Y_6$	6.60	1.63	1.84
$Y - Y_7$	6.56	1.65	1.95
$Y - Y_8$	6.59	1.68	2.03
1969 blue collar: number = 507, mean earnings = 8.68			
Y	2.70	3.38	24.16
$Y - Y_1$	2.66	1.79	11.74
$Y - Y_2$	2.67	3.08	22.69
$Y - Y_3$	2.72	2.93	19.01
$Y - Y_4$	2.65	3.20	24.10
$Y - Y_5$	2.66	3.16	22.73
$Y - Y_6$	2.73	3.18	21.63
$Y - Y_7$	2.68	2.87	19.47
$Y - Y_8$	2.73	3.28	24.44

Table 8 (*contd*).

	Standard error	Skewness	Kurtosis
1969 professional: number = 1001, mean earnings × 14.63			
Y	8.74	3.27	15.45
$Y - Y_1$	6.60	2.60	15.30
$Y - Y_2$	7.96	3.61	18.84
$Y - Y_3$	8.73	3.29	15.60
$Y - Y_4$	8.00	3.18	16.10
$Y - Y_5$	8.65	3.30	15.57
$Y - Y_6$	8.61	3.27	15.55
$Y - Y_7$	8.65	3.19	14.86
$Y - Y_8$	7.86	3.21	16.81
1955 manager + some owner: number = 1281, mean earnings = 8.52			
Y	4.54	3.33	19.82
$Y - Y_1$	4.10	3.27	24.72
$Y - Y_2$	4.52	3.32	19.84
$Y - Y_3$	4.53	3.34	19.97
$Y - Y_4$	4.36	3.29	21.77
$Y - Y_5$	4.47	3.32	19.94
$Y - Y_6$	4.51	3.35	20.49
$Y - Y_7$	4.40	3.33	20.88
$Y - Y_8$	4.54	3.33	19.99
1955 service: number = 96, mean earnings = 5.75			
Y	1.83	1.79	4.85
$Y - Y_1$	1.83	0.93	2.39
$Y - Y_2$	1.79	1.79	5.05
$Y - Y_3$	1.83	1.68	4.41
$Y - Y_4$	1.83	1.47	3.86
$Y - Y_5$	1.85	1.75	4.68
$Y - Y_6$	1.84	1.73	4.50
$Y - Y_7$	1.85	1.35	3.69
$Y - Y_8$	1.85	1.80	5.02
1955 salesman: number = 507, mean earnings = 7.62			
Y	4.19	6.20	70.17
$Y - Y_1$	3.79	5.59	63.16
$Y - Y_2$	4.18	6.23	70.74
$Y - Y_3$	4.16	6.15	69.14

Table 8 (*contd*).

	Standard error	Skewness	Kurtosis
$Y - Y_4$	4.07	6.14	69.62
$Y - Y_5$	4.18	6.23	70.95
$Y - Y_6$	4.18	6.16	69.72
$Y - Y_7$	3.97	5.87	66.68
$Y - Y_8$	4.16	6.11	68.58
1955 office worker: number = 293, mean earnings = 5.12			
Y	1.16	0.97	3.11
$Y - Y_1$	1.29	−0.20	2.31
$Y - Y_2$	1.13	0.96	3.08
$Y - Y_3$	1.14	0.87	2.42
$Y - Y_4$	1.26	0.59	2.46
$Y - Y_5$	1.13	0.85	2.80
$Y - Y_6$	1.16	0.87	2.84
$Y - Y_7$	1.19	0.69	2.37
$Y - Y_8$	1.14	1.09	3.42
1955 technical: number = 98, mean earnings = 6.13			
Y	1.48	1.30	3.84
$Y - Y_1$	1.59	0.92	3.15
$Y - Y_2$	1.49	1.30	3.78
$Y - Y_3$	1.49	1.48	4.58
$Y - Y_4$	1.52	1.25	3.76
$Y - Y_5$	1.49	1.36	3.73
$Y - Y_6$	1.48	1.34	4.20
$Y - Y_7$	1.46	0.90	3.04
$Y - Y_8$	1.55	1.10	2.95
Blue collar: number = 692, mean earnings = 5.79			
Y	1.58	1.78	8.54
$Y - Y_1$	1.59	0.55	2.38
$Y - Y_2$	1.57	1.76	8.29
$Y - Y_3$	1.59	1.60	7.22
$Y - Y_4$	1.55	1.13	4.40
$Y - Y_5$	1.56	1.74	8.32
$Y - Y_6$	1.57	1.73	8.14
$Y - Y_7$	1.65	1.19	6.83
$Y - Y_8$	1.59	1.73	8.27

Table 8 (*contd*).

	Standard error	Skewness	Kurtosis
1955 professional: number = 1547			
number = 1281, mean earnings = 8.52			
Y	3.11	3.33	20.46
$Y - Y_1$	2.78	2.90	19.81
$Y - Y_2$	3.03	3.08	20.20
$Y - Y_3$	3.08	3.41	21.13
$Y - Y_4$	2.99	3.14	19.17
$Y - Y_5$	3.05	3.46	21.84
$Y - Y_6$	3.09	3.35	20.62
$Y - Y_7$	3.09	3.23	19.52
$Y - Y_8$	3.01	3.51	22.31

the occupations are owner, manager, professional, salesman, technical, blue collar, office worker, and service.

The standard error also varies by occupation ranging from \$13.4 for owners to \$2.3 for service workers. The rank order of the occupations are owner, professional, manager, sales, technical, office worker, blue collar, and service worker. This rank order differs from that of the mean only in the reversal of professional and manager and office and blue collar groups, and both the mean and standard error of the professional and managerial groups are close. An unweighted regression of the mean and standard error of the occupational earnings yields

$$1969 \text{ mean} = \underset{(.02)}{1.03}{*}\text{SE} + 5.39 \qquad \bar{R}^2 = .91.$$

In ch. 5, we present and describe equations which use the same variables as in ch. 3 for the first three occupations and the last four combined. We have used those equations to determine what variables, if any, are important determinants of within occupation earnings inequality. For owners, the business asset variable and the SES variable reduce the standard error almost 10 and 5% respectively. No other set of variables reduces the standard error by as much as 2%.

Among managers, the largest reduction of 4% is produced by the SES variables. The education, so-called business assets, work experience, and nonpecuniary variables each reduce the standard error about $2\frac{1}{2}$ to 3%. The picture for professionals is somewhat different. The biggest reduction of 10% is in the miscellany category, which, for programming convenience, happens to include the dummy variable for salaried professionals. The education variables also reduce the standard error by 9%, but most of this reduction is due to the L.L.B. and M.D. categories. No other set of variables reduces the standard error by 2%.

We have one equation for all other workers with dummy variables for all but technical. Although we have estimated the equation for all the occupations, we have examined the inequality within the separate equations. For blue collar workers, we find that no variable reduces the standard error by more than 2%. The technical workers in this overall category yield similar results with no category explaining more than 2% of the standard error. The same pattern holds for office workers. However, for service workers, education reduces the standard error by 6% and the SES variables by 4%.

The results on the standard error suggest that with the possible exception of the SES and asset variables, no set of variables has a large individual effect. However, the results on the standard error do not indicate whether or not the within occupation results are normally distributed. This question can be examined with the data on skewness and kurtosis.

The skewness coefficients range from 1 to 7 with the lowest level for service workers and the highest for office workers. Most bunch around a value of 2 or 3. All these measures are significantly different from the zero of the normal distribution. The kurtosis measures range from 2.0 for technical workers to 60 for office workers. The joint results on skewness and kurtosis for office workers suggest that this (self-indicated) occupational category may be very heterogeneous.

Next, let us consider briefly the sources of skewness and kurtosis. For owners, skewness and kurtosis decrease by 20 and 8%; but the only variable that has a noticeable effect is SES. For managers, skewness decreased by 10% and kurtosis by 2%. The only variable with large effects are work experience for skewness and business assets for kurtosis. For professionals, the skewness decreases by 20% and kurtosis by 1%; but no one variable has a large effect.

For blue collar workers, skewness and kurtosis decrease by nearly

50%. The biggest source for skewness is the SES variables while for kurtosis, ability and nonpecuniary variables are individually important. Technical workers have an increase in kurtosis but an 8% decrease in skewness after holding constant all variables. No one variable is important by itself. Office workers have a 3% decrease in skewness and a 4% decrease in kurtosis with education and SES variables important. Salesmen have no change in skewness but an increase in kurtosis.

Finally, service workers find their skewness dropping 80% to near zero and kurtosis becoming a minus .09. Thus, after adjustment, the earnings in this last category are normally distributed.

9. 1955 occupational inequality

Next, let us consider briefly the within occupation inequality in 1955[31]. As shown in table 8, *A* through *H*, average earnings (in 1958 dollars) range from \$8.5 to \$5.1. The rank order is owner/manager, salesman, professional, technical, blue collar, service, and office worker[32]. The standard error ranges from \$4.5 for owner/managers to \$1.2 for office workers. The complete rank order is owner/manager, salesman, professional, service, blue collar, technical, and office worker. These two orderings correspond except for the switching of technical and service. The rank orderings are also similar to those for 1969.

When we correlate the occupation mean and standard error of earnings, we obtain

$$\text{mean} = \underset{(.01)}{.20}{*}\text{SE} + 5.96 \qquad \bar{R}^2 = .25.$$

Allowing for the doubling of earnings between the two years, the 1955 results are not similar to those of 1969. Indeed, the trade off for risk appears to be more important in 1969.

The three variables which are important in several occupations in 1955 and 1969 are business assets, nonpecuniary trade offs, and education. For

[31]Once more, we remind the reader that the 1955 and 1969 occupation codes were constructed on a different basis. See ch. 2 for a discussion.

[32]Excluding the 86 people who were farmers then but are not separated out in 1969.

owner/managers, 1969 business assets, SES variables, and the nonpecuniary variables explain 4, 2, and 3% of the standard error respectively. For professionals, 1969 business assets reduce the standard error by 3%. In addition, education (including M.D.), nonpecuniary, and the miscellany (including the teacher dummy) reduce this standard error by 2%.

The other occupations were included in a single equation. For the few technicians, none of the variables reduce the standard error by 2%. For office workers, education and nonpecuniary trade offs are the only two variables causing a 2% reduction. For salesman, 1969 assets and the SES variables induce a 2 and 5% reduction in the standard error. Holding education constant reduces the standard error by 3% for service workers, while no variable has a 2% effect for salesman.

The lowest estimate for skewness and for kurtosis are both found in the office worker category. But the 1.0 and 3.1 figures both indicate the office worker distribution is not normal[33]. (The marked difference in results for office workers in 1955 and 1969 may arise because of the differences in the occupational codes. But it is possible that there are few well-paying office jobs, such as supervisor, that are only reached after long experience.) The other within occupation distributions are also not normal. The largest measure of skewness and of kurtosis are the 6.2 and 70.2 of salesmen.

Among the owner/managers, no variable reduces skewness or kurtosis by 2%; and kurtosis in the residuals is greater than in the original series. For professionals, skewness is reduced by more than 2% by education and 1969 business assets, while kurtosis is reduced by the SES variables.

Among technical workers, the business assets, SES variables, and the miscellany reduce skewness by 2% or more. Their kurtosis is also reduced sharply by business assets, SES and nonpecuniary variables. Office workers have substantial reductions in skewness and kurtosis; all but education and the miscellany have large individual effects.

The skewness of earnings of salesmen is reduced 2% by holding constant the SES variables. Their kurtosis is reduced by the same variables and the miscellany. Service worker's skewness is reduced by ability, business assets, and SES variables. The last two also reduce

[33]After adjusting for all the variables in the equation, the skewness measure is about zero; but kurtosis is still 2.31.

kurtosis. Blue collar worker's skewness is reduced by the same items as salesman, but all the variables individually reduce blue collar worker's kurtosis which falls from 8.5 to 2.3.

10. Conclusion

This chapter has examined the distribution of earnings and residual earnings in 1955 and 1969 in the NBER–TH sample. Briefly we found that the distribution of earnings is not normal nor log normal in the whole sample, or in any subset of education, ability, or occupation (except that the self-employed earnings are log normal). We also found that very few variables had a large impact on the standard error except for business assets which is not a 'skill' variable. Holding constant education, SES and other variables do not reduce skewness and kurtosis by much and may increase these moments. Thus, in this sample, the major sources of skewness and kurtosis are not education or the other variables we measure (except business assets). Finally, the shape of the distribution changes markedly between 1955 and 1969. We will try to explain the causes of these changes in ch. 7. In Appendix D, we compare our results with those in the 1960 Census.

CHAPTER 5

Occupations and earnings

Until now we have included everyone in our sample without regard to the occupation the person was in, except some self-employment variables and a pre-college teacher dummy. There are, however, several reasons to be concerned with the relationship between occupations and earnings. For example, our earnings equations have included several variables which we argue are measures of tastes for nonpecuniary rewards. But nonmonetary rewards vary by occupation. Thus, in general, for a person to forego monetary wages for nonmonetary rewards requires him to choose one occupation over others[1]. A person's occupational choice depends in part on the earnings available to him in all occupations, which can be estimated from (within) occupation earnings equations.

There are a number of other reasons to examine the determinants of earnings within occupations. If, for example, 'prefer to be salaried' is a measure of risk aversion, we should expect that variable to have the same sign in and be larger in those occupations in which risk is more important[2]. We would also expect risk averse people to be more concentrated in less risky occupations, *ceteris paribus.* Second, we argued in ch. 1 that certain types of skills or tastes may be more useful in certain occupations. It is interesting to try to determine what skills, if any, are occupation specific rather than general. Third, in TW, it was argued that we can use within occupation regressions to calculate wages available to people with different characteristics in an occupation and to determine if education is

[1]Other means to trade off monetary for nonmonetary rewards include location of a job, and, as Becker has shown, discriminatory behavior within a particular occupation.

[2]If a competitive labor market is in equilibrium, the various occupations must have just the right premium to balance supply and demand for each occupation. With individuals having different degrees of risk aversion, these premiums will not be enough to attract those most risk averse into the higher risk operations; but the premium will increase with riskiness. Rosen demonstrates these and other propositions (in the two occupation case) where the risk is that of occupational specific illness or death.

used as a screening or signalling mechanism[3]. Haspel has used variants of our within occupation regressions to study screening within a broader choice framework than TW. His results are summarized below.

1. Occupational choice

The relationship between occupations and earnings can be separated into the effect of earnings on occupational choice and the differences in earnings within an occupation. Since A. Haspel has written a dissertation on occupational choice using this data set, I will concentrate on the within occupation equations and, where appropriate, summarize his results.

Briefly stated, his model is one in which each occupation offers a vector of nonpecuniary and pecuniary rewards and the individual then chooses that job that maximizes a utility function defined over a set of both nonpecuniary job aspects and consumer goods. This procedure allows Haspel to obtain an occupation demand function which depends on tastes and on relative prices. While the nonpecuniary rewards attached to a job are assumed to be the same for all individuals, tastes which are measured by the variables we use or similar ones, vary. The relative earnings in each occupation are obtained by inserting a person's characteristics into all the estimated within occupation equations and that if an individual receives $X\%$ more earnings than predicted in his actual occupation, he will receive $X\%$ more in all other occupations. Since Haspel uses our within occupation equations to estimate his occupational earnings (in 1969), we will turn first to those equations.

2. What occupations?

In this chapter, we will generally use the following occupational breakdown: self-employed businessman, manager, self-employed and salaried professional, technical, sales, clerical, blue collar, service, farm, and

[3]Two objections that were made to the earlier TW work were that since the within occupation regressions had low R^2, the estimated wages were subject to large error and that there may be differences in nonpecuniary rewards. Our new variables should help meet both these objections.

others. These breakdowns were chosen because they correspond to the crudest one-digit disaggregation in Census data and because we want to have reasonable sample sizes in each group. The last criterion forces us to combine some of these groups when estimating equations although we then include occupation dummies.

The NBER–TH sample contains several not completely consistent sets of occupational information. Specifically, in 1969, there is available information from a 'please check the category that best describes your work' question and a three-digit code based on their separate response to a 'give the title of your job' question. The 1955 occupational code was constructed by Thorndike and Hagen from the information they collected on job descriptions. In my piece, I have indicated that at our level of aggregation the two 1969 pieces of information correspond 70 to 80% of the time and that the Thorndike–Hagen coding system would agree 50 to 60% with the NBER coding system. However, based on (incomplete) job histories coded by the NBER, it appears that 1955–1969 estimates of occupational mobility are not much different whether 1955 is coded by TH or the NBER[4].

We can distinguish self-employed businessmen from managers in 1969 but not in 1955. Since there are enough people in each category, we have estimated separate equations in 1969 for the two groups.

3. *Summary of within occupation results*

The final equations for each occupation, as well as some more preliminary ones, are given at the end of this chapter in tables 5 and 6. It does not seem necessary to overburden the reader with a detailed analysis of the equations in each occupation for 1955 and 1969. Instead we will indicate the effect of particular groups of variables across occupations in both

[4]It is important to note that in a yet unpublished paper, the chief coder of the NBER data has indicated that I may have overstated the conformity because NBER coders 'often' referred to the self-checked items in 1969 and the TH codes in 1955 when there were ambiguities in the job description in 1969 or in the histories. Since even on the basis of my evidence, the conformity is far from perfect, it is clear that the results may be affected by measurement error.

1955 and 1969. Later, we will briefly summarize the results for each occupation.

In judging these results, the reader should keep in mind that the effect of any variable on earnings can be divided into the between and within occupation effects, i.e. the effect of the variable on occupational choice and the effect on earnings within the occupation. Since the between effect in part depends on occupational differences in earnings, the within effect can be much smaller than in ch. 3.

4. Education

We have included both the quantity and quality of education in our equations[5]. In the equations with quality, the education coefficients indicate the difference in earnings for a person who went to a school with a Gourman rating of zero, which is the average for high school students. For this reason, we will discuss the quantity results from the equation without and quality and later discuss quality. (The reader can find the effect of quantity with quality constant, by adding the difference from some college to the particular education level in the quality equation to the some college coefficient in the first equation.)

The quantity and quality results are given in table 1 within which an asterisk indicates the variable is not significant at the 5% level – perhaps because there are relatively few observations. In 1969, the some college variable is always positive but insignificant. The bachelor's coefficient is positive and significant in all but the professional occupation. The some graduate coefficient is almost always greater than the bachelor's coefficient but is only significant in the 'other' group[6]. Earnings are higher for those with a master's degree (except for the 12 people in the 'other' occupation) with the coefficient significant only among the managers. Ph.D.'s also earn more with the coefficients significant among managers

[5]In some occupations, none of the people have advanced graduate work. In several others, there are only a very few people with a given education level. These cases are usually noted in the text.

[6]Within occupations, we would expect nonpecuniary rewards to be about the same by education level. Thus, it is encouraging to find earnings are higher for those with some graduate work.

Table 1.
Effects of education within occupations (thousands of 1958 dollars).

	Self-employed businessman	Managers	Professionals	Other
1969				
Some college	1.33*	.34*	1.99*	.15*
Bachelor's	3.32	1.68	2.51*	1.54
Some graduate	4.09*	1.62*	1.41*	2.34
Master's	6.27*	2.93	2.62*	.76*
Ph.D.	9.04*	5.08	4.34	N.U.
L.L.B.	9.04*	5.08	6.84	N.U.
M.D.	N.U.	N.U.	9.95	N.U.
Gourman rating	.005*	.005	.005	Not run

	Self-employed businessmen and managers	Professionals	Others
1955			
Some college	.42*	.13*	.34*
Bachelor's	1.15	.88	.63
Some graduate	.49*	.89	.50*
Master's	.47*	.78	.07*
Ph.D.	.38*	.76*	.58*
L.L.B.	.38*	.85*	.58*
M.D.	N.U.	4.51	N.U.
Gourman rating	.002	.001*	Not run

*Not significant at the 5% level.
N.U. = not used because too few observations.

and professionals. Finally, among professionals, M.D.'s earn the most and L.L.B.'s the second highest amount. The Gourman quality coefficient is about .005 in the first three occupations and significant among managers and professionals.

A comparison across occupations in table 1 indicates that the effect of education does vary by occupations and is generally greatest for the self-employed.

In 1955, people were in different occupations. Perhaps it is for this reason that the pattern of results changes so much. The only significant variables are bachelor's in the three broad occupations and some graduate, master's, and M.D. in the professional group. The Gourman rating is significant in the owners and managers group and significant at the 5.1% level in the professional group.

5. Mental ability

As shown in table 2, earnings in 1969 generally increase with ability within all the occupation groups used; however, the only variables significant are the top two-fifths in the self-employed equation and the top fifth in the other groups. Each fifth of ability is most important for the self-employed[7]. The general lack of significance may occur because of the relatively small sample sizes in each occupation, because ability is primarily associated with occupational choice, or because within occupations, there are other skills that are relevant. In comparison with a bachelor's degree, the coefficient on the top ability is much smaller in the

Table 2.
Effects of ability in within occupations 1969 and 1955 (thousands of 1958 dollars).

<table>
<tr><th></th><th>Owner</th><th>Manager</th><th>Professional</th><th>Other</th></tr>
<tr><td>1969</td><td></td><td></td><td></td><td></td></tr>
<tr><td>2nd fifth</td><td>1.12*</td><td>−.57*</td><td>.60*</td><td>.61*</td></tr>
<tr><td>3rd fifth</td><td>.94*</td><td>−.43*</td><td>.46*</td><td>.97*</td></tr>
<tr><td>4th fifth</td><td>3.32</td><td>.25*</td><td>1.10*</td><td>.75*</td></tr>
<tr><td>top fifth</td><td>3.06</td><td>1.01*</td><td>1.37*</td><td>1.63</td></tr>
<tr><td>1955</td><td></td><td></td><td></td><td></td></tr>
<tr><td>2nd fifth</td><td colspan="2">.37*</td><td>.23*</td><td>.32*</td></tr>
<tr><td>3rd fifth</td><td colspan="2">.17*</td><td>.26*</td><td>.13*</td></tr>
<tr><td>4th fifth</td><td colspan="2">.53*</td><td>.49</td><td>.29*</td></tr>
<tr><td>top fifth</td><td colspan="2">.53*</td><td>.78</td><td>.98</td></tr>
</table>

*Not significant at the 5% level.

[7]This is at variance with TW. See their ch. 5.

manager and professional occupations but about the same in the other two occupations.

In 1955, the top two-fifths in the professional group and the top fifth in the other group may be significant. The difference in pattern between 1955 and 1969 may indicate that our ability measure is poor; but it must be remembered that there was substantial occupational mobility between the years and, for example, the best and brightest professionals of 1955 may be the managers in 1969 who cause the top two-fifths of ability to be so large and significant.

6. SES variables

Next let us consider the various SES variables used in the overall equation. One of the major determinants of earnings in ch. 3 was religion. In 1969, Jews earn more than Catholics except in the other group in which there are only a few Jews; and Catholics, in turn, earn more than Protestants (except among managers). See table 3. Compared to Protestants, the Jewish coefficients are always significant; but when compared to Catholics, only the manager coefficient is significant. For managers, the Protestant–Catholic difference is nearly significant. In 1955, Jews earn significantly more among owner/managers and the other group, with the latter having the largest coefficient. The Protestant coefficients are small and insignificant.

The frequency of attendance at religious school does not have any significant effects in 1969 or in 1955 although the coefficient of $2000 in the 1969 manager equation is significant at the 10% level.

The time spent in youth variables, which are novel to this study, also have some effects in 1969 within our broad occupations. For example, time spent on a part-time job has a significant, positive effect in the manager equation and is significant at the 6% level in the owner equation. We have suggested that this variable represents willingness to work hard and to achieve financial success. It seems plausible that this variable should be important in these two occupations and that the coefficient should be larger in the owner equation.

The time spent on chores variable has a significant negative effect on earnings of owners and of those in the other occupation, and insignificant

Table 3.
Effects of various SES measures in various occupations in 1969 and 1955 (thousands of 1958 dollars).

	1969				1955		
Variables	Owner	Manager	Professional	Other	Owner/manager	Professional	Other[a]
Biog. 2nd and 3rd fifths	1.15*	.48*	−.23*	.17*	.06*	.31*	.28*
Biog. 4th and 5th fifths	1.40*	1.01*	−.76*	.45*	.62	.54*	.73*
Protestant	−2.65	−.88*	−.70*	−.40*	−.17*	−.03*	.21*
Jewish	1.62*	4.82	.93*	N.U.	1.94	.24*	3.75
Attended religious school several times a week	−1.59*	−1.99*	1.09*	−.18*	−.47*	−.05*	−.18*
Father-in-law's ed. yrs.	−.35	.15	.21	.07*	.07	.04	.04*
Mother-in-law H.S. +	1.19*	.91*	−.77*	.32*	−.05*	−.15*	−.13*
Never moved before H.S.	−1.29*	−.41*	−.05*	−.11*	−.14*	.25*	.06*
Attended private elementary school	−17.68	5.80	3.32*	N.U.	.11*	−1.32*	.15*
Attended private H.S.	7.50	.13*	3.06*	−.84*	2.68	.11*	−.57*
Time spent on sports	.17*	.43	.04*	.19*	.03*	.05*	−.02*
Time spent on chores	−.85	−.15*	.10*	−.25	−.09*	−.01*	−.04*
Time spent on hobbies					.06*	.05*	.10*
Time spent on part-time job	.50*	.28	.21*	.10*	.05*	.05*	.01*
Time spent on reading					−.10*	.03*	−.11*

[a]Equation without quality of college variable.
*Not significant at the 5% level.
N.U. = not used.

coefficients elsewhere. We interpret this variable as representing a family background that stresses conformity. Apparently conformity has more inhibiting effects among owners.

The sports variable has a significant positive effect on managers' earnings. Most of the explanations advanced to explain this variable would also seem to apply to the self-employed, but sports was not significant there. In 1955, none of the time spent variables are significant and the coefficients are substantially smaller than in 1969.

In the overall equations, one of the most important sets of SES variables was private elementary and high school. Nearly all the people who attended private schools are in the first three broad occupations. In 1969, in the owner and manager occupations, one or the other of these two variables is significant and positive. (The significant negative coefficient on private elementary school in the owner group is based on only two persons and probably can be safely ignored.)

In the professional occupation, private high school is significant at about \$5000 when elementary school is omitted. Attendees of a private high school who are owners receive \$7600 more, while those who are professionals earn nearly \$3700 more. Surprisingly, the 44 people who went to private high school and are managers earn no more than others although the 12 people who attended private elementary school earn \$6500 more. Because there are only 29 people who went to private elementary school and since nearly all went to private high school, we have rerun the equations omitting the elementary school variable. The results, which are given in parentheses in table 3, indicate that the coefficient in the professional group is now significant.

In 1955, the only significant coefficient is private high school in the owner/manager group. The results in 1955 and 1969 conform with the overall equations in ch. 3 and do not contradict a nepotism interpretation.

Father-in-law's education has positive significant effects among managers and professionals in 1969, but a negative effect for owners. Mother-in-law's education has a positive effect on managers, which is nearly significant, and a negative effect significant at the 10% level for professionals.

In the overall chapter, we indicated that parental education became insignificant when business assets were included in our equation but that this did not occur for in-law's education, perhaps because the in-law's were not business owners. The above results would seem to confirm that logic and the associated nepotism idea, although the negative result among owners is not encouraging.

In 1955, father-in-law's education is significant and positive in the owner manager and professional occupations. Mother-in-law's education is not significant.

7. Nonpecuniary preferences

In previous chapters, we have laid great stress on variables we designate as indicating nonpecuniary preferences and whose coefficients indicate earnings foregone. These variables are related to occupational choice (see table 4), but they are also significant within several of the broad occupations we are using.

Table 4.
Nonpecuniary trade offs in various occupations in 1955 and 1969 (thousands of 1958 dollars).

	Owner	Manager	Professional	Other
1969				
No = 1 to question on occupation choice				
Future financial success	−3.45	−.85*	−1.47	−1.17
Independence in work	3.97	1.72	.84*	.16*
Helping others	1.00*	.88*	.61*	.56*
Challenging work	−3.50	−1.80	−.51*	−1.00
Job security	.97*	1.14	1.14	.84
Prefer to be salaried	−3.55	−2.00	−.01*	−.28*
1955				
Future financial success	−.47		−.54	−.51
Independence in work	.23*		.19*	.43
Helping others	.82		.40	.23*
Challenging work	−1.00		−.52	−.44
Job security	.54		.34	.06*
Prefer to be salaried	−.43*		−.27*	−.25*

*Not significant at the 5% level.

In 1969, those who prefer to be salaried earn significantly less as owners ($3500) and managers ($2000). Once again, the largest effect is among owners, who probably have more control over their choices and actions and who are subject to the largest amount of variance. In 1955, all the coefficients are negative but insignificant although owner/managers are significant at the 6% level.

Next consider the occupational choice questions. Note first that each variable has the same sign within each occupation as in the overall equation. Those who are not interested in future financial success earn significantly less in 1969 in each of our occupations (except managers) with the effect much bigger for owners[8]. Those not interested in independence in work earn significantly more among owners and managers with the owner coefficient much bigger. (Interestingly, among owners, nearly 90% are interested in independence, while among managers only about 50% are so inclined.)

The help others variable is not significant among any of our occupations. But those not interested in challenging work earn significantly less as owners, managers, or in the other occupations. As we are continuously finding, the biggest impact is for owners which is the group probably having the most control over its destiny and work effort.

Those not interested in job security earn more among managers, professionals and our miscellaneous group. The coefficient is positive but insignificant for owners.

In 1955, those not interested in future financial success earned a significant $500 less in each occupation. Those not interested in independence earned more, but the coefficient is only significant among 'others'. Those who do not want to help others and those who are not interested in job security earn more with the coefficient significant in all but the other group. Those interested in challenging work earn more within each occupation.

All these variables are significant within one or more occupations and the significant variables all have the same sign as in the overall equation. This would tend to reinforce our interpretation of these variables. Also,

[8]Among owners, of those who answered the question, less than 15% were not interested in future financial success; while in the sample, about $\frac{1}{3}$ were not interested in future financial success.

the effects of the variables on the range of earnings are large as compared to those of education.

8. Hours, assets, and city size

Hours worked on main job in 1969 has a significant, positive effect in 1969 within the managerial and professional occupations. The 1969 variables were not used in 1955 since it was not significant overall and since people have changed occupations. The 1969 hours on second job has a negative coefficient within all occupations, with all but the owner and other ones significant. Within each of these groups, those who receive a low wage rate feel compelled, on the average, to moonlight[9].

The 1969 weeks lost from illness variable is significant and negative in the professional and other occupations. This 1969 variable is not significant in any of the 1955 occupations.

The weight variables, which we think measure another aspect of physical fitness, are significant at the 5 or 6% level in each occupation except other; and in each case, the negative coefficient on weight squared indicates that the maximum earnings are obtained by the 200 pounder[10]. In 1955, weight (measured in 1969) is only significant in the professional group.

The 'other' asset (business, real estate) variable is significant in all occupations. Since we do not expect the managers and miscellaneous groups to have business assets (unless the managers included stock of closely-held companies), it seems clear that some of the correlation both here and in ch. 3 occurs because real estate and other nonbusiness assets are held by those who earn more. However, in the manager and other groups, there are only small changes in most coefficients when assets are omitted. The business asset interpretation, however, still seems relevant since the coefficient in this variable is greatest in the two occupational groups in which we include owners.

People in the largest cities earn significantly more in 1969 among all but

[9]The professional category includes more than M.D.'s and L.L.B.'s who do not have second jobs.

[10]The one exception occurs when we examine salesmen by themselves, where the linear term is negative and the quadratic term positive.

professionals. In 1955, the 1969 size of city is significant within each occupation. The post-1955 interregional mobility variable is significant in 1969 in all but the professional group, but is not significant in any occupation in 1955.

9. Work experience

Except for age in the other occupations, neither age nor length of work experience is significant within occupations in 1969. In 1955, both age and year of first job are significant in the owner/manager group, year of first job is significant in the professional group, and neither is significant in the other group.

The formulation of experience as (Age – Year of First Job) assumes that each year of experience prior to 1969 is the same, regardless of the fields in which a person obtained his experience. To examine the question of the generality of experience, we have computed another set of equations for 1969 in which, like TW, we have included dummy variables for the person's occupation in 1955[11]. We find that for 1969 owners, those who were professionals or salesmen in 1955 earn $5000 more and those who were owner/managers $3000 more than those who were blue collar workers then[12]. Among 1969 managers, those who were professionals, salesmen, or owner/managers in 1955 earn about $1300 more than blue collar workers then. In the professional group, only those who were professionals in 1955 earn more ($2000) than 1955 blue collar workers. Finally, in the miscellaneous group, former professionals earn $2100 more and former managers, sales and servicemen about $1500 more than other types of workers.

These results indicate that being in some types of jobs is better for long-run earnings success than being in others. These results, of course, need not occur because of the type of on-the-job training given in an occupation. But to the extent these represent on-the-job training, it appears that the training is not general.

[11]Because the other variables are correlated with and help determine a person's 1955 occupation, their net coefficients are not very meaningful and will not be discussed here.

[12]In 1955, we cannot distinguish owners and managers.

The above presentation enables the reader to compare variables across occupations but tends to obscure comparisons within each occupation. At this point, therefore, we will give a brief summary of the findings within each occupation.

10. Self-employed businessmen in 1969

For the 798 men who are owners in 1969, we have been able to explain 27% of the variance in earnings when we include information on 1955 occupations and 25% without this data. Because the 1955 occupation is correlated with the other variables, a better picture of the effects of education, etc., can be obtained from eqn 1.

In this equation, we find that earnings increase uniformly with education with most of these dummy variables significant. Since there is no reason to suspect that the nonpecuniary rewards differ much by education level within this occupation, the $7800 coefficient on Ph.D. suggests that in our overall equation, the Ph.D. coefficient is much smaller because of other nonmeasured, nonpecuniary rewards. We find that the top two-fifths of ability are highly significant with owners in these groups earning $3000 more[13].

In the final equation, the biography variable is not significant and the pattern is erratic. Other dimensions of SES are important. For example, Jews earn $3000 more and Protestants $3400 less than Catholics.

The asset variable has a coefficient of 14 when private high school is included. The private high school coefficient is large and positive. (The elementary school variable is based on only two people.)

An important finding is that those who are self-employed who prefer to be salaried earn $4000 less. This supports our risk aversion interpretation for this variable. Those who moved interregionally after 1955 received $600 more.

We also find that those not interested in future financial success earn $3400 less, those not wanting challenging work receive $3800 less, and

[13]TW found no effect of ability for owners. The difference in results appears to occur because of the increase in sample size arising from responses in 1970 and from a different set of throw out rules, i.e. we no longer omit people for not giving answers to secondary questions such as father's education.

those not interested in job security receive $1300 more, while those not interested in independent work receive $4000 more.

11. Managers in 1969

For the 1482 managers, we explain about 25% of the variance in 1969 earnings. Earnings increase continuously with education with the B.A., through Ph.D. coefficients significant. The Gourman quality index is also significant. Once again, nonpecuniary rewards are important with the independent, helping others, challenging work, job security, and prefer to be salaried significant. Those in the top ability fifth earn $1000 more than those in the bottom fifth (but the '*t*' value is only 1.4); the other differences are small, sometimes the wrong sign and insignificant[14].

The top two-fifths of the biography variable are significant at about $1300. Once again, we find that religion is important with Jews earning nearly $6300 more and Protestants $1000 less than Catholics et al. The 12 people who attended private elementary school receive $5600 more, perhaps because these people receive high paying positions on account of their family and personal contacts and control of companies. Father-in-law's education is significant.

Post-1955 mobility is important. The amount of work effort is also important; for example, each hour on the job adds a highly significant $200 to earnings, while each hour on a second job is associated with a $100 drop in earnings.

In another equation, we also included the variable we are calling business assets in this equation, and obtained a significant coefficient of about .1. This is a somewhat disturbing finding, given our interpretation of the variable and its coefficients. There are, however, several plausible explanations other than data error. First, as noted earlier on the questionnaire, the variable is entitled 'other assets (own business, real estate)'. It is quite possible that managers own real estate and other nonspecified assets, whose amount is correlated with wage income. Second, a person may have included the value of his share of an owned (controlled) corporation in this category despite our giving him an option listing such

[14]Once again, TW reached opposite results.

assets under 'common stock, mutual funds, other marketable securities'[15]. Third, it is possible that a member of a partnership would check manager rather than self-employed. If the first reason and to a lesser extent the second reason are correct, we would be correct in not including the asset variable in the equation, except perhaps as an indication of family wealth when growing up. However, most coefficients are only changed by a small amount when the asset variable is included.

12. *Professionals*

We can explain about 42% of the variance in 1969 earnings of the 1001 professionals in our sample. The quantity of education variables are not significant except for M.D. and L.L.B.[16]. (The Gourman index is also significant.) While the ability coefficients are positive and generally increase with ability, only the top fifth at 1600 is significant and then only when quality is excluded.

Socioeconomic background plays a role within this occupation. For example, Jews receive \$1700 more than Protestants and \$1000 more than Catholics et al. Also, father-in-law's education is significantly related to earnings. With private elementary school omitted, those who attended private high school receive some \$4000 more than those who did not.

Each hour worked per week on main job adds \$60 to annual earnings, but each hour worked on second job is associated with a decrease in earnings of \$160.

The so-called business assets variable is significant and has a coefficient of .10. Since our category includes self-employed professionals, this finding is not unreasonable. Of the nonpecuniary variables, only the lack of concern for future financial success and job security are significant although the signs on the other variables are the same as in the previous occupation. The self-employed professionals earn \$5000 more than the salaried ones.

[15]There is also a separate line for 'your own home'.

[16]There are high school graduates who are professionals. For example, about $\frac{1}{2}$ of all entrants to the engineering profession in the post-World War II period were just high school graduates.

13. Other occupations

The remaining occupations of technical workers, salesmen, office workers, service, blue collars and others have been combined to obtain 1318 observations. In the equation, we include dummies for the various suboccupations other than blue collar and other. We find that salesmen and technical workers earn about a significant $2000 more, while the other two dummies are insignificant negative amounts. Earnings increase with education with bachelor's and some graduate significant. The Gourman index is negative but insignificant. Ability increases earnings with the third and top fifths significant.

Of the SES variables, the significant variables are the time spent on chores and on sports. The future financial success, challenging work, and job security variables are significant with the same signs as in the overall equation.

14. Occupational choice

As explained in the introduction to this chapter, the within occupation regressions can be used as inputs in a model of occupational choice. A. Haspel has formulated such a model and estimated it using the NBER–TH sample and the earnings equations of this chapter. An oversimplified view of his model is that a person's occupational choice can be derived from a utility maximization procedure in which the arguments of the utility function are the money income a person can earn with a given set of characteristics in each of the N occupations and the various nonpecuniary rewards attached to each occupation. Under certain conditions, demand for occupational functions which depend on relative money and nonmoney wages and tastes can be derived.

Haspel calculates the occupational specific money wage rate for each person on the basis of our equations[17]. He then measures tastes by the types of variables we have used, as well as some additional, all subjected to factor analysis. He estimates equations using the taste variables and

[17]He also assumes that for the ith person in the jth occupation that $u_{ij} = Y_{ij} - X_j B_j = \alpha X_k B_k$ for all k occupations.

Table 5.
1955 earnings equations.

	Managers and self-employed businessmen		Professionals		Other	
Independent variables	Ceof.	*t* value	Coef.	*t* value	Coef.	*t* value
Education:						
Some college	−.36	1.1*	−.21	.8*	.34	1.8*
Bachelor's	.28	.7*	.51	1.9*	.63	2.6
Some grad.	−.36	.6*	.52	1.4*	.50	.9*
Master's	−.39	.6*	.43	1.4*	.07	.1*
Ph.D. + L.L.B. + M.D.	−.44	.5*	.45	1.0*	.59	.7*
L.L.B.			.04	.1*		
M.D.			3.77	6.5		
Ability:						
2nd fifth	.37	1.3*	.23	1.0*	.32	1.4*
3rd fifth	.17	.6*	.26	1.2*	.13	.6*
4th fifth	.53	1.9*	.49	2.3	.29	1.2*
(top) 5th fifth	.53	1.8*	.78	3.7	.99	3.6
Biography:						
2nd fifth, 3rd fifth	.06	.2*	.31	1.8*	.28	1.4*
4th fifth, 5th fifth	.62	2.4	.54	3.0	.73	3.4
Father high school						
Father college						
Religion:						
Jewish	1.94	4.8	.24	.6*	3.75	7.6
Protestant	−.17	.8*	−.03	.2*	.22	1.3
Attended religious school often	−.47	1.1*	−.05	.2*	−.59	1.4
Father-in-law	.07	2.7	.04	2.1	.04	1.5*
Mother-in-law high school	−.05	.2*	.15	1.0*	−.13	.7*
Time spent on sports	.03	.4*	.05	1.1*	−.02	.4*
Time spent on chores	−.09	−1.3*	−.02	.3*	−.04	.6*
Time spent on hobbies	.06	.9*	.05	1.2*	.10	1.7*
Time spent on part-time job	.05	.8*	.05	1.2*	.01	.1*
Time spent on reading	−.10	1.5*	.03	.6*	−.11	1.8*
Never moved before high school	−.14	.7*	.25	1.7*	.06	.3*
Attended private high school	2.68	4.5	.11	.2*	−.57	.8*
Attended private elementary school	.11	.1*	−1.32	.9*	.15	.1*
Factors influenced entering occupation						

Table 5 (*contd*).

	Managers and self-employed businessmen		Professionals		Other	
Independent variables	Coef.	*t* value	Coef.	*t* value	Coef.	*t* value
Future financial prospects, no = 1	−.47	2.0	−.54	3.6	−.51	2.6
Independence, no = 1	.23	1.0*	.19	1.2*	.43	2.1
Challenging work, no = 1	−1.00	3.8	−.52	2.8	−.44	2.0
Help others, no = 1	.82	3.8	.40	2.5	.23	1.2*
Job security, no = 1	.54	2.6	.34	2.3	.07	.4*
Prefers to be salaried	−.44	1.9*	−.28	1.8*	−.25	1.4*
Other assets (own business, real estate), 1969	.04	10.7	.03	8.5		
Self-employed businessman, 1969						
Self-employed professional, 1969						
Teacher, pre-college	−1.40	5.5				
Hours on main job, 1969						
Hours on second job, 1969	−.03	1.8*	−.03	2.3	−.02	1.2*
Weeks lost from illness, 1969	−.04	.9*	−.02	1.1*	−.02	.8*
Mobility 1955 to 1969	.02	.4*	.02	.5*	.07	1.5*
Age	.09	2.3	.02	.6*	.05	1.5*
Year of first job	−.13	3.4	−.08	3.1	−.03	−.9*
Current residence in town of 50, to 1000000	.58	2.6	.13	.8*	.44	2.2
Current resident in excess of 1000000	1.30	3.9	.47	2.1	.68	2.3
College quality (Gourman rating)	.002	3.0	.0009	1.9*		
Weight, 1969	6.13	1.4*	7.01	2.2	3.64	1.0*
Weight squared, 1969	−1.44	1.2	−1.89	2.2	−.88	.9*
Office worker					−.90	3.9
Sales worker					.92	4.3
Service worker					−.32	.9*
Farmer					.04	.1*
Dummy for nonresponse in 1972	1.03	1.9*	.65	1.7*	.39	.9*
Constant	.27	.1*	.89	.2	−.21	.04
R^2	.20		.17		.13	
Stand error	3.87		2.94		3.24	
Degrees of freedom	1935		2198		1729	

Definitions same as in ch. 3.
Occupations taken from I, Q4.

Table 6.
1969 earnings equations.

	Owners		Managers		Professionals		Others	
Independent variables	Coef.	*t* value	Coef.	*t* value	Coef.	*t* value	Coef.	*t* value
Education:								
Some college	−.88	.5*	−2.01	2.1	−.19	.1*	.15	.5*
Bachelor's	.81	.4*	−.85	.8	.35	.2*	1.54	3.5
Some grad.	1.66	.6*	−.88	.7	−.74	−.4*	2.34	2.3
Master's	3.88	1.0*	.48	.4	.49	.3*	.76	.6*
Ph.D. + L.L.B. + M.D.	6.61	1.6*	2.75	1.8	2.27	1.2*		
L.L.B.					2.37	2.2		
M.D.					4.82	3.4		
Ability:								
2nd fifth	1.12	.8	−.57	.8*	.60	.7*	.63	1.7*
3rd fifth	.94	.7	−.43	.6*	.46	.6*	.97	2.4
4th fifth	3.33	2.4	.25	.4*	1.11	1.4*	.75	1.8*
(top) 5th fifth	3.06	2.1	1.01	1.5*	1.37	1.8*	1.63	3.5
Biography:								
2nd fifth, 3rd fifth	1.15	1.0*	.48	.8*	−.24	.4*	.17	.5*
4th fifth, 5th fifth	1.40	1.2*	1.01	1.7*	−.76	1.2*	.46	1.2*
Father high school								
Father college								
Religion:								
Jewish	1.62	1.0*	4.82	5.0	.94	.8*		
Protestant	−2.65	2.6	−.88	1.9*	−.70	1.4*	−.41	1.4*
Attended religious school often	−1.59	.9*	−1.99	1.9*	1.09	1.1*	−.18	.3*
Father-in-law	−.35	2.7	.15	2.6	.21	3.2	.07	1.5*
Mother-in-law high school	1.19	1.2*	.91	1.9*	−.77	1.5	.32	1.0*

Time spent on sports	.17	.6*	.43	2.7	.04	.2*	.19	1.9
Time spent on chores	−.85	2.7	−.15	.9*	.10	.5	−.25	2.2
Time spent on part-time job	.50	1.9*	.28	2.1	.21	1.5*	.11	1.2*
Never moved before high school	−1.29	1.3	−.42	.9*	−.05	.1*	−.11	.4*
Attended private high school	7.50	2.9	.13	.01*	3.06	1.7*	−.84	.6*
Attended private elementary school	−17.68	2.0	5.80	2.4	3.32	1.0*		
Factors influenced entering occupation								
Future financial prospects, no = 1	−3.45	2.4	−.85	1.7*	−1.47	−2.8	−1.17	3.5
Independence, no = 1	3.97	2.6	1.72	3.7	.84	1.5*	.16	.5*
Challenging work, no = 1	−3.50	2.6	−1.80	3.0	−.51	.7*	−1.00	2.7
Help others, no = 1	1.00	1.0*	.88	1.9*	.61	1.0*	.56	1.6*
Job security, no = 1	.97	1.0*	1.14	2.5	1.14	2.2	.84	2.4
Prefers to be salaried	−3.55	2.0	−2.00	4.1	−.01	.01*	−.28	.9*
Other assets (own business, real estate), 1969	.14	10.8	.10	9.2	.11	9.5	.05	5.2*
Self-employed businessman, 1969								
Self-employed professional, 1969					4.99	8.0		
Teacher, pre-college					−.06	.1*		
Hours on main job, 1969	−.01	.3*	.20	7.2	.06	2.0	−.03	1.4*
Hours on second job, 1969	−.11	1.5*	−.13	2.9	−.16	4.0	−.04	1.4*
Weeks lost from illness, 1969	−.19	.6*	−.16	−1.8	−.16	2.3	−.10	2.2
Mobility 1955 to 1969	.60	2.4	.31	3.1	.14	1.2*	.30	3.6
Age	−.20	1.0*	.07	.7*	−.13	1.1*	−.15	2.6
Year of first job	−.43	1.9*	−.16	1.9*	−.07	.9*	−.08	1.3*
Current residence in town of 50, to 1000000	2.46	2.4	.80	1.5*	.58	1.0*	.38	1.1*
Current resident in excess of 1000000	5.99	3.8	2.73	4.0	.87	1.1*	1.76	3.6
College quality (Gourman rating)	.005	1.4*	.005	3.2	.005	2.5		
Weight, 1969	36.78	2.0	31.76	3.1	30.92	2.9	4.35	.7*
Weight squared, 1969	−10.42	2.1	−7.95	2.9	−7.88	2.7	−1.33	.7*
Technical							2.38	6.3

Table 6 (*contd*).

Independent variables	Owners Coef.	Owners t value	Managers Coef.	Managers t value	Professionals Coef.	Professionals t value	Others Coef.	Others t value
Office worker							−1.01	1.7*
Salesman							2.05	5.1
Service worker							−.48	1.0*
Dummy for nonresponse in 1972	1.42	.6*	5.03	4.2	2.23	1.7	.91	1.2*
Constant	8.72	.4*	−28.29	2.5	−13.03	1.1*	14.94	2.0
R^2	.27		.26		.41		.23	
Stand error	11.42		7.49		6.73		4.78	
Degrees of freedom	756		1440		955		12.77	

Definitions same as in ch. 3.

Occupations from II, Job Description, Q1.

relative earnings in various occupations for owner, manager, professional, blue collar, technician, office worker, salesmen, and service workers in 1969 and comparable detail for initial occupations[18].

By including both relative earnings and the taste variables, he is able to separate out the income and taste effects of variables such as education or religion. Generally, he finds that both earnings and most of the so-called taste variables are significant and form a reasonable pattern in most of the occupations[19].

Haspel also re-examines the question of the extent to which the NBER–TH data are consistent with the hypothesis that education is used as a screening device in addition to increasing skills. His basic method is to examine the education coefficients in his occupational choice equations. He finds that if he includes the relative earnings and education variables that the less educated seem to be underrepresented in the higher paying occupations[20]. However, once he includes the taste variables, the education dummies are insignificant, i.e. no screening. Haspel's first result is in accord with the Taubman–Wales finding. His second result obviously is not. However, Taubman–Wales also noted that different tastes for nonmoney rewards could explain their findings, but if that was the explanation that their already low estimates of the rate of return to education would be biased upwards, this has been shown to be the case in the appendices to ch. 3 of this study[21].

[18]He estimates comparable initial earnings equations.

[19]A useful summary of his findings are given in Haspel, pp. 276–281.

[20]See Haspel, p. 275.

[21]Taubman–Wales, p. 167 and 168.

CHAPTER 6

Individual stability in the earnings distribution

In our year-to-year comparisons, we have concentrated on changes in summary statistics such as mean and variance produced by different variables. These comparisons have provided us with a number of interesting and thought provoking findings. While many of the findings are based on variables not previously used in studies of earnings, in principle the same phenomena could be examined for different cohorts in Census or other cross section studies[1]. The longitudinal data in our sample also permit us to examine a different set of questions, to extend our understanding of the dynamic evolution of the earnings distribution and to analyze the relationship of annual to lifetime earnings by examining the stability of an individual's position in the earnings distribution over time.

The empirical facts on stability and change over a long time span are very valuable in themselves since the distribution of lifetime earnings is more important for many purposes than that of any one year's earnings[2]. But equally important, these facts will allow us in the next chapter to test and thus to have a chance to reject certain earnings distribution theories.

1. Individual stability and change in the earnings distribution

Stability and change can be defined and analyzed in several ways, each of which tends to highlight different aspects of the problem. To begin our

[1]Conceptually, the previous results are also comparable with those of, say, T. P. Schultz in which random samples of the same cohort are studied at different points in time but in which individuals are not linked over time. Recently, Schiller and others have begun to use the Social Security Continuous Work History files which provide annual data for a random 1% of people issued Social Security numbers. Unfortunately, the only other data contained in this file is date of birth, sex, and race.

[2]Most studies such as Summers have only examined this problem over a two or three year span during which transitory events may play a large role. Mincer has some analysis of stability over longer periods but was forced to rely on recalled estimates for earlier periods. See also Schiller.

examination of individual stability in the distribution, we have calculated the 'transition probability matrix' for the people who reported earnings in both 1955 and 1969[3]. Table 1 indicates the percentage of people who ended up in any tenth of the 1969 earnings distribution from any given tenth in the 1955 distribution. For example, of the people in the bottom 10% of the earnings distribution in 1955, in 1969 39% were still at the bottom, an additional 30% could be found between the 10 and 30% percentiles, and less than 9% have moved up into the top 30% of the earnings distribution[4]. A more useful summary measure of stability is given in table 2, but as a simple (ordinal) measure we can use the average percentile position, which has risen from 5 to 26% by 1969.

For contrast, consider the people in the top 10% in 1955. In 1969 44% were still in the top 10%, an additional 35% were in the next 20% of the distribution, and only 4% had fallen below the 30th percentile. The average percentile position had fallen from 95 to 80% in 1969.

In the other tenths in 1955, people tend to be close to their starting position with, for example, from 39 to 64% of the people falling within the same or neighboring tenths of the distribution. Not more than 30% of the people in the row lie above the 70th percentile in 1969 until we reach the 60–70% interval in 1955, while at least 30% of the row fall below the 30th percentile in 1969 until we reach the 50–60% interval in 1955. The average percentile standing in 1969 for each tenth in 1955 rises continuously; but, on average, people who were in the bottom 40% in 1955 have a higher percentile standing in 1969 while the reverse is true for those in the top 60% in 1955[5]. In all but one comparison, the KS test would reject the hypothesis

[3]A transition probability matrix indicates what percentage of people in state i in period t will be in state j in period $t+1$. As shown in Anderson and Goodman, the observed ratio, such as $Nijt + 1/Nit$, where N is number of people, is the maximum likelihood estimator of the probabilities. If one assumes that the (conditional) probabilities are invariant over time, then sometimes it is possible to solve for the steady state distribution that will occur in the long run.

[4]There are not exactly 10% of the sample in each row or column for two reasons. First, the dividing points were found for all respondents with nonzero earnings in the sample while some individuals were not included in this table, primarily because they did not report earnings in both years. Secondly, in a few instances, a large number of people reported earnings equal to the dividing point. While we could randomly allocate people to each adjoining class to fill it, it was simpler and not misleading to place people in only one class.

[5]Some of this difference may reflect attenuation since those in the bottom tenth cannot fall but can rise in 1969, etc.

Table 1.
Distribution of earnings in 1969 for 1955 earnings percentile – percent of people.

Percentile in 1955 (%)	Number in 1955	Percentile in 1969 (% of row sum) Bottom 10	10 < 20	20 ≤ 30	30 < 40	40 < 50	50 < 60	60 < 70	70 < 80	80 < 90	90 < 100	Average percentile in 1969
Bottom 10	412	38.7	19.1	10.6	6.5	5.6	6.5	3.9	2.7	3.4	2.6	25.7
10 < 20	484	15.2	21.7	16.5	11.4	10.8	8.9	4.1	2.3	2.0	1.6	29.2
20 < 30	368	16.4	20.4	14.4	10.6	10.0	9.3	7.1	4.8	4.5	1.9	34.6
30 < 40	358	8.9	12.6	16.2	18.1	15.6	11.1	6.7	6.4	2.5	1.7	38.7
40 < 50	516	5.4	13.0	13.2	14.8	16.5	15.2	9.9	7.8	3.1	1.4	42.8
50 < 60	586	4.9	10.0	7.3	13.9	14.6	13.9	11.9	11.1	7.5	4.2	46.9
60 < 70	353	3.1	7.1	3.7	6.8	14.8	16.7	15.3	17.3	11.8	3.3	57.0
70 < 80	565	3.0	2.5	3.5	6.1	11.1	14.0	17.2	17.7	16.1	8.9	62.8
80 < 90	500	1.2	3.2	2.8	4.0	3.8	11.2	9.8	19.0	26.0	19.0	71.3
top 10	462	1.7	1.5	0.8	1.3	3.9	6.9	4.5	10.0	25.5	43.7	80.1
Number 1969	4607	451	492	397	428	491	520	428	470	501	416	

The Cut off points by tenths for 1955 are: 4068, 4788, 5028, 5388, 6000, 6468, 7188, 8028, 8798.
The Cut off points by tenths for 1969 are: 8899, 10000, 12000, 15000, 16510, 19000, 23000, 30000.

Table 2.
Distribution of growth rate in earnings 1955 to 1969 by earnings percentile in 1955 whole sample[a].

1955 percentile	(Y69 − Y55)/Y55 = growth rate <0	0 < .25	.25 < .50	.50 < .75	.75 < 1.00	1.00 < 1.25	1.25 < 1.50	1.50 < 1.75	1.75 < 2.00	2.00 < 2.25	2.25 < 2.50	2.50 < 2.75	2.75 < 3.00	3.00 < 5.00	> 5.00	Mean growth rate	Mean compound annual growth rate (%)
0 < 10	0.000	0.007	0.010	.046	.077	.116	.082	100	107	070	075	043	036	135	092	2.675	6.8
10 < 20	0.002	0.010	.006	.056	.126	.152	.157	118	101	076	037	050	023	064	021	1.759	5.1
20 < 30	0.000	.005	.035	.070	.138	.177	.087	130	065	082	030	026	041	081	030	1.806	4.6
30 < 40	0.000	.000	.039	.064	.128	.131	.193	103	123	050	039	031	036	042	017	1.671	4.8
40 < 50	0.002	.006	.043	.094	.090	.173	.093	125	075	063	053	025	020	057	019	1.550	4.6
50 < 60	0.000	.000	.026	.099	.141	.178	.152	105	089	068	037	031	010	037	026	1.715	4.5
60 < 70	0.006	.020	.059	.057	.105	.150	.142	096	105	102	023	031	031	059	018	1.610	4.6
70 < 80	0.004	.030	.044	.087	.119	.143	.103	127	087	051	053	021	028	071	032	1.702	4.5
80 < 90	0.010	.048	.062	.068	.118	.114	.098	092	082	062	032	052	024	106	030	1.760	4.7
90 < 100	0.086	.043	.110	.087	.089	.087	.089	100	065	041	039	030	024	089	022	1.425	3.6
	.011	.018	.045	.076	.110	.145	.115	.113	.089	.066	.044	.034	.027	.076	.030	1.757	4.7

[a]People with zero earnings in either year excluded.

that each row is distributed the same as its adjacent rows. On average, however, over the 14 years the rich remain the richest and the poor the poorest.

2. The distribution of growth rates in earnings

The average 1969 percentile calculated in table 1 is an ordinal measure which need not correspond with the more useful cardinal measure of the average growth rate in earnings[6]. Growth rates are also needed to implement the tests (in the next chapter) of the theories of the earnings distribution. In table 2, which contains the distribution of growth rates, about 1% of the people suffered a decline in nominal earnings, and 15% had a growth of less than 75%[7]. For almost 50% of the sample, earnings grew between 75 and 175% while for 3% of the sample earnings grew in excess of 500%. Using individual observations, we have calculated both the average percentage change and the average annual compound growth rate between 1955 and 1969. The latter measure gives less weight than the former to large percentage increases in earnings and thus implies a lower (comparable) average increase which is about the only reason to prefer the former measure. The average growth rate is about 175% while the average annual compound growth rate is 4.7%, which, over 14 years is equivalent to an increase of about 90%.

Next let us examine the distributions by 1955 earnings level. Of the people who were in the second tenth of earnings in 1955, 1% had a decrease in (nominal) earnings. Nearly 16% (the mode) had a gain between 125 and 150%, while 8.5% had a growth in excess of 300%. The average growth rate in earnings in this tenth is 176%.

Of the people in the 80th to 90th percentile in 1955, nearly 5% had a decrease in their nominal earnings. The mode is in the 75 to 100% interval,

[6]Alternatively, the average percentile measure treats the difference between each percentile difference as an equal unit. But earnings are distributed more unequally in 1969 than 1955 and in both years, the cut off points given in table 1 are of unequal length.

[7]In this chapter we use nominal earnings rather than the constant dollar ones used in earlier chapters. This change is made because the determination of the cut off points was done, early on, in current dollars. Deflation would not change the pattern or conclusions.

and 14.5% had a growth rate in excess of 300%. The mean growth rate in the next to bottom, and next to top rows are identical; but there are people in both tails of the distribution in the 80th to 90th percentile, and the two distributions are significantly different at the 5% level (K.S. test). (For this reason, the average compound growth rate is slightly less than in the second tenth.)

In all but the two extreme rows, the mean growth in earnings only ranges from 151 to 176% and the compound rates .045 to .051. However, those whose earnings placed them in the top 70 to 90% in 1955 have distributions which are significantly different (K.S. test, 5% level) with more people in both tails than those in the bottom 10–50%. In the bottom tenth, the mean change is 267% with a heavy concentration in the right hand tail. In the top tenth, the mean change is only 143% and there is a heavy concentration in the left hand tail.

3. *Distribution of growth rates by education level*

Tables 3–6 contain the growth rate distributions for each of four education levels[8]. Since in these tables cut off points for the tenths are those for the entire sample, we may compare the corresponding rows. From the total row of the four tables, we observe that the mean growth rate increases with education from 140 to 220%.

In the 10 to 20th percentile about 68, 57, 45, and 36% of people with high school, some college, a bachelor's degree, and at least some graduate training had earnings increases no greater than 150%. Moreover, at this point, the cumulative distributions of growth rates are at a lower height, the higher the education level. Thus, the cumulative distributions are more compact the lower the education level. Also, the average growth in earnings increases with education for people with the same earnings in 1955.

This same pattern emerges at the other 1955 percentile levels. Despite the relatively small sample sizes within each of these 1955 percentiles, the KS test rejects the hypothesis that the cumulative distribution of, say, the

[8]We used education as reported in 1969. The distribution of education in 1955 is different because of the post-1955 education received by about 8% of the sample.

Table 3.
Growth rate in earnings 1955 to 1969 by earnings percentile in 1955 high school graduates.

1955 percentile	<0	0<.25	.25<.50	.50<.75	.75 <1.00	1.00 <1.25	1.25 <.150	1.50 <1.75	1.75 <2.00	2.00 <2.25	2.25 <2.50	2.50 <2.75	2.75 <3.00	3.00 <5.00	>5.00	Mean growth rate	Mean compound annual growth rate
	(Y69 − Y55) = growth rate																
0<10	0.000	.006	.012	.093	0.86	.154	.105	.117	.130	.043	.062	.049	.025	.067	.049	1.875	.056
10<20	0.000	.012	.012	.093	.216	.234	.191	.100	.068	.031	.006	.012	.019	.006	.000	1.246	.037
20<30	0.000	.000	.091	.091	.190	.223	.074	.140	.033	.033	.017	.000	.025	.066	.017	1.559	.037
30<40	0.000	.000	.086	.140	.194	.172	.151	.065	.075	.032	.011	.032	.043	.000	.000	1.234	.041
40<50	0.000	.005	.116	.152	.152	.223	.076	.112	.049	.031	.031	.013	.005	.022	.013	1.260	.036
50<60	0.000	.000	.024	.167	.190	.286	.095	.143	.000	.024	.024	.024	.024	.000	.000	1.238	.034
60<70	0.000	.016	.078	.109	.172	.234	.109	.016	.078	.047	.031	.000	.031	.078	.000	1.377	.038
70<80	0.012	.049	.074	.210	.222	.136	.049	.049	.062	.037	.012	.012	.000	.037	.037	1.354	.034
80<90	0.032	.063	.168	.131	.116	.074	.063	.074	.032	.053	.000	.074	.021	.095	.000	1.307	.029
90<100	0.120	.040	.173	.067	.080	.067	.080	.120	.053	.040	.067	.013	.027	.027	.027	1.199	.033
	.012	.016	.080	.122	.159	.184	.103	.098	.063	.037	.027	.023	.020	.039	.016	1.386	.034

Items in this table are fractions of row sum except the last two columns.

Table 4.
Growth rate in earnings 1955 to 1969 by earnings percentile in 1955 some college.

	(*Y*69 – *Y*55)/*Y*55 = growth rate															
1955 percentile	<0	0<.25	.25<.50	.50<.75	.75 <1.00	1.00 <1.25	1.25 <1.50	1.50 <1.75	1.75 <2.00	2.00 <2.25	2.25 <2.50	2.50 <2.75	2.75 <3.00	3.00 <5.00	>5.00	Mean growth rate	Mean compound annual growth rate
0<10	0.000	.000	.010	.040	.102	.163	.061	.112	.092	.071	.061	.030	.051	.133	.082	2.675	.069
10<20	0.008	.000	.008	.076	.114	.152	.167	.106	.083	.076	.030	.045	.023	.076	.038	1.759	.051
20<30	0.000	.009	.009	.072	.153	.198	.090	.108	.063	.108	.036	.036	.027	.072	.018	1.800	.049
30<40	0.000	.000	.042	.073	.125	.188	.208	.104	.146	.031	.042	.010	.010	.000	.010	1.671	.045
40<50	0.000	.009	.050	.161	.120	.190	.046	.143	.074	.065	.032	.037	.018	.051	.005	1.550	.042
50<60	0.000	.000	.040	.140	.180	.100	.160	.100	.080	.060	.020	.000	.020	.080	.020	1.715	.040
60<70	0.000	.045	.112	.067	.123	.202	.135	.045	.067	.067	.011	.022	.034	.034	.034	1.617	.043
70<80	0.007	.067	.081	.101	.135	.121	.128	.095	.054	.034	.067	.014	.034	.054	.007	1.702	.037
80<90	0.000	.066	.041	.082	.131	.139	.106	.082	.090	.032	.024	.041	.041	.090	.033	1.700	.041
90<100	0.081	.060	.081	.126	.104	.096	.067	.067	.074	.059	.037	.022	.022	.089	.015	1.495	.031
	.011	.022	.049	.099	.126	.158	.108	.101	.081	.061	.032	.029	.028	.067	.024	1.611	.043

Items in this table are fractions of row sum except the last two columns.

Table 5.
Growth rate in earnings 1955 to 1969 by earnings percentile in 1955 bachelor's degree.

	$(Y69 - Y55)/Y55$ = growth rate																
1955 percentile	< 0	0 < .25	.25 < .50	.50 < .75	.75 < 1.00	1.00 < 1.25	1.25 < 1.50	1.50 < 1.75	1.75 < 2.00	2.00 < 2.25	2.25 < 2.50	2.50 < 2.75	2.75 < 3.00	3.00 < 5.00	> 5.00	Mean growth rate	Mean compound annual growth rate
0 < 10	0.000	.015	.015	.015	.105	.045	.060	.075	.119	.105	.105	.015	.045	.164	.120	3.087	.075
10 < 20	0.000	.011	.000	.011	.066	.120	.099	.120	.176	.099	.088	.066	.000	.179	.015	2.044	.059
20 < 30	0.000	.016	.000	.078	.094	.125	.063	.172	.094	.063	.047	.047	.063	.109	.030	1.938	.057
30 < 40	0.000	.000	.000	.032	.138	.053	.213	.138	.106	.096	.043	.043	.043	.074	.021	1.934	.053
40 < 50	0.004	.011	.011	.044	.063	.170	.159	.144	.096	.077	.074	.022	.019	.067	.037	1.754	.053
50 < 60	0.000	.000	.016	.063	.143	.222	.111	.079	.143	.079	.048	.048	.000	.016	.032	1.926	.050
60 < 70	0.008	.008	.031	.039	.086	.094	.180	.117	.141	.164	.016	.023	.008	.078	.008	1.718	.048
70 < 80	0.000	.010	.019	.058	.082	.159	.087	.192	.101	.043	.067	.029	.019	.082	.053	1.923	.053
80 < 90	0.011	.040	.038	.048	.136	.115	.107	.079	.085	.073	.068	.040	.011	.102	.034	1.794	.049
90 < 100	0.072	.039	.112	.086	.065	.112	.112	.119	.066	.033	.033	.026	.026	.105	.007	1.413	.037
	.012	.017	.029	.050	.091	.126	.125	.130	.106	.078	.059	.033	.021	.089	.034	1.877	.050

Items in this table are fractions of row sums except the last two columns.

Table 6.
Growth rate in earnings 1955 to 1969 by earnings percentile in 1955 graduate training.

	(Y69 − Y55)/Y55 = growth rate															
1955 percentile	< 0	0 < .25	.25 < .50	.50 < .75	.75 < 1.00	1.50 < 1.25	1.25 < 1.50	1.50 < 1.75	1.75 < 2.00	2.50 < 2.25	2.25 < 2.50	2.50 < 2.75	2.75 < 3.00	3.00 < 5.00	> 5.00	Mean growth rate	Mean compound annual growth rate
0 < 10	0.000	.012	.000	.000	.012	.047	.082	.071	.071	.094	.094	.071	.035	.247	.165	4.147	.095
10 < 20	0.000	.020	.000	.010	.051	.051	.141	.162	.111	.131	.051	.101	.051	.080	.040	2.176	.063
20 < 30	0.000	.000	.014	.028	.069	.111	.125	.111	.097	.139	.028	.042	.069	.097	.069	2.275	.053
30 < 40	0.000	.000	.027	.000	.040	.107	.200	.107	.173	.040	.067	.040	.053	.120	.027	2.085	.060
40 < 50	0.005	.000	.010	.055	.050	.155	.100	.130	.100	.095	.085	.035	.050	.110	.020	1.766	.057
50 < 60	0.000	.000	.028	.028	.028	.083	.278	.111	.111	.111	.056	.056	.000	.056	.056	2.214	.055
60 < 70	0.014	.014	.028	.028	.056	.111	.111	.194	.111	.083	.042	.083	.070	.042	.014	1.827	.054
70 < 80	0.000	.008	.023	.039	.094	.148	.133	.109	.117	.094	.039	.023	.055	.094	.023	1.879	.050
80 < 90	0.000	.028	.019	.009	.075	.123	.104	.142	.113	.094	.009	.066	.028	.142	.047	2.173	.055
90 < 100	0.080	.030	.100	.050	.110	.080	.090	.100	.060	.030	.030	.060	.020	.110	.050	1.702	.044
	.010	.011	.024	.029	.061	.110	.123	.124	.105	.090	.052	.054	.045	.113	.046	2.191	.057

Items in this table are fractions of row sums except the last two columns.

second and ninth rows are the same in each education level. (The same conclusion would be reached using the other rows in the table.)

For any one educational level, the results are similar to those given for the whole sample in table 2. That is, except for the top and bottom row, the mean percentage change is independent of earnings percentile in 1955[9]. The people at the bottom in 1955 have the highest growth rate, while those at the top in 1955 have the lowest growth rate (except for the high school category). Also, at each education level, those with high earnings in 1955 tend to have distributions with a greater percentage of people in both tails than people with low incomes. Despite the relatively few observations in these tables, the differences in the distribution by row are significant. Thus, we can conclude that results in table 2 do not occur solely because high school graduates are more concentrated in the lower percentiles in 1955.

4. Growth rate equations

The information in tables 1 through 6 indicates that about 50% of the people moved by no more than 10 percentile points in the sample's earnings distribution between 1955 and 1969 but that the distribution of growth rates covers a wide range and varies with the level of 1955 earnings. In this section, we will present equations to determine which characteristics that determine the level of earnings also determine growth rates. These results are interesting in their own right, especially since we have measures of such a wide variety of characteristics. In addition, these equations will help us to refine the tests of the various hypotheses presented in the next chapter.

In table 7, we present several equations in which the dependent variable is $(Y69 - Y55)/Y55$. (The reader who wishes to examine the determinants of $Y69 - Y55$ can do so by subtracting the 1955 regression from the 1969 one as given in ch. 4[10].) The first equation contains all the variables

[9]There is, however, a tendency in each of the tables for the average compound growth rate to decrease with 1955 earnings partly because of the wider variance in growth rates at the higher 1955 percentiles.

[10]With least squares regressions, the estimate of B from $\Delta Y = XB$ is equal to $(X'X)^{-1}(X'\Delta Y)$ which equals $(X'X)^{-1}(X'Y69) - (X'X)^{-1}(X'Y55)$. The last two expressions are the estimates obtained in 1969 and 1955 since X is the same in the two years (except that 8% of the people obtained more education after 1955).

Table 7.
($Y69 - Y55$)/$Y55$ earnings equations.

Independent variables	(1) coef.	(1) t value	(2) coef.	(2) t value	(3) coef.	(3) t value	(4) coef.	(4) t value
Education:								
Some college	.040	.8*	.070	1.5*	.082	1.7*	.116	2.4
Bachelor's	.143	2.8	.214	4.4	.187	3.6	.245	4.8
Some grad.	.122	1.5*	.173	2.2	.142	1.7*	.180	2.2
Master's	.362	4.8	.393	5.4	.332	4.6	.338	4.8
Ph.D. + L.L.B. + M.D.	.487	4.0	.543	4.6	.491	4.1	.511	4.4
L.L.B.	.191	1.3*	.176	1.2*	.464	3.1	.493	3.4
M.D.	.793	3.9	1.114	5.6	1.357	6.8	1.676	8.5
Ability:								
2nd fifth	−.009	.2*	.016	.3*	.013	.2*	.038	.7*
3rd fifth	−.006	.1*	.024	.5*	−.003	.1*	.021	.4*
4th fifth	.013	.2*	.063	1.2*	.020	.4*	.061	1.1*
(top) 5th fifth	.018	.3*	.098	1.8*	.036	.6*	.098	1.8*
Biography:								
2nd fifth, 3rd fifth	.008	.2*	.039	.8*	.016	.3*	.039	.8*
4th fifth, 5th fifth	−.080	1.6*	−.035	.7*	−.063	1.3*	−.028	.6*
Religion:								
Jewish	.037	.4*	.215	2.7	.203	2.4	.376	4.5*
Protestant	−.036	1.0*	−.049	1.4*	−.023	.6*	−.031	.8*
Attended religious school often	−.009	.1*	−.056	.7*	−.032	.4*	−.071	.9*
Attended religious school never	−.037	1.0*	−.042	1.2*	−.035	.9*	−.037	1.0*
Father-in-law high school								
Mother-in-law high school	.075	2.0	.077	2.1	.106	2.7	.113	2.9
Time spent on sports	.014	1.1*	.020	1.6*	.006	.5*	.009	.7*
Time spent on chores	−.030	2.1	−.032	2.4	−.024	1.7*	−.027	2.0
Time spent on hobbies	−.010	.8*	−.006	.6*	−.016	1.3*	−.014	1.1*
Time spent on part-time job	.017	1.6*	.024	2.3	.016	1.5*	.021	1.9*
Never moved before high school	−.012	.3*	−.018	.5*	−.009	.2*	−.013	.4*
Attended private high school	.005	1.5*	−.001	.4*	.114	.9*	.629	2.4

Attended private elementary school	.720	2.9	.790	3.3	.622	2.3	.236	1.9*
Factors influenced entering occupation, no = 1								
Future financial prospects	−.137	3.3	−.188	4.7	−.203	4.8	−.261	6.3
Independence	.065	1.6*	.078	2.0	−.039	.9	−.049	1.2*
challenging work	−.060	1.5*	−.084	2.1	−.052	1.2*	−.069	1.7*
Help others	.019	.5*	.052	1.4*	−.049	1.2*	.083	2.1
Job security	.021	.6*	.069	1.9*	.091	2.3	.139	3.6
Prefers to be salaried	−.066	1.6*	−.102	2.5	−.167	3.9	−.215	5.2
Other assets (own business, real estate), 1969	.005	1.5*	.013	4.4				
Self-employed businessman, 1969	.405	4.7	.443	5.4				
Self-employed professional, 1969	.080	1.5*	.146	2.8				
Teacher, pre-college, 1969	−.08	.9*	−.126	1.5*				
Hours on main job, 1969	.011	5.5	.010	5.2				
Hours on second job, 1969	−.007	2.0	−.010	3.1				
Weeks lost from illness, 1969	−.017	2.6	−.020	3.1	−.018	2.7	−.020	3.1
Mobility 1955 to 1969	.028	3.1	.036	4.1	.022	2.4	.026	2.9
Age	−.029	3.7	−.022	2.9	−.027	3.3	−.021	2.7
Year of first job	.021	3.0	.012	1.8*	.016	2.3	.009	1.3*
Current residence in town of 50, to 1000000	.060	1.4	.105	2.6				
Current resident in excess of 1000000	.211	3.6	.297	5.2				
College quality (Gourman rating)								
Weight, 1969 (100's of lbs.)	1.114	1.4*	1.684	2.2	1.083	1.3*	1.509	1.9*
Weight squared, 1969	−.288	1.3*	−.430	2.0	−.271	1.2*	.376	1.7*
Summy for nonresponse in 1972	.040	.4*	.156	1.6	−.055	.6*	.009	.1*
Entered school age 7+	−.074	.8*	−.116	1.3*	−.077	.8*	−.108	1.2*
$Y55$			−.089	19.1			−.067	14.4
Constant	−.424	.5*	−.494	.6*	.344	.4*	.332	.4*
R^2	.135		.200		.084		.124	
Stand error	1.109		1.067		1.142		1.117	
Degrees of freedom	4547		4546		4555		4554	

*Not significant at the 5% level.
Variables are defined in ch. 3, tables 6 and 7.

used in the final equations for 1955 and 1969 in ch. 4. The second equation adds $Y55$ to the first. In both these equations, we have included a number of variables, such as 1969 business assets, where we do not have comparable 1955 variables. In eqns 3 and 4, we have omitted the variables measured exclusively in 1969 except weeks lost because of illness, which probably is not highly correlated with the comparable 1955 variable.

We will concentrate first on the second equation which contains $Y55$ and which has an R^2 of .20. We have established that $Y55$ is determined by nearly all the other variables in the equation. We can think of $Y55$ as equal to Ze plus Xb where X is all the included variables and Z are all the other determinants of $Y55$. We demonstrated in ch. 3 that if we were to compare the estimates of

$$Y = Xd + Ze$$

and

$$Y = Xf + (Z + Xb)g,$$

that our estimates of g and e would be identical while the estimate of f would equal that of $d - bg$. Thus, the inclusion of $Y55$ in our equation means that we have held constant all the other determinants of Y including luck and $K55 - I55$ where $K55$ is the stock of investment in on-the-job training and $I55$ is the investment in that year[11]. The coefficients or the other variables in this equation represent the effect of each variable on the growth rate, net of the effects passed on through $Y55$.

As might be expected from the results in tables 1 and 2, the higher a person's 1955 earnings are, the slower his growth rate. The coefficient of $-.09$ is highly significant with a 't' value of 19. (Table 2 would make us suspect that the effect of $Y55$ is concentrated in the two extreme rows or, in other words, that the coefficient on $Y55$ varies by level of $Y55$.) As just explained, the coefficient on the earnings variable represents the effect of all the unmeasured variables. Results presented later suggest that one of the important unmeasured variables is luck. The on-the-job training variable, $K55 - I55$, may also be important although tests of the theory presented below tend to conflict with Mincer's theory.

[11]We have expressed the on-the-job training variable in this way to be in accord with Mincer's model, as explained below.

Previous research based on cross section data has shown that age earnings profiles tend to be steeper for the more educated. Using the same people at different points of time, we also find that the average growth rate increases continuously with education (except for some graduate) with most of the difference from high school graduates being statistically significant[12]. The coefficients on the education variables are larger than most of the other coefficients although attending private elementary school is the single largest coefficient.

While the average growth rate increases monotonically with ability, none of the coefficients are significant at the 5% level. Indeed, many other variables that determine *Y*55 or *Y*69 do not have a significant effect on the growth rate. There are, however, several interesting variables, which have significant and large effects. For example, those who are Jewish have a growth rate 21% points above that of Catholics[13]. Several other SES variables are also significant. For example, those who attended private elementary school have a growth rate 80% greater than those who did not. Also, mother-in-law's and father-in-law's education are both significant and positive.

Of the time spent in youth variables, sports and part-time job have significant positive effects (a 10 percentage point difference between no time and most time) while chores have a significant negative effect (of 12 percentage points). With the exception of helping others and job security, which is significant at the 6% level, the other nonpecuniary variables are all significant. Those not interested in future financial prospects nor in challenging work have a slower growth rate which also is true for those interested in independence in their work. The people who prefer to be salaried have a 10 percentage point slower growth rate.

The age variable has a negative coefficient implying a concave earnings function. The positive sign on the year of first job also implies concavity, but this coefficient is only significant at the 7% level.

Those who were self-employed in 1969 have a faster growth in earnings. Increased hours on first job in 1969 also lead to a faster growth

[12]A word of caution is in order. The cross section results are based on the percentage change in average earnings over various cohorts but our results are based on the average of percentage changes. The two are not necessarily compatible. For example, the M.D. result appears to be dominated by a few people who were interns in 1955.

[13]When *Y*55 is excluded, the Jewish coefficient is only .04 and not significant.

rate, but the opposite is true for hours on second job[14]. Those who moved interregionally after 1955 have a faster growth rate as do those who live in bigger cities in 1969. Good health in 1969, as reflected in weeks lost from illness and weight, is associated with higher growth rates.

The other equations in table 7 give similar results although some coefficients fluctuate between equations, and many fewer coefficients are significant when *Y*55 is not included in the equation.

The equations clearly indicate that there are important systematic elements in the distribution of growth rates from 1955 to 1969. An interesting question is whether there is an underlying structure that explains which of the determinants of earnings in 1955 and 1969 are also significant in the growth rate equations. We will discuss this issue more formally in the next chapter, but a brief survey seems appropriate here.

In Mincer's theory, differential growth rates reflect differential investments in O.J.T. Thus in his framework the more educated, those whose in-laws have high education, those who attended private elementary school, those who do not want to be self-employed, do not want to be independent, are not interested in future financial success, and who are Jewish all invest more than the omitted categories. Mincer may be right, but one still wonders why these groups are different.

An alternative explanation is that because of uncertainty, people have to demonstrate their competence on the job which determines how quickly they ascend their career ladder. There are different carrer ladders with different characteristics. Some careers are relatively safe or undemanding but as a consequence have both a relatively low ceiling on earnings and a narrow distribution of outcomes. Other careers have higher earning ceilings, and perhaps more risk[15]. Because people are relatively risk averse, the latter careers have higher average earnings[16]. The difference in earnings between ladders is greater for older persons

[14]This may be because the 1969 earnings are only for main job while the 1955 earnings may include all jobs. However, this variable seems to represent those people with low wage rates who work hard. Thus it may represent some of the same forces in *Y*55.

[15]The ceilings may be related to span of control, degree of responsibility, and the cost and benefits of decisions. See Mayer or Reder.

[16]For example, we have already shown that the mean and variance (adjusted for personal characteristics) of earnings are correlated across occupations.

because the sorting process takes place *sequentially* over time and people only gradually reach the upper parts of the hierarchy.

This explanation can be applied easily to the risk preference and other nonpecuniary variables. The same model can explain the in-law, religion, private school, and education findings. For example, the in-law and private school variables can be interpreted as proxies for nepotism. But, in an uncertain world, a nepotistic system may function by giving a person a secure job and then, only if he has the ability, promoting him. Since there are pay scales within a firm, even the owner's son or son-in-law will only receive very high earnings if he holds an important job.

We have argued earlier that the religious variable is associated with drive and hard work, but such effort only pays off cumulatively. Finally, the education findings reflect the types of career ladders chosen by the more educated. That is, relatively few of our college graduates worked at any job but owner, manager, salesman, or professional. Their choice may have been based on opportunities or preferences; but, in any event, these are the careers within which sorting is important and ceiling earnings are high[17,18].

Even if this alternative explanation is correct, Mincer's theory may be correct in a formal sense. That is, lifetime earnings within career ladders can be adjusted to be the same, net of risk premiums and nonpecuniary rewards. But even here, the increase in earnings need not be due to on-the-job training but could solely reflect the firm's learning by observation, although a combination of the two learning mechanisms seems more likely.

5. Implications for the permanent income and life cycle hypotheses

Both Friedman and Modigliani, Brumberg, and Ando have presented consumption theories in which individuals plan their current consumption on the basis of expected income over a horizon that can be as long as

[17]Of course, there are subgroups within these broad occupations that are more or less risky, etc.

[18]For a discussion of riskiness by occupation, see ch. 5.

expected remaining life. Since in a cross section, we generally have only one or a few consecutive years of income, the expected long run income has been constructed either as an average of the few adjacent years or from equations that related earnings to personal characteristics such as age, education, occupation, etc.

The information on the relationship between earnings in 1955 and 1969 can be used to assess the appropriateness of such long run income estimates. For example, our finding that 40 to 60% of the people are found within the same or adjacent decile groups suggests that while there is a large amount of stability, that (presumably independent) transitory elements can still be fairly large relative to systematic elements. Moreover, the percentage change regressions, which include the same types of variables used by others to predict long run income, indicate that most of the change is not explainable by such variables. Indeed, since our most powerful explanatory variable, $Y55$, can be negatively correlated with $(Y69 - Y55)/Y55$ because of the presence of either measurement error or transitory events in $Y55$, we can be sure that we explain less than 20% of the dispersion in the growth in earnings. Unless variables such as occupation explain much of the growth rate in earnings, the long run variables constructed from earnings equations are far from perfect measures of long run income[19]. However, our growth rate equations eliminate constant multiplicative 'personal' variables which would appear as residuals in 1955 and 1969. Some people who construct long run income series from cross section data incorporate such residuals in their measures.

6. Conclusion

In this chapter we have examined the stability in the distribution of earnings between 1955 and 1969. While we find most people remain about in the same position, many moved from their starting point. Some of the variables we have used to explain the levels of earnings also explain the growth rate. Higher growths are related to education, in-law's education,

[19]Occupations have not been included because of the substantial degree of occupational mobility between 1955 and 1969.

preferring not to be self-employed, not wanting independence in work, not being interested in future financial success and being Jewish. Also, *Y*55 has a significant negative coefficient. Many of these variables seem to be related to drive, motivation and climbing career ladders. Since occupational choice is related to education and since earnings in various occupations differ, it appears that career ladders in a broad sense are important. Finally, it might be noted that while the R^2's of .1 to .2 indicate that we do not explain much of the dispersion in growth rates, these R^2's compare favorably with those for the 1955 earnings equations.

CHAPTER 7

Additional tests of some earnings distribution theories

In ch. 1, we indicated that a number of not necessarily inconsistent theories have been proposed to explain all or parts of the features of the distribution of earnings. To a large degree, our empirical work has been guided by these theories in the sense that we have tried to include empirical counterparts or proxies for the variables suggested by the several theories. At least as long as we have a good proxy, we cannot accept a theory as being correct if the suggested variable is not significant in our earnings equation[1]. But often, some of the key variables suggested by a theory are not measurable in our sample. Still, we may be able to test the theory if it yields predictions about the distribution of the residuals at a point of time or over time[2]. In this chapter, we will try to test various predictions made by several theories. Specifically, we shall examine versions of the stochastic theory, Mincer's on-the-job training model, and a sorting uncertainty theory. Before doing so, we remind the reader that we have tested and tentatively accepted certain theories (such as risk aversion) where we have used and found significant an empirical measure of the theoretical construct[3].

[1]Recent work by Goldberger also suggests that we can determine how much measurement error there is in the proxy. We have not, however, incorporated these techniques.

[2]Many of these predictions are of the nature of 'if A is true, then B must happen' where A is not observed. But even here some testing may be possible if the theory also predicts some other aspect of the problem such as 'if A is true, then C must happen, while if D is true, then E must happen'. If D and A are mutually exclusive, we should not observe both C and B.

[3]We are still assuming the empirical measures do represent the theoretical construct. We examine this issue in ch. 8.

1. Stochastic theories

We begin the discussion with the stochastic theories in which an individual's earnings depend cumulatively on random events[4]. In these models initial earnings depend on an individual's capacity, but the change in earnings depends on luck. For each individual, all previous rolls of the dice plus initial earnings determine earnings at any time. Let the earnings of the ith individual in year t be represented by Y_{it} and the random event by e_{it}, which is assumed to be independent of Y_{it-1}. The stochastic theories can be written as:

$$Y_{it} = Y_{it-1} + e_{it} = Y_{io} + \sum_{j=0}^{N} e_{it-j}. \tag{7.1}$$

$$\ln Y_{it} = \ln Y_{it-1} + e_{it} = \ln Y_{io} + \sum_{j=0}^{N} e_{it-j}. \tag{7.1a}$$

The variance of Y_t can be expressed as

$$\sigma^2_{Y_t} = \sigma^2_{Y_o} + \sum \sigma^2_{e_{t-j}} + 2\sum \sigma_{Y_o e_{t-j}} + 2\sum_{j>k} \sigma_{e_{t-j}e_{t-k}}. \tag{7.2}$$

There is a similar expression for $\sigma^2_{\ln Y}$.

An important case, which is the one generally but not exclusively studied, arises if the e's are serially independent. Then, after a long enough passage of time, the distribution of Y_t will depend solely on the distribution of e_t. Moreover, with this assumption the last two terms in (7.2) will be zero and σ^2_{YT} will increase each year by the addition of σ^2_{et}. Thus, this version of the stochastic theory predicts that the variance of earnings (or of its log) will increase continuously with age for a cohort. In addition, since the theories either assume or imply that e_t is distributed independent of Y_{it-1} and its systematic determinants, σ^2_e should be independent of X_t e.g. σ^2_e should be homoskedastic over the different education levels.

In some stochastic models only luck is involved and there should be no systematic determinants of Y_{io} or Y_{it}. But other stochastic models assume

[4]See Mincer (1970) for an interesting survey and analysis of these theories. The original work in this area is due to Aitcheson and Brown, Champernowne, Rutherford, and Mandelbrot. Various assumptions about the distribution of the e's and about the validity of (7.1) and (7.1a) can lead to the normal, log normal of Pareto or other distributions.

that Y_{io} is determined by education, etc. and then luck is added on. In this version, the correlations of education, etc., with Y should decline over time since the variance of Y_t increases while that of Y_o is constant[5]. Moreover, a hypothesis of stochastic models is that e_{it}, which is the difference in earnings (or its log), should be distributed independently of Y_{it-1} for Y_{io}.

How do these predictions of the stochastic theory with the e's serially independent compare with our findings? In ch. 4, we examined the standard error in earnings in 1955 and 1969 for the sample as a whole and various subdivisions. As shown in tables 1, 4, and 6 of that chapter, the standard error of earnings and its log increased between 1955 and 1969 in the whole sample and in each of the education and ability groups[6]. However, contrary to predictions of the model, the errors display heteroskedasticity in both years with respect to both education and mental ability[7].

The stochastic theories require that either the difference or the percentage changes in earnings be independent of the level of earnings. But table 2 in ch. 6 indicates that the mean growth in earnings is different at the highest and lowest levels of 1955 earnings[8]. The difference in mean growth rates might be attributable to transitory effects that do not become impounded into a person's earnings base, but such an explanation is not in accord with the Markov assumptions of the stochastic models. As is evident from the pattern of the percentage changes and has been confirmed by direct calculations, the *average difference* in earnings increases with the level of $Y55$. Thus models expressed as eqn (7.1) are also rejected by our data.

Education, ability, family background, nonpecuniary preferences, and other characteristics yield an R^2 of about four points higher in 1969 than in 1955 even when we exclude the information such as business assets which pertain directly to 1969. This is contrary to the model's prediction.

[5]The stochastic processes theories also provide no explanation of why age earnings profiles slope upwards or why the steepness of the profiles varies with education.

[6]This need not indicate a continuous increase. Mincer, for example, has found more complicated patterns in Census data.

[7]The variances also differ by occupation, but what occupation a person is in could be determined by luck.

[8]Those with high earnings in 1955 also have distributions with fatter tails for which the theory offers no explanation although no prediction is failed.

All in all, the particular version of the stochastic model that we are testing does not seem to fit the data well. But it can be objected that other versions that make different assumptions about either the pattern of serial correlations of the e's or the relationship of the e's and the determinants of Y_o could be in accord with the facts. Indeed, Kalecki has demonstrated that with different assumptions, the stochastic model produces other results such as σ_e^2 remaining constant as people age. But I have yet to see a version of the stochastic theory that can be made consistent with all the findings presented above, unless the sorting model described below is thought of as a stochastic model.

2. *Investment in on-the-job training models*

Next let us consider the investment in on-the-job training theory. Mincer has greatly broadened the pioneering work of Becker and Schultz on investment in human capital by superimposing a general equilibrium framework on a learning-by-doing model. His model can be thought of in the following terms. Suppose skills learned on the job increase a person's marginal productivity to many employers. If an employee who receives general on-the-job training is legally free to accept any job offer at any time, after finishing his training he will be paid a wage equal to his new, higher marginal product (in a competitive market). Next, suppose occupation A gives no general training and will pay a person the same wage rate throughout his lifetime; but occupation B involves general training and has a rising age earnings profile for an individual. A rational person would choose the occupation whose earnings streams has the larger present discounted value. But Mincer argues that with free entry into both occupations, the present value of the two earnings streams will be equalized[9]. Since a person will receive a real wage equal to his marginal

[9]However, some people may be receiving quasi-rents if education or any skill does not augment skills by the same percentage in all occupations. For example, suppose I.Q. augments a person's skills more in cognitive than physical based occupations. If the people with high I.Q. are $X\%$ more efficient than those with low I.Q., then the high I.Q. people will receive $X\%$ higher wages. If I.Q. is more important in B than in A, all the high I.Q. people will choose B; but if B also hired some low I.Q. people, then it is only for this marginal group that present values are equated.

product after training, he must be paid less than his marginal product while being trained[10].

Mincer expresses his theory as:

$$Y_{it} = Y_i^* + r\left[\sum_{j=0}^{t} \lambda_{ij} Y_j - \lambda_{it} Y_t\right], \tag{7.3}$$

where Y^* which depends on schooling, ability, etc., is the constant earnings of a person who never invests on the job; λ is the fraction of earnings invested or k_t/Y_t where k_t is the amount of the investment; r is the rate of return on investments in on-the-job training; and Y is observed earnings. Since λ_j is not observable directly, eqn (7.3) becomes a tautology if no restrictions are placed on the λ_j's. Mincer avoids this by assuming that investments are monotonically decreasing function of age. The change in earnings, $Y_{t+1} - Y_t$, can be written as $rk_{t+1} - (K_{t+1} - k_t)$ which certainly will be positive if k decreases with age.

Equation (7.3) is a complicated difference equation which is difficult to analyze directly. Mincer, however, introduces several modifications that simplify the problem. One such modification is that there is some peak level of earnings, Y_p, at which $\lambda_{it} = 0$ (or perhaps λ_{it} just equals depreciation). Another important concept Mincer uses is the overtaking point, which is designated as the year in which $r \sum \lambda_{it} Y_t$ equals $\lambda_t Y_t$ or when $Y_t = Y^*$. Let us write $\sum \lambda_{it} Y_t$ as K_t and $\lambda_t Y_t$ as I_t.

At the peak earning period, the variance in earnings will be

$$\sigma^2_{Y_p} = \sigma^2_{Y^*} + r^2 \sigma^2_{Kt} + 2r\rho_{Y^*K_p} \sigma_{Y^*} \sigma_{K_p}, \tag{7.4}$$

where ρ_{YK} is the correlation between Y and K. While at the overtaking point, which for the moment we will assume to be the same for all, and which we designated as j,

$$\sigma^2_{Y_j} = \sigma^2_{Y^*}. \tag{7.5}$$

In eqn (7.4), the variance over individuals in observed earnings depends on the variance of Y^*, the variance of investments in OJT and the

[10]This agument is based on the proposition that the discounted value of wages will be equalized in all occupations. This equilibrium condition should hold if the age earnings profile is upward sloping because of institutional phenomena, or for any reason. Even if no learning-by-doing is involved, we can if we wish call the positive difference between a flat and a rising profile 'investment'.

correlation between Y^* and K. At the overtaking point, $rK_t = \lambda I_t$ and the variance in observed earnings equals the variance in Y^* (and the variance in this is due to variances and covariances in innate ability and in abilities acquired off the job). If r and ρ are nonnegative, Mincer's model indicates that the variance in earnings should increase from the overtaking to the peak year. Also, since individual variation in investment in OJT is not measured, the contribution of the measured variables to observed earnings should be greater in the overtaking year[11].

The above conclusions are conditional on the sign of ρ and on our having observations corresponding to the overtaking and peak periods. We will argue below that 1955 and 1969 do correspond at least roughly to those years. We cannot eliminate the other conditional aspects but we can derive other tests which also depend on the sign of ρ or in which ρ does not enter.

For example, suppose we rank individuals by earnings in the overtaking period and calculate mean earnings for people in the bottom tenth, second tenth, . . . top tenth in 1955. Now, for the people who fall into a 1955 cell, calculate average earnings in 1955 and 1969. Then, using eqn (7.3), we can calculate that the mean change in a cell between the overtaking and peak year is

$$\bar{Y}_p - \bar{Y}_j = r\bar{K}_p, \tag{7.6}$$

(assuming r is the same for all).

Now, if $\bar{K}_p$ and $\bar{Y}^*$ are not correlated, the expected value of $r\bar{K}$ should be the same for each cell. If, however, $\bar{K}_p$ is positively correlated with Y^*, the $r\bar{K}$ will increase with $\bar{Y}_j$. But the correlation of Y^* and $\bar{K}_p$ is the 'between cell' estimate of ρ. The model, of course, could be expressed in terms of ln Y in which case (7.5) can be approximated by $(\bar{Y}_p - \bar{Y}_j)/\bar{Y}_j$. The ln Y and Y answers could be different since $\bar{K}$ could be positively related to $\bar{Y}$ but ln $\bar{K}$ could be negatively related to ln $\bar{Y}$.

It may be helpful to view this problem in another way. If the distribution of K_p is independent of Y^*, then when examined at the overtaking point, Mincer's theory yields the same testable hypothesis on

[11]Unless the individual variation in OJT is perfectly correlated with some measured variables.

[12]Note that $\bar{Y}_j$ and $\bar{K}_j$ would be uncorrelated at times since every value of K_j can be found at any one value of Y^*. This does not rule out K_p and Y^* being correlated.

growth rates as the stochastic theory expressed in eqn (7.1a). Mincer's model, however, yields different predications when growth rates are calculated from a year that is not the overtaking point. We can see this best if we specify the on-the-job training investment function. Mincer in his analysis often assumes that the individual's investment paths are exponential as in eqn (7.7):

$$\lambda_{it} = A_i^{-b_i t} e \qquad 0 < A_i < 1, \, b_i > 0. \tag{7.7}$$

The implications of this investment equation (as well as one with a linear time trend) for testing his hypothesis are derived in Appendix F and will be summarized here. Mincer usually restricts b_i to be the same for all individuals while letting A_i vary. In this case the length of the overtaking period (for people who can borrow at the rate r) is the same for all A_i although the actual overtaking year will vary for people of the same age because of differences in time spent in school and perhaps military service. Mincer's model, therefore, predicts that those with the higher A_i will always have higher growth rates in earnings.

If we knew A_i for each person, we could test the theory directly. We can, of course, calculate the average earnings a person with a given set of measurable skills would receive. But the difference between an individual's actual earnings and this average would also include the effects of other unmeasured skills, etc.

Suppose, however, in a year prior to the overtaking period we were to order people by observed earnings and then calculate average earnings within each of successive tenths in the distribution. By reasoning similar to that of Friedman's as to why the bottom and top observed income groups contain more individuals with large negative and positive transitory income, we can establish that those in the bottom deciles must be investing more. That is, for each individual $Y_i - \bar{Y}$ would be equal to $(rK_t - I_t) + Y^*$, where these last terms are calculated about their mean values. A person can fall into the lowest tenth of the distribution for any one of the following reasons. First, Y^* may be very negative and $(rK_t - I_t)$ not a large enough positive number to offset Y^*. Second, both terms may be at least moderately negative; and third, $rK_t - I_t$ may be a large negative and Y^* not large enough positive to offset it. If one thinks of drawings from distributions of $(rK - I)$ and of Y^*, it is clear that the average value of each of these variables must be negative in the lowest decile of observed earnings. Similar analysis indicates that the average of $rK - I$ will increase monotonically with average observed earnings. Note that no mention was made of any correlation between $(rK - I)$ and Y^*. Positive or negative correlation would offset the average levels of $(rK - I)$ and Y^* in each tenth, but would not affect the statements about the qualitative pattern of the change in the average as earnings increase. That is, if $(rK - I)$ and Y^* are positively correlated rather than uncorrelated, it will be less likely to find someone with positive Y^* in the bottom tenth of the distribution but some can still be there. Moreover, it would be more likely to find people with low Y^* and low $(rK - I)$ concentrated in this area.

Since grouping by average earnings separates people by average level of $(rK - I)$, it is possible to determine whether those who have been investing more in pre-overtaking years and for whom $rK - I$ is smaller, are the ones with the greater increase in earnings. Similarly, it is shown in Appendix F that if b varies in eqn (7.6), those who invest more will have a higher growth rate in earnings. Moreover, those who have below average earnings in the pre-overtaking years will have above average earnings after overtaking.

Now let us test the predictions of the investment in the on-the-job training model. According to Mincer, the overtaking point occurs in no more than $1/r$ years of work experience or probably less than a decade. In 1955 in the NBER–TH sample, the length of time in the civilian post-World War II labor market is 8 to 10 years for most high school graduates, 7 to 9 years for most of those with some college work and 5 to 8 years for those with one or more degrees[13]. As a first approximation, let us assume that everyone was at the overtaking point in 1955. It also appears that 1969, when the men ranged in age from 45 to 52, corresponds to the peak earnings period. This conclusion is based not only on the age of the people but also on the finding that the 1969 and recalled 1968 earnings estimates are almost identical.

Earlier, we observed that Mincer's model predicts an increase in the variance in observed earnings from overtaking to peak period, for positive (and for small negative) values of ρ. As indicated in ch. 4, the

[13]About $\frac{1}{2}$ of the high school graduates and $\frac{1}{3}$ of the some college attendees began work before 1942.

variance does increase in the whole sample and in every education and ability group for Y and for $\ln Y$. The model also predicts that the R^2 explained by the measured variables should decrease with age, which is contrary to our results in ch. 3. Of course, the equations in ch. 3 include several important variables that are only measured in 1969 and must have been different in 1955; but the R^2 exceeds that in 1955 even excluding such variables.

Our previous chapters also provide additional information on the sign of ρ. First of all, in Mincer's theory, coefficients on all skills other than those produced by OJT would remain constant if OJT did not change; and the change in coefficients occurs only because of differentials in average investment in OJT. (This can be proven using omitted variable theorems.) The $Y69 - Y55$ coefficients can be obtained by subtracting the two comparable equations in ch. 3. As indicated in the text of that chapter, nearly every variable that has a positive effect on $Y69$ or $Y55$ has a positive effect on the change in earnings, i.e. ρ would be positive for all of these variables. Similarly, the equations in ch. 6 for the growth rate in earnings revealed a number of variables which had positive and significant effects on earnings and which were positively related to the level of earnings.

The material on the distribution of growth rates in ch. 6 reveals a different picture. The average growth rate in the whole sample or in the education subgroups indicate that ρ is zero over much of the range but negative if the highest and lowest values of $Y55$ are included. Negative values of ρ can be consistent with growth in the variance, but such a finding seems strange given the above discussion of ρ from regression results and especially since those tables do not hold constant the variables with a positive ρ. The tables in ch. 6 are based on the percentage change in earnings. Comparable tables for $Y69 - Y55$ indicate that the average change and the (redefined) ρ is positive.

Until now, we have assumed that everyone was at the overtaking point in 1955. But because the more educated have worked fewer years and because individuals follow different investment paths, this assumption is unlikely to hold for *all* individuals. Mincer often specifies in his investment function that bi is equal to $\bar{b}$ for all persons. For this investment function, the overtaking period is the same for people with the *same education* (who begin work in the same year). But when we examine the distribution of growth rates within education groups, as in tables 3–6 in ch. 4, we find the same pattern of results as above; and this pattern is unaltered if we standardize the observed growth rates or the 1955 level of earnings for differences in age and time on the job. Thus, if on average, we are at or before the overtaking point within each education group, ρ, in the ln form would be negative or zero.

There is another possibility to consider. Suppose that, contrary to Mincer, the b's differ; but, on average, people in all educational levels were at the overtaking point in 1955. At every education level, there will be a dispersion of b's about $\bar{b}$. Since earnings increase with education, on the average people with high education but low earnings in 1955 must be investing more than people with less education and the same earnings[14]. But those people with less education and high earnings in 1955 must be investing less than the more educated. Thus, at each level of 1955 earnings, the mean growth rate should increase with education, as is found in tables 3–6 in ch. 6. But under the assumption that A_i and Y_i^* are not correlated, the same argument would suggest that within an education class, those with smaller earnings in 1955 must on average have been investing more than those with more earnings, implying that the mean growth rates should be inversely related to 1955 earnings *within* each education group[15]. But in tables 3–6, the mean growth rates are constant except for the very top and bottom tenths again suggesting negative or zero correlation[16].

[14]This argument assumes that the other positive determinants of earnings are not negatively correlated with education. However, we have recalculation tables 2–6 in ch. 6, adjusting Y and $\Delta Y/Y$ for differences in all significant variables (e.g. we subtract out the average difference in earnings between those in the bachelor's and high school group or the top and bottom fifth, etc.) The adjusted tables yield comparable results.

[15]This tends to happen in the compound growth rates but the differences are not significant.

[16]Mincer has suggested that the more educated invest more, i.e. b declines with educational attainment. But the above test would still be valid because the more educated can only have the same below average earnings if they invest *more* than the less educated. Also, in Appendix F it is demonstrated that if the investment function is $\lambda_{it} = C_i + bt$, Mincer's model yields the same hypothesis tested and rejected above. However, it is also shown in the appendix that if, in this equation, b also varies by individual, it is not possible to obtain a testable hypothesis without knowledge of the parameters C_i and b_i. Thus, there may be some investment function that would reconcile table 2 with Mincer's investment model; but the theory is empty without knowledge of this function. Moreover, the linear and exponential investment functions are the ones used by Mincer in his empirical work.

It is possible that high school graduates are beyond the overtaking point – especially since $\frac{1}{2}$ of this group began work before World War II while those with one or more degrees have not yet reached the overtaking point. When either A or b vary in eqn (7.6), the profiles will continue to fan out beyond the overtaking point (as long as investment continues). While for those people not yet at the overtaking point, those investing more in 1955 should have the higher growth rate. Thus, in this case the correlation between mean growth rates and 1955 earnings level should be positive for high school graduates and negative for college graduates. But in ch. 6, once the top and bottom fifths are eliminated, there is no correlation at any education level in the average growth rates and a slight negative correlation at any education level in the compound growth rates.

The classification by observed percentiles in 1955 may be affecting the test of Mincer's theory since his formulation does not deny that an individual's earnings in a year may be affected by random events. Suppose such events are transitory so that, ignoring on-the-job investments, $Y_t = \bar{Y} + e_t$. Then, as in Friedman, we would expect the top and bottom tenth of 1955 earnings to include a larger proportion of those with large positive and negative e's. But with transitory events uncorrelated over 14 years, we would also expect those at the top in 1955 because of large positive e's to have low growth rates, etc. Replacing the observed fraction of people in the top tenth in the left-hand cell with the overall sample percentage, the average growth rate becomes about 1.8 while a comparable adjustment for the right-hand cell for the bottom tenth reduces its average growth rate to about 2.2. If these numbers are to be trusted, table 2 in ch. 6 would yield a U-shaped pattern of average growth rates which is not consistent with either the Mincer or luck theories. However, if transitory events are found in varying amounts throughout the distribution, Friedman's analysis would suggest that the estimates of ρ would be biased towards zero. Thus, the tendency towards ρ being negative might be more pronounced if we could eliminate transitory earnings.

The essence of Mincer's argument is that labor markets function well. There are several reasons why our data might reject the investment hypothesis, although Mincer's theory might be a partial explanation of earnings and the labor market. By 1955 the market might have adjusted for *expected* wage changes that were *not* realized. But if forecasts are generally incorrect, it is difficult to consider how investment models can ever be verified with either cross section or time series samples; or more importantly, how can such samples be analyzed within the context of equilibrium investment models.

Second, Mincer's formulation only applies to general on-the-job training. We presented some evidence in ch. 5 that suggests that nongeneral training is important in this sample. No one has yet analyzed the implications of firm specific training on earnings profiles although some arrangements must lead to rising profiles. Personally, however, I suspect that there is too much uncertainty, lack of information, and barriers to competition to let markets function well.

3. *Sorting uncertainty and hierarchy models*

Suppose that employers are uncertain about a person's productivity because performance depends on many skills some of which are difficult to test for in advance. The firm can react to uncertainty in many ways. Of course, the firm could let a person fill any job and use a piecework system to pay him. But on most jobs a piecework system is (or can) not be used because of the difficulty in measuring an individual's output and because of the possibility of negative outputs associated with bad decisions. An alternative procedure, which may be very relevant in a hierarchical structure where errors can be more costly the higher a person's position is for the firm to learn by observing. In this model, firms initially place an individual in a job which is an entry position for one or more career paths. Then firms make successive decisions to fire, retain or promote on the basis of both the observed and required competency in the particular position held and the number of job openings in the next rung. People will be promoted faster the more competence they demonstrate and the quicker positions they are qualified for open up.

Ross has recently analyzed this model. He represents the model as one in which firms, who use an expected discounted profit criteria, acquire information by sampling on initial and subsequent assignments. While he assumes that an individual's skill level remains constant, the solution of this model indicates that on average, earnings will rise with time on the job. The importance of this finding is that rising age earnings profiles need not imply that skills are being created on the job[17].

Without more information, it does not appear to be possible to specify the optimal assignment path. Instead, I will postulate a partial adjustment model that is built up of several elements. The peak earnings a person can earn can be represented as:

$$Y^* = f(x), \tag{7.8}$$

where x is a vector of inherited and acquired skills. Progress along a career path can be represented as

$$Y_T^N = Y^* \frac{b}{T-t} \qquad \text{for } t < T, \quad 0 > b. \tag{7.9}$$

Actual earnings in any year depend on random events and on performance versus normal performance

$$Y_t = \alpha Y_T^N + (1-\alpha) Y_{t-1} + u_t, \qquad 0 \quad \alpha \quad 1. \tag{7.10}$$

If b is the same along all ladders, then the coefficients of the X's should change proportionately over time. However, there is every reason to believe that some career ladders are steeper than others or that b varies. Similarly, α can also vary by occupations.

While this model has certain similarities with the previous two, it yields some different predictions. Consider first the R^2 between Y and X. As in the stochastic models, if u_t are distributed independently, the variance of u will increase with t. To determine the change in R^2 as people age, we must examine the variance of the independent variables times their coefficient in comparison with the growth of the variance of

$$\sum_{j=0}^{t} \alpha^j u_{t-j}.$$

Since in our empirical work, we generally do not include Y_{t-1}, the estimated coefficients on the X's will be those implied by eqn (7.9). This equation can be written as Xd_t. In our equations the variance of the X's is

[17]Of course, a person may only exercise certain skills when he reaches particular rungs on the ladder. But in this model the person always had the skill, and it was not created on the job.

a constant as the people age, but the coefficients, and thus their contribution to the variance of Xd_t, alter. It is possible, therefore, for the R^2 to increase or decrease as people age. As just noted, when the u's are independent, this model postulates a growth in the residual variance in Y. The model also indicates that σ_y^2 will grow as people age as long as the d's have the same sign and increase with time.

Next, let us consider the change in earnings as people age. From eqn (7.10) we see that

$$\mathrm{d}Y_t/\mathrm{d}t = \alpha bY^*(1/T - t)^2 + (1-\alpha)\,\mathrm{d}Y_{t-1}/\mathrm{d}t, \tag{7.11}$$

which for most purposes we can treat as $b(1/T - t)$. As noted early, b probably varies by career ladder or occupation. In general, we would expect people who work in jobs such as manager and professionals to have the highest b. Because the x's help determine the occupation a person is in, we would expect that those x's that determine Y^* would influence b in the same direction, e.g. education would increase earnings and lead to a faster growth in earnings.

Over a 14 year period, $(1-\alpha)^j\,\mathrm{d}Y_{t-1}$ can be treated as close to zero except for large $\mathrm{d}Y_{t-1}$[18]. Thus, ignoring the last term in (7.9), $\mathrm{d}Yt$ should be positively related to Y^* and Y^N in 1955; and it can be shown that the percentage change in Y should be independent of the 1955 value of Y. However, the larger $\mathrm{d}Y_{t-1}$ terms which cannot be ignored will be more concentrated among those with the highest and lowest 1955 earnings. Since the model indicates that Y_t will grow faster the more Y^N exceeds Y_{t-1}, those with very low earnings would grow fastest over a 14 year period.

Alternatively, the model could be expressed in terms of ln Y in place of Y. The only major difference in the above analysis is that the percentage change in earnings from the equivalent of (7.9) would be dependent on b and could vary by education, etc.

None of these predictions are contradicted by the results given in previous chapters and used in the tests of the other theories. But since the theory is not tightly specified, especially in comparison with Mincer's, these tests are relatively weak. A more definitive test of this theory and Mincer's could be made if more years of earnings were available since for

[18]For example, if $\alpha = .1$, $(1-\alpha)^{14}$ is less than .2.

those the dynamic implications vary. But such tests await more and better data.

4. Conclusion

In this chapter, we have attempted to test aspects of those theories for which it is not possible to construct empirical counterparts of theoretical constructs by examining various predictions made by the model. As demonstrated in the OJT and sorting model sections, the hypotheses to be tested are too often too flexible to be subjected to a definitive test. That is, in the models there are several unknown relationships or correlations which can be chosen so as to explain practically any empirical observations. Still, this chapter has not been an exercise in futility since we have been able to indicate what some of the unknown relationships must be for the models to be correct. For example, in the stochastic models, u must be correlated over time which seems peculiar if only luck is involved. In Mincer's model, we need to have a negative correlation between the omitted variables and investment in on-the-job training although all the variables we have measured have a positive correlation.

Finally, we have been examining each of these theories in isolation. It seems likely that all of them are partially true – especially since we have already found so many variables suggested by different theories to be significant. Given the difficulties of testing a pure theory, it seems clear that to test a mixed theory and to separate out the roles of the various elements will be an imposing task.

CHAPTER 8

Validation of nonpecuniary tastes and family environment variables

Many of the important variables in our earnings equations are based on survey responses to questions not normally or even previously used in econometric analysis. Throughout our discussion, we have been treating these variables as measures of preferences towards various nonpecuniary rewards, family environment, etc. In this chapter, we will try to fulfill our earlier promise to justify the use of these labels by examining regressions in which the variables to be discussed either explain or are explained by other variables. While the results of these equations are often of interest in themselves, we will postpone a complete discussion until ch. 9.

1. Validation

A problem common to empirical work in the social sciences and elsewhere is the translation of theoretical constructs into empirical counterparts. The converse of this problem is the determination that an empirical measure is the counterpart of a particular theoretical construct. In general, such a determination involves two issues which can be expressed in the following way. Suppose our empirical measure, X, has a measurement error, u, and a systematic part x where $X = x + u$. The first question is the noise to signal ratio i.e. the variance of u divided by the variance of x. The second question is what exactly is x. That is, can we identify which theoretical construct x is and can we determine there is only one (dimension of) systematic variation or alternatively is $X = x_1 + x_2 + u$?

Certain techniques have been developed to answer these equations. Most of these involve comparisons of subjective classifications made by experts and objective classifications yielded by indices or tests, or comparisons of results on a series of tests given during a short period of time or on odd and even questions on a given test[1]. Unfortunately, these options are not open to us although the survey questions we use could be so tested in the future.

The primary validation technique we will use is based instead on the hypothesis that the x's under consideration are or, in case of family environments produce, latent traits. By a latent trait we mean that x will affect behavior or choices in a wide variety of areas. For example if a person is risk averse in occupational choice, we are assuming he will also be risk averse in many other activities such as whether or not to migrate, what to invest in, etc. It is worth noting that some traits need not be latent, e.g. people need not be risk averse in all choice situations[2]. Thus, our test is a conservative one.

The validation test we propose to use can be expressed as follows. We will estimate a variety of equations in which we will include the variables we wish to validate as well as those that should be included for other reasons. We will then examine the results to determine if the coefficients on the variables we are interested in have the right sign and are significant in the equations they should be and insignificant elsewhere. We will then consider the proportion of findings that are correct for each variable.

In principle, it would be possible to estimate equations for any item on which people make choices; but we have decided to restrict our analysis to: mental ability, educational attainment, quality of college, probability of migrating, and the earlier examined earnings. These choices were made for two reasons. First of all, since some traits, skills or tastes are almost surely not important for some choices, we probably have a better chance to reject our interpretations if we examine these variables which we think are strongly determined by the true variables we are trying to measure. Second, many of the variables we use can be important in an analysis of the direct and indirect effects of variables such as education.

[1]Goldberger recently has been exploring methods to estimate the noise to signal ratio. We have not used his methods because they are expensive and because in this first round we are more interested in establishing which variables appear to be useful proxies.

[2]A college professor may be averse in his choice of his investment portfolio but not in his choice of research projects. It is hard to investigate this problem because actual choices depend on opportunities as well as preferences. Morgan et al. have tried to construct a measure of risk aversion in an interesting recent Survey Research Center Study. The measure, which is based on answers to questions on use of seat belts, purchase of insurance, etc., is not significant perhaps because traits are not latent.

A few words on what we expect to find in the various equations are in order. First, scores on tests measure learned knowledge which depends on innate ability, quality of schooling, family environment, and pressures or incentives to learn. Thus we would expect traits that are related to hard work or drive to be related to test scores. Similarly, we would expect family variables to be proxies for genetic abilities and family environments that affect learning. The quantity of education obtained can be treated like the quantity of any good that can be purchased. The demand curve for education can be related to family income, prices, rates of return, and tastes. Our trait and ability measures are related to rates of return and tastes, while family background is related to at least income and tastes. Similar comments apply to the quantity of college education variable. Finally, the probability of migrating should be related to returns from migration and tastes or traits, but since we cannot find any effect of migration on earnings we will only examine traits and taste type variables.

Table 1 presents a comparison of results from the ability, educational attainment, college quality equations (which are described in ch. 9) and the 1969 earnings equations (described in ch. 3). We do not show the migration equation because so few variables are significant. These will be discussed in the text. Many other variables are included in each of these equations besides those shown in the table.

One of the most common proxies for SES is father's education. Father's education is positively and significantly related to test scores and the quantity and quality of educational attainment. However, father's education is not significantly related to earnings, unless business assets are excluded from the equation.

We could rationalize the ability and education results from a genetic, environmental, and taste viewpoint. The nonsignificance in the earnings equation is more enlightening. If, as is sometimes argued, the more educated spend more time or are more efficient in training their children and if this training increases abilities other than that held constant by our test score variables and schooling, we would expect father's education to be significant in the earnings equation[3]. Thus, training related to father's

[3]Others who have not included business assets have found father's education to be significant even after including ability. See Taubman–Wales or Sewell.

Table 1.
Comparison of coefficients in 1969 earnings, 1969 educational attainment, and mental ability equations.

Variable	Ability	Education	Earnings	College quality
Father's education	+ sig. (coll.)	+ sig.	+ not sig.	+ sig.
Mother's education	+ sig.	+ sig.	+ not sig.	+ not sig.
Father's occupation (SES)	not sig.	not sig.	+ not sig.	not used
Protestant	+ not sig.	− not sig.	− sig.	− not sig.
Jewish	+ sig.	+ not sig.	+ sig.	+ sig.
Private elementary school	+ not sig.	+ not sig.	+ not sig.	+ sig.
Private high school	+ not sig.	+ sig.	+ sig.	+ sig.
Raised on farm	− not sig.	+ sig.	not sig.	not used
Area high school	not sig.	not sig.	not sig.	not used
No move before high school	− not sig.	0	− not sig.	+ not sig.
Time spent on sports	− not sig.	0	+ sig.	− not sig.
Time spent on hobbies	− not sig.	− sig.	− not sig.	− not sig.
Time spent on reading	+ sig.	+ sig.	0	+ not sig.
Time spent on chores	− sig.	− not sig.	− sig.	− not sig.
Time spent on part-time job	− not sig.	− not sig.	+ sig.	− not sig.
Prefers to be salaried	+ not sig.	− sig.	+ sig.	− not sig.
Factors influencing occup. choices, no = 1				
Future financial success	− sig.	+ sig.	− sig.	− not sig.
Independence	+ sig.	+ not sig.	+ sig.	− not sig.
Help others	+ not sig.	− sig.	+ sig.	+ sig.
Challenging work	+ sig.	− sig.	− sig.	− not sig.
Job security	+ sig.	+ sig.	+ sig.	+ sig.
Grew up middle size city	+ not sig.	+ sig.	+ sig.	+ not sig.
Grew up large city	+ sig.	0	+ sig.	+ sig.

[a]Significantly different from Protestant.

The ability results taken from table 2, eqn 1, ch. 9. The education results from table 3, eqn 1, ch. 9. The earnings results from table 7, eqn 2 or earlier versions where not shown in ch. 3. The college quality results from table 4, eqn 1 in ch. 9. In all these equations, many other variables have been included.

education has a direct effect on earnings except that allowed for in our ability measure[4,5].

Mother's education has a similar pattern – a positive significant effect on test scores and educational attainment and an insignificant effect on earnings and college quality. The mother's work history results also are not in accord with the time spent on training argument (although the recalled information may be inaccurate).

Next let us consider the religious variable. The Jews in the sample score higher on ability, obtain more education (than Protestants), go to much higher quality schools, and receive higher earnings, *ceteris paribus.* While the ability results may only be a reflection of the nonrandomness of the sample, it seems likely that it reflects an environment in Jewish homes that emphasizes intellectual achievement. This same emphasis would explain the extra educational attainment and much higher college quality which has also been found in more random samples such as Eckland. Jews may be earning more because the drive for intellectual achievement is transferred to other activities or Jews acquired more knowledge (not included in our ability measure) that is useful on the job in their education[6].

Those who attended a private high school earn nearly $5000 more in 1969 than those who attended public or parochial school. We argued in ch. 3 that this huge differential represented either nepotism or the environmental effects of large family income, and not the quality of the education. That the variable does not represent quality is supported by our finding of a positive but not significant effect on ability and an insignificant effect on the quantity of education[7]. The family income and nepotism possibilities are in accord with the much higher quality schools attended.

Since most of the 29 people who attended private elementary school

[4]Unless the training is incorporated in other variables such as time on sports.

[5]We also find that her (recalled) work history while the respondent was 0 to 5 or 6 to 14 has no effect on his earnings. It is worth noting that there is a wide range in mother's education and that about 70 to 90% of the mothers did not work while the child was growing up or in elementary and high school.

[6]Our respondents were born around 1920; hence, the Jews must have been children or grandchildren of immigrants who, like many other recent immigrants, were greatly concerned with financial success and worked hard to achieve it.

[7]As discussed below, the test questions may be ones on which quality is unimportant.

(exclusively) also attended private high school, the elementary school variable indicates the effect, net of attending private high school. While the elementary school coefficients are always positive, they are only significant in the college quality equation[8].

The area of high school attendance has no effect on any of the variables. This would seem to rule out regional differences in the quality of pre-college education, etc., which affects earnings, education or test scores. However, the size of the town in which the respondent grew up affects test scores, educational attainment, college quality and earnings. All of these results may indicate differences in (be proxies for) the quality of education, tastes molded by the respondent's environment, or the availability of nearby colleges[9].

People who never moved before high school graduation have significantly lower intelligence and earnings but the same schooling and college quality. There are several possible explanations for this pattern. For example, if able people achieve success gradually, over time it might be expected that they would move occasionally as their incomes rose. Since there are very few Rockefellers, the stable group may include mostly those whose parents were never successful, and who have 'lesser' genes. The educational differences, in this interpretation, work primarily through differences in mental ability which are allowed for in the equation. Earnings are less, however, because the relevant genes for which the variable is a proxy span more than intelligence. An alternative view is that the stable group lived in small towns, etc. and did not have challenges to their intellectual curiosity or had relatively low quality schooling. Education is not affected for the same reasons as above. Low earnings in this view arise from lack of curiosity, a tendency to stay in small communities in which we have shown earnings are less, and perhaps less emphasis on material success.

Now let us consider the effects of time spent on various activities. Those who were sports minded have insignificantly less intelligence and college quality, the same schooling and more earnings, and were less

[8]The variance of the coefficient of a zero, one dummy variable is dependent on the number of people in each of the two categories. A variable with only $\frac{1}{2}$ of 1% of the people in a group will always have a very wide variance on its coefficient.

[9]It is not clear why 'large cities' has no effect on educational attainment.

likely to have left their high school states by 1969. The intelligence result may simply indicate lack of time for homework. The schooling result is not too surprising. People who are active and have (had) a great deal of physical energy are likely to engage in sports. This energy would stand them in good stead in business world as would physical fitness at age 47. In addition, sports involve both a competitive and cooperative learning situation, both lessons which can be valuable. The migration result is not clear to the author.

That reading is positively associated with the test scores and educational attainment is hardly surprising although we must realize that interest in reading is partly caused by intelligence as well as fostering intellectual interests. The absence of an earnings effect probably means that reading does not develop skills or knowledge useful on the job. Somewhat surprising, reading does not affect college quality.

There is a presumption that people who had a part-time job while growing up came from poorer families and ones which stressed a work ethic. Thus, it is not surprising that either because of drive and/or impatience, these people have achieved financial success by age 47 although they have less schooling and went to lower quality schools. The insignificant positive effect on intelligence may be a further reflection of drive to succeed partly offset by lack of time to study and perhaps poor genes.

People who remember spending much time on chores when growing up have significantly smaller test scores and earnings, significantly positive additions to schooling, but insignificant decreases in college quality. Following Merton, we argued that families that insist upon children doing chores (*ceteris paribus*) are on average of a lower middle income class that prizes conformity and frowns upon risk taking[10]. If this is a correct explanation, the ability results would occur because of poor genes and a family environment which would not encourage intellectual curiosity. The schooling result can also be interpreted along the same lines.

The next variable we will discuss is the prefer to be salaried response made in 1969. The people who so responded we consider to be risk averse and to earn less for that reason. There is no reason for such a characteris-

[10]Below we indicate that those who want job security or prefer to be salaried spent more time on chores although the coefficients are not significant.

tic to be related to test scores which is our finding. These people also have significantly less education. Weiss has shown that risk averse individuals choose less variable occupations. Since risk associated with income increases with education, the result may be plausible. The college quality differences are insignificant.

1.1. Other nonpecuniary preference variables

In our earnings equations we found that yes/no answers to factors affecting occupational choice were related to earnings. Those not interested in future financial success (whom we think are either less motivated or interested in monetary compensation) score less, go to lesser but not significantly different quality schools, but achieve more education. The ability result is in conformity with the motivation idea while the education result is in conformity with the monetary preferences idea.

Those not interested in independence score more and have insignificantly more schooling. If those wanting work independence maintained such behavior in school, it is possible for them not to have studied to have mastered tests, etc., and so score less.

Those who do not want to help others have less education, and lower college quality, more earnings, and insignificantly higher scores. If those who do not want to help others are more self-centered and desirous of monetary success, it seems possible that they would value less the nonmonetary aspects of education, but that there be little effect on test scores.

Those who do not want challenging work score more, go to school less and earn less. They also are less likely to have migrated. The ability and desire to work hard and to solve difficult tasks would explain the earnings, education, and migration results. The test scores can be explained in a way similar to the independence result, i.e. those who do not want challenging work master the things tested for rather than the important parts of knowledge.

Finally, those not interested in job security earn more, learn more, get more schooling, go to higher quality college, and migrate less. The one difficult item to reconcile here – especially given the previous paragraphs – is the ability result.

2. Additional comments on nonpecuniary reward and time spent variables

In the previous section, we indicated that our nonpecuniary reward and time spent variables generally yielded consistent results in equations other than earnings. In this section we will discuss some other evidence that bears on the meaning and usefulness of these variables. The major questions asked here are the extent to which the answers represent differences in preferences rather than past and current opportunities and the extent to which there is internal consistency between the variables.

2.1. Preferences and opportunities

Most of our so-called nonpecuniary variables are derived from the yes/no answers to the set of questions asked in 1972 that read, 'as best as you can remember, what factors influenced your decision to enter the occupational field you are in at the present time?' Several important and interrelated questions that arise with respect to these questions are first, whether yes/no answers to them could measure differences in preferences; second, how should the coefficients be interpreted assuming these are valid questions; and third, whether the responses to such questions asked of 47 year old men contain a substantial amount of ex post rationalization of their actual economic success?

Let us consider the first two questions simultaneously. Suppose that every occupation has a (discounted lifetime) pecuniary and nonpecuniary reward attached to it. Then an individual could construct an opportunity locus, such as AA' in fig. 1. The individual could also determine indifference curves such as BB' between pecuniary and nonpecuniary rewards and select that occupation at point C which yields the most utility. Suppose there is another person with the same opportunity curve but a different set of preferences. He would choose a different reward structure such as at D along the opportunity curve. For these two persons, the difference in monetary earnings, $Y_D - Y_C$, would indicate the effect of both the taste differences and the trade off opportunities available, although in a fundamental sense the differences arise because of variations in taste.

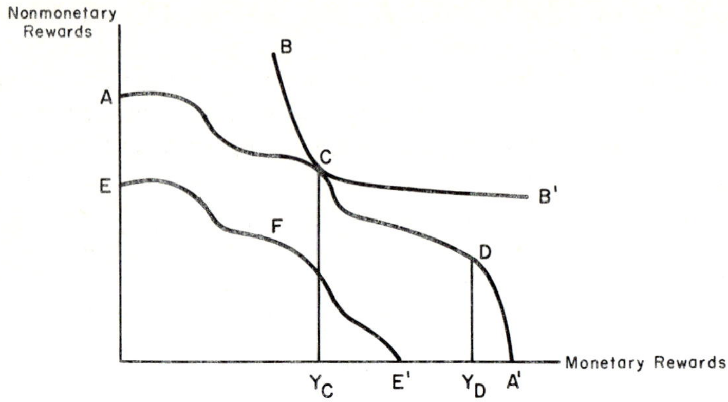

Fig. 1. Monetary and nonmonetary rewards.

For the moment, let us assume everyone in our sample has the same opportunity set. Then each person would choose a point along AA'. Now what does a yes/no answer indicate in the context of the wording of the question? One possibility is that a person compared C with other points along AA' and answered yes if monetary rewards were sacrificed to a significant extent in choosing the occupation entered. Suppose, therefore, that a person's opportunities are described by $E'E$ with his equilibrium at F. If the person at F said no and the one at C said yes, would it be true that $Y_F - Y_C$ represented differences in monetary rewards arising from differences in tastes? To this question, the answer is no since both preferences and opportunities differ between C and F. However, along a given opportunity curve, the yes/no answers can indicate something about preferences even if interpreted within a formal framework.

This formal approach, however, may be too rigid. In answering the question, the people may have been telling us something about themselves and their preferences patterns without regard to opportunity costs. For example, those who want job security may be indicating that they are conservative, cautious, and risk averse. Alternatively, the variables may also measure other skills; for example, those who want to help others may be saying that they know that they do not have the personality, drive, and commitment to be a top level manager. If this is true, we are not measuring nonpecuniary rewards but we are measuring other skills which help determine earnings.

One possible objection to interpreting our nonpecuniary variables as reflecting taste differences is that the responses may have been contaminated by the person's experience. That is, a person who at the beginning of his career was a risk lover may have failed at a risky job and is currently interested in job security and a salaried job. Similarly, a person may say he is interested in helping others as a means of rationalizing his lack of financial success.

The best way to handle this objection would be to use a sample in which the variables were asked prior to a person's leaving school. While this option is not available to us, we do have some information on how well people succeeded compared to their expectations. In 1969 we asked the people to indicate how their current financial compensation from work compared to their expectations when they began to work. The people could check the responses of 1 (actual well below expectations), to 5 (actual well above expectations). It seems very likely that these responses do measure the (major) differences between expected and actual income since this one–five variable alone explains 25% of the variance of *Y*69. A second piece of information is contained in the responses to questions on 'how important luck was in achieving success in your occupation'. It seems possible that those who consider themselves to have been treated unkindly by the fates would indicate luck is very important and circle the 5.

We have used the financial expectations and luck responses (both divided into dummy variables), as independent variables in equations for the nonpecuniary variables and the time spent variables[11]. When we use just the financial outcome variable, the highest R^2 in our ten equations is .006 and only 3 of the 40 dummies are significant at the 5% level. (If 4 or 5 were circled, people spent more time on a part-time job. If 5 were checked, people were less likely to be uninterested in a challenging job.) When the luck responses are added to these equations, the same two financial outcome dummies are significant in the part-time job equation

[11]Since in later equations we will correlate the nonpecuniary variables against one another, we have excluded those people who did not answer the 1972 questionnaire as well as those whose *Y*55 or *Y*69 was zero.

and 6 of the luck dummies are significant. But the luck responses do not follow a meaningful pattern since the dummy variable for luck 3 is significant in 4 equations, while the other luck coefficients in these equations do not follow a monotonic pattern. We obtain the same type of results when other variables are added to the equation. Thus, it seems safe to conclude that the responses to the nonpecuniary and time spent variables have hardly been affected, if at all, by work experiences.

Another possible worry about our variables is whether they form a consistent pattern among themselves. To study this question, we have correlated each of the variables with each other, as well as with the financial outcome variables. These descriptive equations, numbers 1 through 10 in table 5, ch. 9 can be summarized briefly as follows[12]. First, the only time the financial outcomes dummies are significant at the 5% level is in the part-time job equation although several of the dummies have '*t*' values in excess of 1.5. Thus, it still appears that we do not need to worry about 'sour grapes' contaminating the results.

Next let us consider which variables are significantly related to one another. Time spent on sports increases significantly with time spent on hobbies, but decreases with time spent on part-time job and chores. Thus people with more leisure time divided it between sports and hobbies. Also those now not interested in future financial prospects, nor in helping others spent less time on sports, which results are in accord with the cooperative/competitive interpretation in the earnings equation.

Other than time spent on sports, the time spent on hobbies is only significantly related to not being interested in job security, a result which does not clear up the author's confusion about this response.

The chore equation is more encouraging. Time spent on a part-time job is positively and time on sports negatively correlated with time spent on chores. The first result suggests that some people progress from within family to outside paid work. The opposite coefficients in the earnings equations on part-time job and chores also suggest differences in values inculcated in part by the family. The sports result indicates availability of leisure time. Of more interest is the finding that those interested in job

[12]Because the yes/no answers are scaled as zero/one dummies and because we have used many variables including continuous ones, we estimated the final equations by the probit method. See the next chapter for details. Also note that the equations have a few more variables than those discussed here.

security spent more time on chores, *ceteris paribus*[13]. This is in accord with our conformist interpretation in the earnings equation. However, the prefer to be salaried variable is insignificant. Those interested in helping others also spent more time on chores.

The part-time job variable is negatively correlated to sports and positively related to chores but to nothing else (although challenging work is nearly significant).

The percentage who prefer to be salaried is greater among those not interested in future financial prospects, and not interested in independence in work, but interested in job security. The last finding is hardly surprising since we interpret job security as another dimension of risk preference. The financial prospects answer may also be related to risk preference, especially since it can be indicative of diminishing marginal utility of income (a definition of risk aversion). Also, people not interested in future financial prospects may not want to work the long, hard hours often associated with self employment. The independence result is not surprising since being your own boss is one aspect of independence and the people who choose independence also prefer self employment.

The probability of not being interested in future financial prospects decreases with time spent on sports. The probability increases for those who prefer to be salaried, who are not interested in independence in their work, who are interested in helping others, who do not want challenging work and those not interested in job security. The salary preference relationship was just discussed. The independence and helping other results reinforce the idea of a lack of concern about material success. Since the financial prospects answer may be indicative of the person's attitudes towards hard work or an easy life, the 'challenging' result is not surprising. It might be thought that people not interested in future financial success would be interested in job security and vice versa. Our opposite finding suggests that since the people are less interested in money, they are willing to throw over a job to do interesting work, etc., and are unconcerned about both income stability and income level. To be consistent with this, the prefer to be salaried coefficient in this equation perhaps should be interpreted as the self-employed being people who work hard and are tied down to one job, rather than our usual risk aversion approach.

[13]In the part-time job equation, job security has the opposite coefficient although not significant.

The probability of not wanting independence increases for people who prefer to be salaried, are not interested in future financial success, do not want to help others, do not want challenging work, but are interested in job security.

The probability of not being interested in helping others decreases with time spent on chores (and is nearly significant for sports) which was discussed above. The probability increases for those not interested in independence, not interested in challenging work, not interested in job security, but interested in future financial success. These last four results suggest that those interested in money or in succeeding on the job are not as interested in helping others (at least as indicated by their occupation choices).

The probability of not being interested in challenging work increases for those not interested in future financial success, not interested in independence and not interested in helping others. This probability decreases with time spent on hobbies, chores, and part-time job. These correlations are not surprising.

Finally, the probability of those *not* being interested in job security increases with time spent on hobbies. Also, the probability decreases for those who prefer to be salaried, who are interested in future financial success, who are not interested in helping others, those not interested in independence, and those not interested in challenging work. All of these results have been discussed above.

While the R^2 in these equations are not very high, and while the discussion suggests that some of the variables may embody several somewhat different ideas, the overall impression one gets from these equations is that our interpretation of the findings in the earnings equations is not unreasonable.

3. Conclusion

The results in this chapter support our position that the simple measures we have employed to represent tastes and traits are likely to be related to the theoretical constructs. But certainly we agree that future research should be conducted both to confirm our findings and to refine the measures we have used.

CHAPTER 9

Determinants of education, ability, nonpecuniary, and other variables

In the equations in chs. 3 and 5, we explained earnings differences by such variables as education, health, work experience, personal characteristics, mental ability, nonpecuniary preferences, and several dimensions of socioeconomic background of the respondent's and his wife's family. The coefficients in these earnings equations represent the *direct* effect of variations in one variable with all other variables held constant. The variables can be divided into ones subject to the individual's control and those beyond his control or exogenous. Since the levels of attainment of some of the personally controllable variables are partly determined by some of the exogenous determinants, these exogenous variables also have an *indirect* effect. For example, the quantity of educational attainment is related to a person's mental ability level. If this is the only variable in the earnings equation causally related to earnings, the indirect effect of mental ability on earnings is equal to the extra education induced by mental ability times the effect of education on earnings.

In ch. 8, we discussed coefficients in particular variables, e.g. the time spent ones, in several of these equations. Our purpose there was to examine the reasonableness of our interpretations of these variables. In this chapter, we will concentrate on each equation at a time and, where appropriate, will refer the reader back to ch. 8 for comparisons and qualifications.

The variables studied in this chapter include the quantity and quality of education, the test scores on our ability measure, the probability of migrating, the nonpecuniary preferences, and time spent variables. The equations for the latter group for the most part represent association rather than causation.

A few words of caution before we begin our examination. First, the ability measure is derived from tests that, judging by other studies, may well be related to the quantity and quality of pre-test education, both of which varied over individuals in 1943 in mostly unknown ways. Though we cannot observe directly the effects of pre-test differences in the quantity of education, Taubman–Wales have concluded that such pre-test differences apparently have little effect on the test scores in this sample. Their conclusion is based on various pieces of evidence, but the most important element derives from the following observations[1]. For people with more than a high school education in 1969, the older ones on average should have more education prior to 1943. Thus, under some fairly weak assumptions, we should expect a bigger test score differential in favor of the older people among the more educated if pre-test education is important. The following table, taken from TW, indicates that the older members have a lower average score (apparently because of the lapse in time between completing pre-World War II schooling and tests) but with the differential the same at each education level[2]. Thus, the learned knowledge component associated with pre-test differences in years of schooling is not very important in our measure[3]. Since the recursive model seems as appropriate in our sample as in others, we will treat ability scores as the first rung in our recursive ladder.

There is one other minor matter. The biography variable, which we have used in the earnings equation, contains some information on pre-test education and grades, as well as family background data. Since we cannot separate out the contribution of such education or grades, we have computed ability equations with and without this variable. Finally, since the equations to follow are a bit tangential to our main theme, we have not explored issues as thoroughly as in the earnings chapter. Thus, we have not searched for interactions and we tended not to use variables already rejected in the more preliminary earnings equations.

1. Ability equations

While in our earnings equations we represent the ability measures by the sample fifth into which the person falls, in this section, for convenience,

[1]See their ch. 4 for the other evidence.

[2]TW only used about 80% of the sample.

[3]Thus, if we wish to estimate a recursive structure with ability 'causing' education, we would be justified.

Table 1.
Average score on mathematics *B* test by age and education.

	Education					
Age in 1969	High school	Some college	Undergraduate degree	Some graduate	M.A.	Ph.D. and L.L.B.
43	14.0	0.0	28.3	0.0	25.7	0.0
	2.	0.	3.	0.	3.	0.
44	18.5	23.4	31.6	31.1	32.9	33.2
	95.	115.	183.	34.	37.	45.
45	17.2	24.1	32.3	31.3	32.7	31.5
	193.	230.	328.	68.	88.	81.
46	16.9	23.4	28.5	30.9	29.0	34.2
	195.	263.	286.	49.	102.	73.
47	16.6	21.2	29.7	32.5	31.7	32.6
	155.	151.	198.	38.	59.	58.
48	16.3	21.5	30.1	31.6	29.6	28.4
	91.	122.	111.	19.	56.	39.
49	15.4	21.1	27.7	26.6	24.1	29.5
	80.	68.	43.	14.	24.	16.
50	14.7	19.4	32.7	35.9	26.1	26.6
	81.	55.	35.	7.	21.	8.
51	16.3	21.8	27.3	23.3	34.0	23.2
	61.	49.	29.	6.	7.	9.
52	15.6	17.9	27.2	26.8	32.2	19.0
	73.	48.	24.	5.	6.	2.
53	13.8	14.8	29.3	22.0	20.8	49.0
	22.	19.	8.	2.	4.	2.
Average age	47.3	46.9	46.3	46.3	46.6	46.3

Source: Taubman–Wales.
The second row for each age group is the sample size.

we use a continuous variable. Since the original test scores are scaled arbitrarily, we have tried two different scales. In the first, ability ranges from 1 (bottom fifth) to 5 (top fifth). Most of our results are based on this scaling. Below, we will compare these results to those obtained when the fifths are scaled so as to represent the midpoints of fifths of a unit normal curve.

The best fitting equations include the biography variables which, as just pointed out, are not unambiguous in interpretation. But since their introduction only changes other SES variables which were included in the biography index, we will concentrate on this equation. Of the two ability equations presented in table 2, the second contains the nonpecuniary reward variables which may be significant because of noncausal reasons. Thus, we will initially discuss the first equation. Perhaps the most

Table 2.
Ability equations.

	Eqn 1		Eqn 2	
	Coef.	*t* value	Coef.	*t* value
Factors influencing entering occupation, no = 1				
Future financial prospects			−0.15	2.99
Independence			0.12	2.51
Help others			0.02	0.47*
Challenging work			0.17	2.81
Job security			0.15	3.19
Age	−.02	2.33	−.01	1.48*
Area high school, West	.07	.74*	.07	.82*
Area high school, South	.34	1.20*	.34	1.19*
Religion:				
Protestant	.15	.01*	.07	1.52*
Jewish	.33	3.49	.34	3.46
Prefers to be salaried	.02	.43*	.02	.48*
Father high school	.06	1.23	.05	1.05*
Father college	.20	3.24	.19	3.08
Mother's education	.17	3.20	.16	2.95
Mother's education 13+	.19	2.86	.17	2.52
Mother's education don't know	.17	1.49	.18	1.56*
Private high school	.08	.01*	.24	1.60*
Private elementary school	.24	.75	.25	.81*
Biog. 2	.06	.87*	.06	.95*
Biog. 3	.15	2.31	.15	2.34
Biog. 4	.21	3.22	.20	3.09
Biog. 5	.58	8.77	.56	8.49
No response '72	−.12	.80*	−.02	.10*
# of older siblings	−.03	.52*	−.04	.71*
# of younger siblings	.05	.95*	.05	.97*
Raised by grandparents	−1.76	1.83*	−1.97	2.04*

Table 2 (*contd*).

	Eqn 1		Eqn 2	
	Coef.	*t* value	Coef.	*t* value
Town grew up in:				
Less than 10000	−0.03	.45*	−.02	.39*
Between 10–5000000	.07	1.14*	.07	1.30*
Over 500000	.11	1.50*	.13	1.79*
Entered school 6 or 7	−.17	3.65	−.16	3.53
Raised on a farm	−.16	1.05*	−.17	1.05*
Never moved before H.S. grad.	−.09	1.99	−.08	1.83*
Time spent on sports	−.03	1.78*	−.03	1.77*
Time spent on chores	−.02	1.34*	−.02	1.21*
Time spent on part-time job	−.03	2.02	−.02	1.79*
Time spent on reading	.07	4.54	.07	4.53
Time spent on hobbies	−.03	1.81*	−.03	1.73*
Circumstances present when began working full time:				
Marriage			−.12	2.31
Children			.05	.81*
Exceptional job offer			.08	1.51*
Self-employed	.34	7.42	.28	5.13
Financial pressure	−.18	4.30	−.18	3.95
Much time looking for job			.04	.76*
Regret leaving school.			.01	.29*
Specific vocational training	−.18	5.78	−.20	5.94
Constant	3.85	8.35	3.35	7.09
R^2	.0735		.0807	
Standard error	1.3578		1.3525	
Degrees of freedom	4560		4550	

*Not significant at 5% level.

Ability scale 1 to 5.

Most variables defined in ch. 3, tables 6 and 7. The new ones are:

Number of siblings – source III, Q7, no response treated as zero.

Raised by grandparents – volunteered by respondents in IV.

Size of town grew up in – source III, Q3, no response dummy was included but not shown.

Age entered school – source IV, Family Background Section, Q5.

Raised on a farm – volunteered by respondents in IV.

Circumstances present when began working full time – source IV, Occupational History Section, Q2, Yes = 1.

astonishing aspect of this equation is the low R^2, .07[4]. Almost as surprising is the lack of significance and small size of most of the coefficients. There are, however, some substantial and significant variables.

Measured ability increases monotonically with parent's education, with the coefficients on the father attending college and mother attending high school or college being quite significant although the coefficients are only .2 or less. It is hardly surprising that parental education affects test scores, especially since Sewell et al. have reported similar results. But, from our viewpoint, it is an important finding because parental education is not related to the respondent's earnings, once other things are held constant. SES variables, in general, may reflect differences in genetic endowments or in family environment including those derivable from greater income. But since 80% or more of the respondent's mothers did not work while the veterans were growing up, and since there are no large differences in her labor force participation by mother's education level, the effect of mother's education presumably represents genetic or nonincome related aspects of environment[5].

The test scores also increase significantly with our biography index, with those in the top fifth registering half a point more than those in the bottom fifth. As noted before, the biography variable incorporates prior education differences, grades in school, and family SES, but these two findings are certainly not inconsistent.

[4]Without the biography variables the R^2 is about .06.

[5]The percentage of mothers who *never worked* in particular intervals are:

Education of mother	Respondent's age (%) 0–5	Respondent's age (%) 6–14
0–4 years	81	70
5–8 years	88	79
9–11 years	86	76
Finished high school	90	82
Attended college	90	83
Bachelors or more	84	75
Don't know	91	82

In ch. 3 and especially in 8, we argued that religious upbringing was associated with different family environment and that Jews had more drive in general and especially for acquiring knowledge. Thus, it is not surprising that Jews score a significant .4 higher than Catholics. However, contrary to our findings on earnings, Protestants score higher than Catholics although the difference is not significant. Several caveats about these results are contained in ch. 8.

In ch. 3, we indicated that how the individual spent his time while growing up was related to earnings and argued that some of the responses were indicative of family status and environment. We find that ability scores increase significantly with time spent on reading and decrease significantly with time spent on chores and hobbies. The reading variable presumably reflects both individual and family attitudes towards intellectual activity, learned knowledge, and speed in doing each question. However, to some extent the causation may be reverse of what is assumed in the equation. It was argued earlier that the time on chores variable primarily reflects lower middle class status and attitudes which involve both family environment and genetic elements. No good explanations for the hobby result are forthcoming.

The attended private high school and elementary school coefficients are each about 125 although neither is significant[6]. As noted in chs. 3 and 8, these variables could represent any of the following: higher quality education, family taste for education and pressure for intellectual achievement; higher family income used to buy private education, and better environmental and better genetic endowments which are the cause of higher family income. Given that the test score differences are insignificant and small, it seems likely that quality of education can be ruled out, which is comforting given that this varied at time of test taking[7].

The never having moved before high school variables may reflect living in certain environments, such as a small town, which do not encourage intellectual activity. In the 1971 questionnaire, which was only returned by 3400 respondents, we asked for the size of town people were raised in.

[6]There are only 29 people in the private elementary category and 121 in the high school group. The variance of a coefficient of a dummy variable which in part depends on the number of people in a category, may be a very large one for these small groups.

[7]The 'production function' literature spawned by the Coleman report finds little effect of school inputs on change in test scores.

We find that the scores increase with size, with the difference between rural/small towns and major metropolitan areas being a significant 17 points. (We included a dummy for no response.) While this is consistent with the above statements, we cannot rule out the possibility of differences by size of town in quality of pre-test education nor of differential selection as with the religious variables. The quality argument seems less likely, however, since when we used a five region breakdown of area in which respondent attended high school, none of the regions are significant although those from the Northeast and North Central score .4 less than those from the Pacific area[8,9].

In the second ability equation, we have included variables that were interpreted as measures of preferences towards risk and other nonpecuniary rewards in the earnings equations as well as a variable that is related to academic/vocational training in school. Many of these variables probably reflect associations rather than causation although it is possible that preference variables are measures of underlying traits which affect how hard a person works in school.

In this equation, we find that the prefer to be salaried variable has a very small and insignificant coefficient. But those who are not interested in future financial success score less, while those who do not want independence in their work, job security, or challenging work score higher. The result would suggest that those who are conformist or nonrebellious, i.e. not interested in independent or challenging work, do better on the particular tests used. However, the job security result would appear to conflict with this interpretation.

We asked the people to answer yes or no as to whether each of a set of reasons were operative at the time he stopped school to begin work full time. One such question was specific vocational training. As worded, the question could include engineers who did not go on to graduate school or high school students in the vocational tract who did not go to college. In

[8]For those who did not give area of high school we assigned the area on the basis of social security number, when available. Taubman has indicated that such assignments were right 90% of the time. When no information was available, the people were assigned to the omitted category. About 400 people did not give area of high school data, but over half had social security numbers. Alaska, Hawaii, and the rest of the world are the omitted area.

[9]We have also explored several other variables. For example, those raised by grandparents score nearly 2 points lower although the variable is not quite significant at the 5% level. Also, such things as type of house lived in, or whether the respondent shared a room are not significant. Those reared on a farm also have a negative, but not significant, coefficient.

any event, when this variable is added to our ability equations, we find that those who answered yes score a highly significant .2 less. This may reflect self selection on the part of people as to what type of schooling they will benefit from, but may also represent the differences in subjects taught and the importance of learned knowledge in the tests used.

Several other questions that related to circumstances at time of leaving school are also related to ability. Those married then have .1 lower scores, while those under financial pressure to work have .2 lower scores, and those self-employed have .3 higher scores. These results may be indicative of the financial position of the respondent's parents with those coming from wealthier parents scoring better because of genes or home environment. But it is also possible that the brighter student had fellowships to graduate school and postponed marriage until school was completed, i.e. the responses represent self selection rather than causation.

As noted earlier, all these results are based on a variable which was arbitrarily scaled 1–5 depending on a person's fifth in the ability distribution. As an alternative, we assumed that the ability was distributed normally and used the midpoints of each fifth of the unit normal curve to form a new continuous variable. Since this variable only ranges from -1.28 to 1.28, the coefficients are reduced in size. But other than this scale effect, we find little difference in our results with only 3 out of 50 variables significant in one equation and not in the other. Thus, the results do not seem too sensitive to the particular scaling used.

In discussing the implications of the above results, we must keep in mind that we are using a particular (weighted) set of test scores. As described and discussed in Thorndike and Hagen and TW, the particular tests employed do not rely very heavily on learned information, and the conclusions seem to be borne out by the low R^2, etc. in the equations. But our findings do not tell us much about the determinants or importance of learned knowledge. This is an important omission since we know of no study which indicates whether earnings depend on innate ability, various types of learned knowledge, or a combination thereof[10].

[10]Although the test scores in our earnings equation are more important than in studies such as Griliches and Mason which use AFQT scores and Wolfle–Smith which use ACE scores, both of which rely on more learned facts, our earnings are mostly from a later period of life and the effect of ability on earnings changes during the life cycle. See Sewell and Hauser.

2. Years of schooling

In this section we will measure schooling by years obtained as of 1969, with high school as 12, bachelor's 16, Ph.D. M.D., etc. as 19[11,12]. In this analysis we have always included the biography and ability variables and most of the variables in the ability equations. In addition, we have included responses (from 4400 persons) to questions related to why they left school when they did.

The results in eqn 1 are rather interesting. As would be expected, schooling increased continuously with mental ability with the top three-fifths very significant. Those in the top fifth achieve 1.3 years more schooling than those in the bottom fifth, everything else (including G.I. benefits) constant.

Various aspects of SES also influence educational attainment. Those whose father went to high school and to college have .2 and .7 years more schooling respectively. Those whose mother attended high school and college have .15 and .25 years more education respectively[13]. Mother's work status (from zero to five years old) had no effect on educational attainment. The biography variable, which contains SES and ability inputs, is also strongly related to schooling with those in the top fifth achieving almost half a year more than those in the bottom fifth. The Jewish/Protestant difference in educational attainment by religion is significant in this sample. (Eckland and others have found that Jews receive more education, *ceteris paribus.*)

Several results in the equation suggest that older persons may have felt that they had to settle down and that persons with more financial obligations felt they could not postpone going to work even though the G.I. bill would have substantially reduced the cost of education[14]. For

[11]While this method makes it somewhat impractical to calculate the indirect effects of education since our earnings equations use dummy variables for education, it is too costly to use *N* chotomous probit analysis.

[12]TW found that about 8% of the sample received more education after 1955. There is also some measurement error between 1955 and 1969 response but all such errors have treated the 1969 response as correct, since this treatment explains more of 1955 and 1969 earnings.

[13]If the respondent did not know his mother's education, he had .6 years less. This may mean either that the education of the mother was low or not discussed at home since education was not highly valued.

[14]In retrospect, it appears that the monetary rate of return on education is in excess of 15% when due allowance is made for the G.I. bill.

Table 3.
Years of schooling.

	Eqn 1		Eqn 2	
	Coef.	*t* value	Coef.	*t* value
Factors influencing entering occupation, no = 1				
Future financial prospects	0.33	4.27	0.35	4.67
Independence	0.04	0.48*	0.02	0.31*
Help others	−0.93	12.41	−0.87	11.93
Challenging work	−0.19	−2.08	−0.19	2.14
Job security	0.36	5.06	0.32	4.60
Age	−0.13	9.11	−0.07	4.44
Area high school, West	0.39	0.89*	0.27	0.62*
Area high school, South	0.30	0.96*	0.20	0.65*
Area high school, Northeast	0.21	0.64*	0.05	0.14*
Religion:				
Protestant	−0.07	1.06*	−0.09	1.29*
Jewish	0.18	1.19*	0.05	0.34*
Prefers to be salaried	−0.16	2.11	−0.13	1.68*
Father high school	0.23	3.05	0.21	2.86
Father college	0.70	7.31	0.62	6.64
Mother's education high school	0.15	1.92*	0.12	1.52*
Mother's education college	0.25	2.50	0.17	1.81*
Biog. 2	0.12	1.22*	0.14	1.43*
Biog. 3	0.25	2.50	0.25	2.57
Biog. 4	0.20	2.02	0.20	1.97
Biog. 5	0.48	4.70	0.44	4.35
No response '72	−1.32	5.25	−1.19	4.80
Town grew up in:				
Less than 10000	0.08	0.98*	0.12	1.49*
Between 10–500000	0.22	2.60	0.28	3.41
Over 500000	0.07	0.61*	0.15	1.36*
Raised on a farm	0.82	3.46	0.81	3.49
Time spent on sports	0.01	0.26*	0.00	0.05*
Time spent on chores	−0.04	1.52*	−0.04	1.68*
Time spent on part-time job	−0.01	0.52*	−0.00	0.21*
Time spent on reading	0.18	8.02	0.18	8.21
Time spent on hobbies	−0.05	2.13	−0.04	1.99
Circumstances present when began working full time:				
Marriage	−0.71	8.87	−0.55	6.95
Children	0.22	0.19*	0.00	0.04*
Exceptional job offer	0.11	1.32*	0.12	1.51*
Self-employed	0.23	2.72	0.23	2.85

Table 3 (*contd*).

	Eqn 1		Eqn 2	
	Coef.	*t* value	Coef.	*t* value
Financial pressure	−0.04	0.52*	−0.07	0.99*
Much time looking for job	0.15	2.07	0.09	1.19*
Regret leaving school	−0.04	1.02*	−0.06	1.55*
Specific vocational training	−0.62	11.89	−0.56	10.91
Ability:				
2nd fifth	0.18	1.76*	0.23	2.29
3rd fifth	0.61	6.04	0.65	6.51
4th fifth	0.89	8.90	0.91	9.27
5th fifth	1.27	12.49	1.31	13.16
Mother did not work when respondent 0 to 5	−0.06	0.69*	−0.07	0.79*
Rent single family house	−0.07	0.99*	−0.06	0.82*
Rent apartment	0.07	0.51*	0.06	0.43*
Other than owned single family	0.25	1.74*	0.21	1.46*
Constant	21.20	28.81	18.24	24.33
R^2	.2456		0.2778	
Standard error	2.0828		2.0378	
Degrees of freedom	4549		4548	

*Not significant at the 5% level.

Most variables defined in ch. 3, tables 6 and 7, or ch. 9, table 2.

New variables:

Mother did not work – source IV, Family Background Section, Q7, dummy variable = 1, if did not work at all.

Home ownership/rent – source IV, Family Background Section, Q1, owned single family house omitted.

example, schooling decreases by .1 with each year of age. Also, if the person was married when he finished schooling, his educational attainment was .6 less[15,16].

The question on marriage was part of a set designed to look at forces that lead to a person stopping his education and beginning full-time work. With dummy variables taking on a value of 1 if the person answered yes

[15] To enter the program in 1943, a person was supposed to be single.

[16] Interestingly, this variable is also significant and negative in our ability equations. Thus, the more able apparently postponed marriage to stay in school.

(and missing answers treated as 'no')[17], we find significant and positive coefficients on 'self-employed then', 'spending too much time looking for a job' and having a 'specific vocational training for the job'. The answer to 'spending too much time looking for a job' becomes insignificant when number of pre-World War II jobs are included.

The vocational training answer, which is the largest and most significant variable in the set, suggests several possibilities. First, the people with vocational training are (were) less interested in the nonmonetary consequences of education and were more willing to start work, once they were trained. Second, these people may have been able to command higher salaries because of their training and thus could not afford to go to, say, graduate school. Third, people who were in the vocational tract of high school may have stopped after high school as they had planned[18]. As noted earlier, these people score lower on our ability measures; but even given ability, they have less schooling probably because of their job interest.

Those who at age 50 would prefer to be salaried have .2 years less education. This may indicate the choice of the (already) risk averse, e.g. Weiss has argued that college education has a wider variance in earnings and that people respond to this extra riskiness. But education may be determining risk preference.

The other measures of SES produce some intriguing figures. For example, while attendance at a private high school or elementary school leads to more education, the coefficients are not significant. As we shall see shortly, however, college quality is significantly related to private school. Age at entering school is negatively but not significantly related to amount of schooling. Those in this sample who were reared on a farm received a significant .8 years more schooling[19]. We also find that those who spent the least amount of time on reading obtained .18 years less, while the corresponding differences for chores is .04 years less[20]. In the

[17]If some should be yes's, this makes it more difficult to find significant differences.

[18]All the people in the sample were in the top half of the I.Q. distribution.

[19]These people receive lower test scores. This may mean that the scores do not reflect the innate ability of people raised on a farm because of cultural bias in the test or that educational attainment is partially determined by ability relative to a local reference group.

[20]Other variables that were not significant include having children, area of residence during high school, financial pressure to work. and regret leaving school although the latter is nearly significant.

next equation, we find that the more jobs a person held before high school, the less schooling he had. The coefficient of −.7 is highly significant with a t value of 14.

3. College quality

Gourman publishes an academic and an overall index, which are highly correlated, of college 'quality'. We are using the 1955 version of the academic index, which is based on such things as college board scores of undergraduates, quality of faculty, and facilities of the respondent's undergraduate school[21]. As acknowledged in ch. 3, this is not necessarily the only or best measure of quality, especially given the work of Solmon and Wachtel; but it is the only one we have used. In judging the coefficients, the reader should note that Gourman scales his index to have a mean of 500, a standard error of 100, and to be normally distributed over a range of 200 to 800. The people in this sample, all of whom are in the top half of the I.Q. distribution and nearly all of whom are eligible for the G.I. benefits, attended school with scores ranging from below 300 to in excess of 750.

Table 4.
College quality.

	Eqn 1		Eqn 2	
	Coef.	t value	Coef.	t value
Factors influencing entering occupation, no = 1				
Future financial prospects			−3.77	0.77*
Independence			−4.84	1.03*
Help others			7.64	1.64*
Challenging work			−6.78	1.16*
Job security			13.15	3.02
Age	−1.05	1.11*	−2.07	2.15
Religion				
Protestant	−1.35	0.31*	.40	.09*
Jewish	46.68	5.19	50.58	5.57

[21]The ETS supplied estimates of some schools not rated. 1955 is the earliest year the index is available.

Table 4 (*contd*).

	Eqn 1 Coef.	Eqn 1 t value	Eqn 2 Coef.	Eqn 2 t value
Prefers to be salaried	−5.34	1.08*		
Father high school	2.85	0.60*	6.47	1.40*
Father college	15.42	2.61	20.66	3.58
Mother's education 12	8.87	1.56*	11.02	1.96
Mother's education 13+	−1.14	0.17*	1.65	0.25*
Mother's education don't know	2.62	0.21*	−2.92	0.23*
Private high school	35.66	2.78	41.37	3.21
Private elementary school	71.72	2.74	69.68	2.65
Biog. 2	−0.26	0.04*	−0.99	0.15*
Biog. 3	4.61	0.71*	3.31	0.50*
Biog. 4	1.59	0.25*	0.32	0.05*
Biog. 5	9.47	1.48*	9.71	1.50*
No response '72	−2.64	0.22*	−18.75	1.36*
Town grew up in:				
Less than 10000	−4.20	0.82*	−3.74	0.73*
Between 10–500000	6.21	1.22*	6.47	1.26*
Over 500000	18.81	2.76	17.21	2.50
Never moved before H.S. grad.	3.21	0.75*		
Time spent on sports	−0.85	0.58*	−0.14	0.10*
Time spent on chores	−0.15	0.09*	−0.13	0.08*
Time spent on part-time job	−2.69	2.10	−2.82	2.20
Time spent on reading	2.05	1.42*	1.96	0.04*
Time spent on hobbies	−1.80	1.28*	−2.13	1.49*
Circumstances present when began working full time:				
Marriage			7.22	1.41*
Children			−10.06	1.68*
Exceptional job offer			−14.05	2.33
Self-employed			11.85	1.86*
Financial pressure			−2.20	0.46*
Much time looking for job			−14.25	2.61
Regret leaving school.			20.07	0.01*
Specific vocational training			−6.72	1.57
Constant	480.34	10.20	560.41	11.73
R^2	0.10		0.09	
Standard error	110.84		111.46	
Degrees of freedom	3383		3383	

*Not significant at 5% level.

All variables are defined in ch. 3, tables 6 and 7 or ch. 9, tables 2 and 3.

For the 3436 people who attended college with a nonzero Gourman rating, we have estimated several equations. We discuss first the ones without the quantity of education since the interpretation of all the coefficients in that equation is not clear[22].

As should be expected, the quality of college attended increases monotonically with ability with the top three-fifths significant. The difference between those in the top and bottom fifths of more than 50 points is about $\frac{1}{2}$ of the (population) standard error in the index. While the effect of ability is nonlinear on the college quality variable, it must be recognized that the quality index is scaled arbitrarily and that there are monotonic rescalings that could make the ability effects linear, etc.

The individual's SES is also an important determinant of the quality of college attended although some dimensions of SES are not significant. In the equations that omit the quantity of education, father's education has small and insignificant effects. However, when the respondent's quantity of education is included, both variables are significant with the father in college variable having a coefficient close to 15.

The respondent's religion is also strongly related to the Gourman index. Jews go to much higher quality schools (45 points) than Catholics or Protestants, ability and other SES measures constant. Others such as Eckland have also found that Jews go to better schools given ability and other things.

Another element of SES that helps determine school quality is attendance at a private elementary school. Those 29 persons who we argue come from well established and wealthy families, go to schools with an index value of 70 points more than those who did not. Moreover, those who attended private high school attend colleges of nearly 40 points higher quality. Thus the 22 people who attended private elementary and high school went to a college more than 100 points higher in the index.

Our other measure of SES, including the time spent variables, have very small and insignificant effects on quality of undergraduate school attended. But the part-time job coefficient is a significant −.2.

The prefer to be salaried variable is insignificant. Of the nonpecuniary factors involved in occupational choice, three variables are significant. Those not interested in helping others or in job security go to colleges with 10 and 17 points higher scores. Thus, it appears that those more

[22]The coefficients are *not* estimates of substitutability. See Neudecker and Theil.

interested in monetary rewards – certain or uncertain – receive a higher quality education as well as higher earnings[23].

The other equation presented in the table also includes the quantity of education. It can be shown that those variables do not necessarily indicate the substitution between quantity and quality. The equations, however, do describe the quality of undergraduate schools attended by people with various levels of educational attainment. Those who are just college graduates went to schools 30 points higher than dropouts. Those at the various graduate levels (except M.D.) also go to better schools than dropouts; but the average level of quality declines for people with some graduate work, master's, and Ph.D., but with the 50 or so M.D.'s coming from schools about 15 points less than college dropouts. This result is consistent with the findings in Astin that, given individual ability and other school characteristics, lower quality undergraduate schools over-produce Ph.D.'s.

4. Nonpecuniary and time spent variables

In ch. 8, we discussed in detail the interrelationships of the various nonpecuniary and time spent variables. We will not repeat that discussion here but merely examine the coefficients on the other variables we have included in some supplementary equations.

A question of some concern to many people is why education affects earnings or what skills, etc. are produced by education. Besides cognitive skills, education may produce the types of nonpecuniary preferences we have just explored. For this reason, we have added our education dummies as well as our religious dummies to each of the above equations. We are, of course, well aware that the differences observed in the equation may well reflect self selection in terms of who obtains more education rather than skills produced by education. For this reason, we will only comment briefly on eqns 11 through 20 and only indicate the significant coefficients[24].

[23]It is not clear from the equations, however, if the answers to job security etc. are related to innate (predetermined) traits or if the quality of education affects our measures of these preferences.

[24]We have not distinguished between Ph.D.'s, L.L.B.'s and M.D.'s.

The dependent variables in these equations can only take on the value of zero or one. As is well known, ordinary least squares will lead to inefficient and inconsistent estimates when the independent variables include continuous variables. We have used probit analysis to estimate the final form of the equations although preliminary analysis was based on the ordinary least squares results which are given in Appendix G. A comparison of the corresponding equations indicates that the two estimating techniques yield similar results as to signs and levels of significance. Since in the probit analysis, the effect of a unit change in a variable varies throughout the normal distribution, we will only discuss the sign of the coefficients.

The probability of a person preferring to be salaried decreases continuously with education (except master's). The response on not being interested in future financial success is more complicated. The probability decreases for some college and bachelor's, but the coefficients are positive on the graduate coefficients with master's significant. The probability of not being interested in independence is higher for those with master's degrees but lower for those with Ph.D.'s, L.L.B.'s and M.D.'s. The probability of not being interested in challenging work is not significantly related to education. The probability of *not* being interested in job security increases continuously with education (except for master's degree).

We have also included the education variables in the time spent equations. For these equations, the sequential order of the variables indicates that we are picking up self selection by education level. We find that only for hobbies and chores are there any significant variables. Time spent previously on hobbies increases with educational attainment (except Ph.D. and equivalent) and time spent on chores is less for Ph.D.'s, L.L.B.'s, and M.D.'s.

As an indication of how home environment might transform skills and tastes, we have included the Jewish and Protestant variables in the above equations. Compared to Catholics, Jews spent more time on sports and less time on chores. Jews also are more likely to prefer to be self-employed, be interested in future financial prospects and in independence, or to be uninterested in job security. Compared to Catholics, Protestants spend less time on sports and more on chores, Protestants are also more likely to take a job because it is challenging work.

Time spent and preference equations.

Independent variable	(1) Time spent on sports Coef.	t value	(2) Time spent on hobbies Coef.	t value	(3) Time spent on chores Coef.	t value	(4) Time spent on part-time job Coef.	t value
Time spent on:								
Sports			.06	3.3	−.09	6.0	−.09	5.0
Hobbies	.05	3.3			.01	.9*	−.002	.1*
Chores	−.10	6.0	.02	.9*			.13	6.5
Part-time job	−.07	5.0	−.002	.1*	.08	6.5		
Prefer to be salaried	−.07	1.3*	.02	.4*	.04	.7*	−.02	.3*
When entered occup., did following factors influence you? no = 1								
Future financial success	−.13	2.5	.04	.7*	.08	1.7*	−.02	.3*
Independent work	.06	1.1*	.03	.6*	.04	.9*	−.07	1.1*
Help others	−.11	2.3	−.03	.6*	−.14	3.0	.01	.2*
Challenging work	.03	.7*	−.04	.8*	.004	.1*	−.09	1.7*
Job security	.07	1.5*	.21	4.3	−.08	2.0	.08	1.4*
Some college								
Bachelor's								
Some graduate								
Master's								
Ph.D., L.L.B., M.D.								
Jewish								
Protestant								
Financial opport. in 1969 compared to expectations when started (1 = low, 3 = about same, 5 = high)								
Biog. 2	.08	.6*	.02	.1*	−.15	1.1*	.30	1.8*
Biog. 3	.08	.6*	.15*	1.1*	−.05	.4*	.20	1.3*
Biog. 4	.01	1.*	−.11	.8*	−.15	1.2*	.31	2.0
Biog. 5	.03	.2*	−.12	.8*	−.02	1.7*	.36	2.3
Constant	4.01	27.3	2.23	13.6	3.15	22.3	2.13	11.8
R^2	.020		.006	1.5	.025		.019	
S.E.	1.41				1.33		1.63	

*Not significant at the 5% level.

There are 4022 observations.

The financial opportunities variable source is II, Attitude Toward Job Section, Q1.

Table 5 (*contd*).

Independent variable	(1) Prefer to be salaried		(2) Future fin. prospects, no		(3) Independence no		(4) Help others, no	
	Coef.	t value	Coef.	t value	Coef.	t value	Coef.	t value
Time spent on:								
Sports	−.001	1.3*	−.01	2.5	.01	1.1*	−.01	2.3
Hobbies	.002	.4*	.003	.7*	.002	.6*	−.003	.6*
Chores	.003	.7*	.01	1.7*	.004	.9*	−.017	3.0
Part-time job	−.001	.3*	.001	.3*	−.005	1.1*	.001	.2*
Prefer to be salaried			.06	3.7	.11	6.5	.018	1.0*
When entered occup., did following factors influence you? no = 1								
Future financial success	.05	3.7			.22	14.0	−.05	2.8
Independent work	.09	6.5	.22	14.0				
Help others	.01	1.0*	−.04	−2.7	.29	20.3	.32	20.3
Challenging work	.01	.8*	.09	6.0	.09	6.0	.18	11.4
Job security	−.09	7.2*	.06	4.2	−.04	2.7	.13	8.6
Some college								
Bachelor's								
Some graduate								
Master's								
Ph.D., L.L.B., M.D.								
Jewish								
Protestant								
Financial opport. in 1969 compared to expectations when started (1 = low, 3 = about same, 5 = high)								
Biog. 2	.007	.2*	−.001	.02*	.08	1.8*	−.03	.7*
Biog. 3	.04	1.2*	.02	.5*	.07	1.8*	−.05	1.2
Biog. 4	.07	1.9*	−.04	.9*	.08	1.9*	−.04	.9
Biog. 5	.04	1.0*	−.07	1.4*	.06	1.4*	−.06	1.5
Constant	.16	3.5	.19	3.9	.03	.6*	.43	8.3
R^2	.035		.078		.179		.151	
S.E.	.40		.44		.44		.46	

*Not significant at the 5% level.

Table 5 (*contd*).

Independent variable	(1) Challenging work, no		(2) Job security		(3) Time spent on sports		(4) Time spent on hobbies	
	Coef.	*t* value	Coef.	*t* value	Coef.	*t* value	Coef.	*t* value
Time spent on:								
Sports	.003	.7*	.01	1.5*			.05	3.1
Hobbies	.004	.8*	.02	4.3	.05	3.1		
Chores	.001	.1*	−.01	2.0	−.09	5.5	.02	.9*
Part-time job	−.007	1.7*	.01	1.4*	−.07	4.9	−.003	.2*
Prefer to be salaried	−.015	.8*	−.14	7.2	−.06	1.0*	.04	.6*
When entered occup., did following factors influence you? no = 1								
Future financial success	−.10	6.0	.07	4.2	−.12	2.4	.04	.7*
Independent work	.10	6.0	−.05	2.7	.06	1.1	.02	.4*
Help others	.18	11.4	.14	8.6	−.11	2.1	−.01	.2*
Challenging work			−.13	7.8	.02	.5*	.05	.9*
Job security	−.11	7.8			.05	1.2*	.18	3.8
Some college					.12	1.8*	.19	2.8
Bachelor's					.10	1.7*	.19	2.8
Some graduate					.07	.7*	.25	2.2
Master's					.21	2.4	.31	3.3
Ph.D., L.L.B., M.D.					−.08	.1*	−.003	−.02*
Jewish					.22	2.0	.13	1.1*
Protestant					−.15	3.1	.08	1.6*
Financial opport. in 1969 compared to expectations when started (1 = low, 3 = about same, 5 = high)								
Biog. 2	−.04	.8*	−.01	.2*	.09	.6*	.003	.02*
Biog. 3	−.06	1.5*	−.01	.2*	.10	.7*	−.16	1.2*
Biog. 4	−.07	1.5*	.01	.2	.02	.1*	−.13	.9*
Biog. 5	−.07	1.7*	.03	.8	.04	.3*	−.11	.8*
Constant	.30	5.9	.40	7.4	4.0	26.0	2.05	11.9
R^2	.082		.048		.026		.010	
S.E.	.46		.49		1.41		1.49	

*Not significant at the 5% level.
There are 4022 observations.

Table 5 (*contd*).

Independent variable	(1) Time spent on chores Coef.	t value	(2) Time spent part-time job Coef.	t value	(3) Prefers to be salaried[a] Coef.	t value	(4) Future financial success, no[a] Coef.	t value
Time spent on:								
Sports	−.08	5.5	−.09	4.9	−0.02	−1.43	−0.03	−2.04
Hobbies	.01	.9*	−.003	.2*	0.01	.055	0.02	1.28
Chores			.12	6.4	0.003	0.18	0.02	1.40
Part-time job	.08	6.4			−0.01	−0.36	0.01	0.67
Prefer to be salaried	.01	.1*	−.02	.4*			0.20	3.78
When entered occup., did following factors influence you? no = 1								
Future financial success	.05	1.1*	.01	.2*	0.19	3.68		
Independent work	.01	.3*	−.07	1.3*	0.30	5.92	0.56	11.58
Help others	−.13	2.9	.003	.1*	0.05	0.92	−0.11	−2.11
Challenging work	.02	.5*	−.09	1.6*	−0.02	−0.31	0.40	8.61
Job security	−.05	1.2*	.08	1.5*	−0.36	−7.04	0.35	7.45
Some college	−.09	1.4*	−.04	.6*	−0.18	−2.89	−0.19	−2.97
Bachelor's	−.09	1.5*	−.02	.2*	−0.22	−3.53	−0.33	−5.32
Some graduate	−.16	1.6*	.15	1.3*	−0.23	−2.09	0.15	1.52
Master's	.09	1.0*	−.02	.2*	−0.14	−1.61	0.43	5.27
Ph.D., L.L.B., M.D.	−.27	−2.8	−.19	.2*	−0.37	−3.27	0.11	1.09
Jewish	−.64	6.4	.02	.2*	−0.47	−3.59	−0.37	−3.18
Protestant	.10	2.3	.04	.7*	−0.07	−1.39	0.05	0.98
Financial opport. in 1969 compared to expectations when started (1 = low, 3 = about same, 5 = high)								
Biog. 2	−.14	.02*	.29	1.7*	0.04	0.24	−0.02	−0.13
Biog. 3	−.03	−1.2*	.19	1.3*	0.17	1.21	0.04	0.29
Biog. 4	−.12	.9*	.30	2.0	0.28	1.98	−0.14	−1.08
Biog. 5	−.17	.8*	.36	2.4	0.16	1.11	−0.25	−1.93
Constant	3.13	21.4	2.15	11.4	−0.80	−4.62	−0.86	−5.28
R^2	.041		.019		0.10		0.20	
S.E.	1.32		1.63					

*Not significant at the 5% level.

There are 4022 observations.

[a]Estimated by probit.

Table 5 (*contd*).

Independent variable	(1) Independent work, no[a] Coef.	t value	(2) Help others no[a] Coef.	t value	(3) Challenging work, no[a] Coef.	t value	(4) Job security, no[a] Coef.	t value
Time spent on:								
Sports	0.02	1.34	−.02	−1.49	−0.02	−0.85	−0.01	−0.95
Hobbies	0.01	0.89	0.002	0.20	−0.03	−1.72	0.03	2.27
Chores	0.13	0.78	−0.04	−2.41	−0.03	−1.55	−0.01	−0.34
Part-time job	−0.01	−0.81	0.01	0.39	−0.05	−3.02	0.02	1.29
Prefers to be salaried	0.31	5.89	0.05	0.98	−0.02	−0.33	−0.39	−7.12
When entered occup., did following factors influence you? no = 1								
Future financial success	0.57	11.71	−0.13	−2.56	0.47	8.61	0.36	7.47
Independent work			0.82	16.84	0.55	10.12	−0.24	−5.02
Help others	0.82	16.98			0.96	15.65	0.52	10.93
Challenging work	0.58	10.12	1.02	15.45			−0.06	−0.99
Job security	−0.22	−4.66	0.51	10.77	−0.02	−0.35		
Some college	−0.09	−1.40	0.04	0.63	−0.06	−0.89	0.22	3.57
Bachelor's	0.07	1.22	−0.12	−1.90	−0.18	−2.65	0.43	7.22
Some graduate	0.15	1.49	−0.46	−4.54	−0.11	−0.93	0.45	4.58
Master's	0.32	3.80	−0.93	−10.43	−0.29	−2.66	0.25	2.98
Ph.D., L.L.B., M.D.	−0.29	−2.65	−0.98	−9.38	−0.07	−0.57	0.59	6.29
Jewish	−0.31	−2.78	0.04	0.39	0.25	2.16	0.27	2.82
Protestant	0.05	0.99	−0.03	−0.62	−0.26	−4.69	−0.07	−1.51
Financial opport. in 1969 compared to expectations when started, (1 = low, 3 = about same, 5 = high)								
Biog. 2	0.23	1.58	−0.03	−0.19	−0.07	−0.43	−0.10	−0.73
Biog. 3	0.18	1.42	−0.09	−0.67	0.01	0.06	−0.15	−1.25
Biog. 4	0.22	1.69	−0.01	−0.07	−0.10	−0.71	−0.06	−0.52
Biog. 5	0.20	1.52	−0.09	−0.72	−0.19	−1.29	0.04	0.33
Constant	−1.42	−8.45	−0.12	−0.74	−1.24	−6.56	−0.82	−5.27
R^2	0.31		0.38		0.35		0.13	
S.E.								

[a]Estimated by probit.

It is worth repeating at this point that in our earnings equations, the religious effects are net of those transmitted indirectly by the above variables; hence, some other skills or preferences are involved.

5. Probability in migrating

As indicated in Appendix C, the people in this sample are more mobile than the population as a whole. That appendix also indicates that migration – 1969 state not equal to state of high school education – has little, if any, effect on earnings in 1969. If we assume 1969 earnings were, on average, expected at time of move, we would have to explain migration by differences in tastes, etc. However, the equations used, whether estimated by ordinary least squares or probit techniques, have an R^2 of about .02 with few variables significant. Thus we find migration increases with education, decreases with ability, decreases with time spent on sports, wanting challenging work and not wanting job security.

6. Conclusion

This chapter began with a discussion of direct and indirect effects on earnings. The equations in this chapter suggest that variables which we think reflect latent traits and family environment have strong effects on educational attainment, college quality, and test scores. Thus, it appears that the personal characteristics that determine earnings directly also have important indirect effects. However, we cannot determine if education produced or is associated with most of these characteristic variables.

CHAPTER 10

Conclusions and questions

In this chapter, we will try to sum up what we consider to be our major findings and indicate what important questions are raised by our research. Our findings are of three types – substantive empirical results, methodological advances, and tests of or information on the relevance of certain theories on the distribution of earnings.

1. Empirical results

In our regressions, we have found a number of significant variables, many of which have never been examined before. Nearly all of these variables have the same sign in the 1955 and 1969 earnings equations, most of these coefficients remain significant in within occupation earnings equations, and generally have what we consider to be consistent signs in equations explaining educational attainment, college quality, and test scores.

In the earnings equations, we find that educational quantity and quality, mental ability, business assets, certain aspects of family background, preferences towards risk and towards nonmonetary aspects of a job, locational information, hours of work, health, and work experience, and age are significant determinants of earnings. Among this list of items are several which to my knowledge have not been included previously in earnings, equations, but yield empirical results in accord with economic and social science theory. For example, economists and others have long recognized that people can trade off earnings for nonpecuniary rewards. We do not have measures of nonpecuniary rewards but we do have crude measures of character traits or taste differences towards nonpecuniary rewards. We find that people earn less for displaying or wanting any of the following traits, *ceteris paribus*: helping others, doing independent work, having job security, avoiding risk, and doing unchallenging work. The percentage reduction in earnings associated with each of these traits becomes progressively larger as people age.

Our family background variables are much different than in most other studies. For example, parents', or especially fathers', education and occupation are often used as the major index of SES. Although we started off using these variables, we found that they became insignificant, especially when business assets were held constant[1]. This suggests to me that education and occupation act primarily as proxies for financial and business inheritance, perhaps tinged with nepotism, and not for home training. (Since parental education is associated with the educational attainment and test scores of respondents, we are only speaking of direct effects on earnings.)

While the traditional SES variables are not significant, we have found others that seem to be related to the types of family life and child rearing processes people have in mind when they talk of training and taste formation. For example, we find that Jews earn significantly more than and Protestants significantly less than Catholics (and the few atheists and agnostics). Other studies have found that Jews of this and succeeding generations have more drive and motivation for financial success – perhaps because of fear engendered by centuries of economic insecurity and because most of them were children or grandchildren of immigrants who were poor and wanted to succeed. The Protestant–Catholic result may indicate that the Protestants in this group come from wealthier families who did not need to emphasize economic success. While this conclusion may seem contrary to the Protestant ethic, others in small samples have found that some Catholic groups – such as German or French – do better than the average Protestant. Given the education cut off in our sample and in the cohort involved, it seems likely that we have drawn Catholics from the above average earnings group.

We also find that attending private elementary school and high school affects earnings with the 29 people who attended private school earning \$3000 a year more and the 121 who attended high school (including 22 of

[1]Parental occupation and education is contained with unknown weight in our biography variable. As argued in ch. 3, when one variable, X, is already included in another one variable Z with a weight of b, the estimate coefficient on X is equal to $c - bd$ where c is the true effect of X and d the true effect of Z. Thus, the estimated coefficient is a net effect. But these were significant before business assets were added.

the 29) $3000 more in 1969 (in 1958 prices). While there are a number of explanations for this result, the one that appeals to me is that these people come from very wealthy families who use pull to advance their sons.

Another aspect of religious upbringing that affects earnings is frequency of attendance at religious (not parochial) school with those attending most often earning the least and those never attending earning the most. The ones who attended more than twice a week are probably certain subgroups of Catholics and more orthodox Jews. This variable may help to distinguish those less interested in a material life. The nonattendees are more difficult to explain although nonattendance in the 1920s or early 1930s may represent a very atypical family.

We also find that those who spent their time differently on various activities while growing up earn different amounts. The explanations for these findings include indication of respondent's tastes and attitudes, as well as certain types of family rearing. For example, we argued that respondents who remembered spending time on chores came from families that are interested in conformity and produce people who enter into bureaucracies and safe jobs.

We also find that the more educated earn more although the graduate coefficients are not always higher than the bachelor's coefficients[2]. The effects of education increase with age and the age earnings profiles are steeper for education than most other variables. However, in this sample which is stratified differently than the population and has a truncated distribution of education and ability, the (average) range in earnings arising from education are dwarfed by the range arising from the combination of SES or of trade offs for nonpecuniary rewards and are only of the same magnitude as the range associated with mental ability.

Mental ability has a continuous direct effect on earnings (as well as indirect effects through educational attainment). Its age earnings profile slope upward with only a tendency for the more able to have significantly steeper profiles.

Time on the job is important, especially early in a person's career; but experience in some types of work is more transferable than in other types. However, people generally do best when they do not switch occupations.

[2]The inclusion of various nonpecuniary and attitude variables generally raises the coefficients on graduate education.

It also appears that hours worked is an important determinant of earnings (although the data is only available for 1969). However, there are a large group of men with low earnings who moonlight.

Business assets as measured in 1969 are one of the most important variables in our equation explaining 10% of the variance in earnings by itself. The coefficient is .11 in 1969 which is not extremely high on a before tax basis.

We have also calculated the same equations within various occupations. Since many of the above variables are related to occupational choice, coefficients tend to be smaller and less often significant. But we do find clear evidence that some skills, attributes, etc. are more important in some occupations than others. For example, intelligence is more important for the self-employed. Moreover, the self-employed who are the ones having more control over their work environment, have larger coefficients on the various nonpecuniary measures.

2. *Sources of the standard error, skewness, and kurtosis*

The variables we use in our equation indicate some of the reasons why people have different earnings. We can, of course, calculate the R^2 for all the variables in the equation or a partial R^2 for any subset. Similarly, we can estimate the contribution of all or part of our variables to the skewness and kurtosis observed in the sample[3,4].

Our findings, which are detailed in ch. 4, are the following. We can explain more of the variance in earnings in 1969 than 1955 even when we restrict our attention to variables equally accurate in both years, i.e. when we ignore business assets, etc. Second, the truncated education variable has a partial R^2 of about .05 although some of the effects of education may be impounded in the nonpecuniary and other variables. The biggest

[3]The skewness or kurtosis measures are divided by σ^3 and σ^4, respectively, which we allow to vary by what is held constant in the numerator. Also, we subtract 3, the expected value of the normal curve in the kurtosis measure.

[4]The R^2, etc. may not generalize to the population because our sample is a stratified sample, with unknown weights, and with trucated ability and education distributions. However, comparisons between years are valid and the distribution of the residuals may generalize to the population.

partial R^2 in each year is attached to the 1969 business asset variable. This result probably does not generalize to the population since we have a high proportion of self-employed, and several with large amounts of business assets. The SES variables (including all the time spent variables) and the nonpecuniary variables (including preferred to be salaried) each explain about 3% of the variance in the two years.

3. Methodology

Perhaps the simplest way to describe the methodological advances we have made is that many phenomena, skills, and attitudes that economists, sociologists, biographers, and others have hypothesized should be related to earnings, can be represented or captured by simple questions that can be included in mail surveys. It seems likely that more systematic efforts would allow us to incorporate many other skills, attitudes, and preferences, or to refine existing measures. The payoff from our work in understanding the earnings distribution appears large and promises adequate payoffs for other work in the area.

4. Relationship of theory to empirical work

At the beginning of this book, there was a lengthy discussion of various theories, hypotheses, and ideas that have been advanced to explain various features of the distribution of earnings. Our empirical results do shed some light on the validity and importance of many of these. For example, Friedman suggested that skewness arose because of differences in risk preferences. In our regressions, we have several variables which related to risk preference. These include the prefer to be salaried item, the entered occupation because of job security item, and (if our interpretation is accepted), the spent time on chores item[5]. In each year, we find that those who want to avoid risk earn significantly less and that the differential grows with age and is a greater percentage of average earnings (of high school graduates) as people age. Finally, we find that risk

[5]Our argument is that the people came from homes that bred conformity.

preferences have an indirect effect, with those who want to avoid risk obtaining less education. These conclusions are reinforced by the corresponding findings on the role of business assets.

Avoidance of risk can be considered one type of nonpecuniary reward. We find that tastes towards other types of nonmonetary returns also show up as a reduction in earnings – presumably primarily through the type of occupation in which a person chooses to work. We find that those who want interesting work, or to help others, or who are not interested in future financial success earn less and that these differentials increase with age. But these variables do not contribute to skewness and kurtosis.

We also find evidence that those who are willing to work hard or have drive or concern for financial success receive much more earnings. These conclusions are based on the effects of religion, part-time job while growing up, and entered occupation because it (work) was challenging. These variables have larger effects over time.

These last several sets of results also suggest that models which emphasize that training and taste formation (on earnings related aspects) occur in the family, religious institutions, and within peer groups have a large grain of truth to them. However, the lack of significance of parental education and occupation suggest that education is too crude an indicator of the difference in upbringing.

Many people have argued that a good portion of earnings differentials arise because of family pull. While we have no variable which is an unambiguous measure of nepotism, we have several which lend themselves to that interpretation. This, for example, is the simplest explanation of the in-law's education results and why the inclusion of business assets wipes out the father's education coefficients. Nepotism and/or inheritance of a controlling interest in a business seem to be likely explanations of why the 22 people who went to private elementary and high school earn, on average, up to 50% more than people who went to public or parochial school[6].

Some theories such as the one that goes under the general title of human capital are more general in nature. To the extent that the human capital model means that people can improve their earnings capacity by

[6]There are also indirect intergenerational earnings transfers via educational attainment and inherited intelligence.

expending time and resources on schooling or informal training, we find strong support in our analyses. The education coefficients are significant and large. Certain types of family environment and childhood activities are also significant. But the human capital model often is presented as one in which people invest rationally, i.e. invest to the point where the rate of return on the last dollar equals the cost of capital. This proposition is very difficult to test because the many nonmonetary returns to education have not been examined in this study, and are not easy to convert into monetary equivalents.

Mincer, in a brilliant series of pieces, has demonstrated that if all on-the-job training is general, that all returns to such training are in monetary terms, and if the market functions as a competitive market would, then the human capital model would predict that age earnings profiles would rise with age for investors and that the more investment the steeper the profile. His model also predicts that the labor market adjusts occupational wages so that the present discounted value of lifetime earnings would be the same (to marginal choosers) in relevant occupations. In its most general form, this theory is a tautology with, for example, the amount invested in a year adjusting to make equations into identities. But, with restrictions, the theory can be tested. We have performed certain tests. We find evidence in ch. 7 that is at variance with the Mincer model, unless certain unmeasured variables are negatively correlated with investment in on-the-job training. We also find some evidence that skills learned in one occupation may not be as transferable to another occupation as 'home grown' skills. This suggests that all training is not general.

We have also examined stochastic models. Since these can be represented as difference equations or Markov chains, it is also true that these models can be used to explain any age profile of variances of earnings as well as generating skewed models. But the most common stochastic models assume that errors are uncorrelated. We find several pieces of evidence at variance with this view. For example, the percentage change in earnings from 1955 to 1969 is not independent of 1955 earnings levels and the R^2 of the systematic elements increases over time although the stochastic model implies a decrease.

The sorting–uncertainty model, which I believe in, receives some support from these findings. In part, this support is in the growth in importance of the effects of education and ability since these determine potential earnings. Additional support comes from the growth in the differentials associated with drive, risk aversion, willingness to work hard, etc., as summarized above. That is, these subjective measures are best displayed on the job. The differential of 1955 experience on 1969 earnings would be consistent with this model.

5. Problems and extensions

Several different types of problems remain. First, our interpretation of many of the new variables we have used may be wrong. It would be very useful for someone else, perhaps a psychologist or sociologist, to test, validate, and improve our measures of risk aversion, eleemosynary behavior, etc. Second, we have spent very little time examining interactions which may be very important and whose omission may be biasing some of our results. Third, we have not related our various cross section periods to macro, time series developments. Fourth, the results are only generated within an atypical sample of a cohort which in turn may be atypical because of war and depression experiences and because the economy and society are much altered now. Thus, many of our findings must be subject to replication in other groups before being accepted as not false. Finally, we have not made much progress on evaluating the nature/nurture or genetic/environment explanations of the distribution. The author hopes to report progress on this issue soon using a large sample of twins.

APPENDIX A

Survey of Post-War Education and Employment

1. Name ______
2. Present Address ______
3. (a) What schooling have you had since your first separation from the Armed Forces? If none, check here. ______

Example:

Place	Major subject	Dates attended From	Dates attended To	Degree, certificate, or diploma earned
University of Maryland	Mathematics	Sept. 1946	June 1950	B. A.

(b) Have you had any on-the-job training since you were separated from the Armed Forces?
Yes ______ No ______ If yes, what kind? ______

(c) If your schooling or on-the-job training was taken under the GI Bill, under what public law did you receive education benefits?
PL 16 (for disabled veterans) ______ PL 346 (other veterans) ______

4. What jobs have you had since your separation from the Armed Forces? (Pleast list your present job first, the one before that next, etc.)

Examples:

Title of job	Dates Starting	Dates Ending	Kind of business or industry	Last monthly salary (confidential)
(a) Welder	Feb. 1949	Present	Aircraft factory	$290
(b) Sheet metal worker	June 1947	Feb. 1949	Automobile factory	$270
1				

3. ______ ______ ______ ______

5. (a) Describe what you do in your present job ______
______
______

(b) How many employees do you supervise? ______

(c) How well do you think you are performing in your present work? (Check one box)

Barely satisfactory ☐	About as well as average ☐	Better than average ☐	Outstandingly successful ☐

(d) How well do you like the type of work you are now doing? (Check one box)

Dislike it ☐	O.K. it's a job ☐	Like it very much ☒	Better than any other ☐

6. Do you have a license or have you passed a certifying examination of any kind? (Example – Master Plumber License, CPA, Licensed Electrician, Teacher, etc.) Yes ______ No ______ If yes, what kind? ______

7. (a) When were you first separated from the Armed Forces? ______

(b) Have you had any tours of extended active duty since your first separation from the Armed Forces? (Do not count short tours of duty for reserve training.) Yes ______ No ______ If yes, please give dates:

1. From ______ to ______
2. From ______ to ______

8. Did you ever receive vocational counseling through the Veterans Administration? Yes ______ No ______

9. Please give your Social Security number if it is readily available ______

(Use the other side of the blank for any comments that you think will give us a better picture of your post-World War II career.)

Questionnaire sent to all men in survey sample by Thorndike and Hagen.

A Twenty-Five Year Follow-Up Survey

Sponsored by the National Bureau of Economic Research, New York, New York

1969, 5086 People

We plan to begin tabulations by July 1, and would appreciate your returning the questionnaire as soon as possible.

Identification

Disregard the small numbers to the right of the boxes; they are for tabulation purposes.

GENERAL INFORMATION

1. What is your age (last birthday)? .... years. 6–7

2. Please check X below to indicate your marital status.

Single .... ☐ 8–1
Married .... ☐ –2
Divorced .... ☐ –3
Widower .... ☐ –4
Other .... ☐ –5

Date
.... 19 9–10

3. How many children do you have?

None .... ☐ 15–1
1 .... ☐ –2
2 .... ☐ –3
3 .... ☐ –4
4 .... ☐ –5
5 .... ☐ –6
6 or more .... ☐ –7

4. Do you own your own home or co-operative apartment?

Yes – house .... ☐ 16–1
Yes – apartment .... ☐ –2
No .... ☐ –3

5. What is the state of your general health?

Excellent .... ☐ 28–1
Good .... ☐ –2
Fair .... ☐ –3
Poor .... ☐ –4

6. What is your approximate height?

.... ft. .... inches 29–31

7. What is your approximate weight?

.... lbs. 32–34

EDUCATIONAL BACKGROUND

1. Please fill in the following form. We have included an illustrative set of responses in dark type.

Schools Attended	Dates attended	Graduated (X if yes)	Type of degree received	Date degree received
High school				
Locust Valley, Pennsylvania	**1938–42**	**X**		
....	....			
....	 17–18	☐ 19–1		
Vocational Training				
Automotive Repair School	**1946**	**X**		
....	....	☐ 20–1		
Undergraduate college or University				
U. of Colorado, Boulder	**1943, 45–48**	**X**	**B.A.**	**1948**
....	....			
....	....	☐ 21–1	.... 22–1 –2	 23–24
Graduate School				
....	....	☐	....	....
....	....	☐ 25–1	....	 26–27

2. Please indicate the highest grade of schooling completed by each of the following family members: (High school graduate would be 12, college graduate 16, etc.):

	Highest grade completed	
Wife	.... yrs.	61–62
Your father	.... yrs.	63–64
Wife's father	.... yrs.	65–66

3. Based on your own personal experience, what do you think high schools and colleges should concentrate on? Indicate your choice by circling the appropriate number on the scale from 5 (very great importance) to 1 (very little importance).

	Great importance ←				→ Little importance	
Basic skills (reading, mathematics, etc.)	5	4	3	2	1	67
General knowledge (history, literature, science, etc.)	5	4	3	2	1	68
Career preparation (vocational, professional, etc.)	5	4	3	2	1	69
Activities (school clubs, newspapers, sports, etc.)	5	4	3	2	1	70
Social awareness (current social problems, community action, etc.)	5	4	3	2	1	71

WORK EXPERIENCE, EARNINGS, AND INCOME

1. We would like you to describe your work experience below, starting with your present job. An illustrative set of responses have been included in dark type.

For the earnings information, even very rough estimates will be helpful. If you are self-employed, mark column 1 as self-employed and interpret the salary columns as total income. If you have more than one job, please report salary on main job only.

	Position held	Years worked	Beginning salary (Annual full time)	Ending salary (Annual full time)	Pension plan (X if yes)	Average weekly hours during last year: Main job	Average weekly hours during last year: Other jobs
	Foreman	**1961–69**	**$7500**	**$9600**	**X**	**42**	**4**
Present job	....	....	....	....	☐	....	....
Previous jobs	....	....	....	....	☐		
	....	....	....	....	☐		
	....	....	....	....	☐		
	....	....	....	....	☐		
	....	....	....	....	☐		
	....	....	....	....	☐		
	....	....	....	....	☐		
First job (full-time, after finishing school)	....	....	....	....	☐		

Office use	
....	6–10
....	11–15
....	16–17
....	18–19
....	20–21
....	22–1

2. For the past year, please indicate the number of weeks spent doing each of the following:

	Number of weeks	Card III
Full-time work (or both full and part-time)	....	6–7
Part-time work	....	8–9
Paid vacation	....	10–11
Out of work or on layoff	....	12–13
Check ☐ if seasonal		14–1
Unable to work due to illness	....	15–16
Other (please specify)	....	17–18
Total	52	

3. Please indicate your total household income for the following years. If your income was unusually high or low in these years, please indicate the average for surrounding years (e.g. 1967–68–69).

Year	Your total earnings	Total earnings of other household members	Other income (dividends, capital gains, etc.)	Total family income
1968	$.........	$.........	$.........	$.........
1958	$.........	$.........	$.........	$.........

19–40

41–62

OCCUPATIONAL INFORMATION

A number of job descriptions are listed below. Please indicate X which of these best describes your own job (A), and which best describes the type of job held by your father (B), and your wife's father (C) during most of their working lives.

JOB DESCRIPTION

	A Your own job	B Father's job	Card IV C Wife's father's job
Business proprietor (owner)	☐ 6–1	☐ 8–1	☐ 10–1
Check X if farm operator: A ☐ 12–1 B ☐ 13–1 C ☐ 14–1			
Managerial (executive, office manager, etc.)	☐ –2	☐ –2	☐ –2
Professional (doctor, lawyer, accountant, teacher, etc.)			
Self-employed	☐ –3	☐ –3	☐ –3
Salaried	☐ –4	☐ –4	☐ –4
Check X if teacher: A ☐ 15–1 B ☐ 16–1 C ☐ 17–1			
Technical, (draftsman, surveyor, medical, etc.)	☐ –5	☐ –5	☐ –5
Office worker	☐ –6	☐ –6	☐ –6
Salesman	☐ –7	☐ –7	☐ –7
Service worker	☐ –8	☐ –8	☐ –8
Protective (policeman, etc.)	☐	☐	☐
Retail or wholesale trade	☐	☐	☐
Other	☐	☐	☐
'Blue-collar' employee			
Foreman or supervisor	☐ 7–1	☐ 9–1	☐ 11–1
Skilled	☐ –2	☐ –2	☐ –2
Semi-skilled	☐ –3	☐ –3	☐ –3
Unskilled	☐ –4	☐ –4	☐ –4
Other (please specify)	☐ –5	☐ –5	☐ –5
Don't know	☐ –6	☐ –6	☐ –6
Not applicable	☐ –7	☐ –7	☐ –7

ATTITUDE TOWARD JOB

In this section we want to find out how people feel about their work. Just circle the number that best describes your own evaluation. The numbers constitute a scale ranging from five (highest, best, etc.) to one (lowest, worst, etc.)

	High ←				→ Low	
Do you enjoy your work?	5	4	3	2	1	18
Does your work provide a challenge?	5	4	3	2	1	19
Is your work interesting?	5	4	3	2	1	20

For the items listed below, how does your total work experience to date compare with what you expected when you first started? (3 = about as expected)

Financial compensation	5	4	3	2	1	21
Requirement for independent judgment	5	4	3	2	1	22
Responsibility	5	4	3	2	1	23
Prospects for advancement	5	4	3	2	1	24

Below is a list of possible requirements for achieving success in a particular job or profession. Indicate on the scale where your own type of work should be ranked. That is, to what degree does success in your work depend on: (3 = average importance for success)

Your own performance	5	4	3	2	1	25
Having the right connections	5	4	3	2	1	26
Being able to get along with people	5	4	3	2	1	27
Being lucky or unlucky	5	4	3	2	1	28
Having a college diploma	5	4	3	2	1	29
Working hard	5	4	3	2	1	30

ACTIVITIES

In this section we would like you to indicate X the extent of your participation in social, civic, religious, and other similar activities.

1. Which of the following types of groups, if any, do you devote some amount of time to, either as a member, an active participant, or an officer.

	Type of participation (X)			No. of hours during last month	
	Member-ship	Active partici-pant	Leader-ship		
Service organizations (Rotary, Chamber of Commerce, etc.)	□ 31–1	□ –2	□ –3	....	32–33
Youth organizations (scouting, Little League, etc.)	□ 34–1	□ –2	□ –3	....	35–36
Veterans' organizations	□ 37–1	□ –2	□ –3	....	38–39
Professional and trade associations	□ 40–1	□ –2	□ –3	....	41–42
Political organizations	□ 43–1	□ –2	□ –3	....	44–45
Educational organizations (PTA, etc.)	□ 46–1	□ –2	□ –4	....	47–48
Church or church related organizations					
Religious activity	□ 49–1	□ –2	□ –3	....	50–51
Educational activity	□ 52–1	□ –2	□ –3	....	53–54
Social action	□ 55–1	□ –2	□ –3	....	56–57
Community and social action groups	□ 58–1	□ –2	□ –3	....	59–60
Organized volunteer work (hospital, etc.)	□ 61–1	□ –2	□ –3	....	62–63
Fund raising	□ 64–1	□ –2	□ –3	....	65–66
Personal service	□ 67–1	□ –2	□ –3	....	68–69
Informal helping out – friends, neighbors, or relatives		□ 70–2		....	71–72
Household tasks		□ 73–2		....	74–75

2. Please check X below to indicate your religious preference.

		Card V
Protestant	□	50–1
Catholic	□	–2
Jewish	□	–3
Other	□	–4
None	□	–5

3. Please indicate X which of the following best describes your right – considering the welfare of the country as a whole?

Always vote in local, state, and national elections	□	51–1
Always vote in national elections, sometimes in state and local ones	□	–2
Usually vote in national elections	□	–3
Sometimes vote in national elections	□	–4
Seldom vote in any elections	□	–5

4. Do you think of yourself as politically conservative or liberal?

Very conservative	□	52–1
Moderately conservative	□	–2
Sometimes conservative, sometimes liberal	□	–3
Moderately liberal	□	–4
Very liberal	□	–5

SOCIAL, ECONOMIC, AND POLITICAL ATTITUDES

In this section we would like you to indicate your attitude about various social and economic problems. Please check X the appropriate box, and feel free to add additional explanation where necessary.

1. Do you feel that young people today have too much freedom, too little, or about the right amount?

Too much ... □ 53–3 About right ... □ 53–2 Too little ... □ 53–1

2. Do you feel that people today are too much concerned with financial security, too little, or what?

Too much ... □ 54–3 About right ... □ 54–2 Too little ... □ 54–1

3. During the past ten years or so, do you think that the pace of racial integration has been too fast, too slow, or about right – considering the welfare of the country as a whole?

Too fast ... ☐ 55–3 About right ... ☐ 55–2 Too slow ... ☐ 55–1

4. Assuming you thought that the financial possibilities were about the same, would you prefer to work for yourself or for somebody else?

Prefer self-employment	☐	56–3
No preference	☐	–2
Prefer salaried employment	☐	–1

5. Suppose you thought that the financial advantages were, on the average, slightly favorable if you worked for yourself rather than for someone else. Would you then prefer:

Self employment	☐	57–3
No preference	☐	–2
Salaried employment	☐	–1

ASSETS, DEBTS, SAVINGS, AND PURCHASES - OPTIONAL

The following questions are of considerable interest to us, but we know that some people regard financial information of this sort as very personal. If that is your feeling, just skip this section. Please return the form, since the other information will be of great help in the study. Once again, let us note that all replies will be treated with the strictest confidence.

1. Please check X to indicate the approximate amount of your household's assets or debts in each of the following categories:

Card V

	Don't have	Approximate amount (dollars) Under $1000	$1000–2000	$2000–5000	$5000–10000	$10000–20000	$20000–40000	$40000–80000	Over $80000
Checking accounts	☐ 6–1	☐ –2	☐ –3	☐ –4	☐ –5	☐ –6	☐ –7	☐ –8	☐ –9
Savings accounts and government savings bonds	☐ 7–1	☐ –2	☐ –3	☐ –4	☐ –5	☐ –6	☐ –7	☐ –8	☐ –9
Common stock, mutual funds, other marketable securities (current market value)	☐ 8–1	☐ –2	☐ –3	☐ –4	☐ –5	☐ –6	☐ –7	☐ –8	☐ –9
Value of your home (what it would currently sell for)	☐ 10–1	☐ –2	☐ –3	☐ –4	☐ –5	☐ –6	☐ –7	☐ –8	☐ –9
Equity in annuities and life insurance (cash surrender value)	☐ 11–1	☐ –2	☐ –3	☐ –4	☐ –5	☐ –6	☐ –7	☐ –8	☐ –9
Equity in pension plan (other than Social Security)	☐ 12–1	☐ –2	☐ –3	☐ –4	☐ –5	☐ –6	☐ –7	☐ –8	☐ –9
Other assets (own business, real estate)	☐ 13–1	☐ –2	☐ –3	☐ –4	☐ –5	☐ –6	☐ –7	☐ –8	☐ –9
Mortgage on your home	☐ 14–1	☐ –2	☐ –3	☐ –4	☐ –5	☐ –6	☐ –7	☐ –8	☐ –9
Other personal debt (installment, etc.)	☐ 15–1	☐ –2	☐ –3	☐ –4	☐ –5	☐ –6	☐ –7	☐ –8	☐ –9

2. Please indicate the approximate change (either increase or decrease) over the past 12 months in each of the following:

	Amount of decrease ←			No change	Amount of increase →			
	Over $2000	$1000–2000	$500–1000	Under $500		Under $500	$500–1000	$1000–2000	Over $2000
Checking and savings accounts, government bonds	☐ 16–1	☐ –2	☐ –3	☐ –4	☐ –5	☐ –6	☐ –7	☐ –8	☐ –9
Common stock, mutual funds, other marketable securities (count only net new money put in or taken out)	☐ 17–1	☐ –2	☐ –3	☐ –4	☐ –5	☐ –6	☐ –7	☐ –8	☐ –9
Equity in annuities and life insurance (cash surrender value)	☐ 19–1	☐ –2	☐ –3	☐ –4	☐ –5	☐ –6	☐ –7	☐ –8	☐ –9
Equity in a pension plan (other than Social Security)	☐ 20–1	☐ –2	☐ –3	☐ –4	☐ –5	☐ –6	☐ –7	☐ –8	☐ –9
Other assets (count only net purchases or sales)	☐ 21–1	☐ –2	☐ –3	☐ –4	☐ –5	☐ –6	☐ –7	☐ –8	☐ –9
Mortgage balance outstanding	☐ 22–1	☐ –2	☐ –3	☐ –4	☐ –5	☐ –6	☐ –7	☐ –8	☐ –9
Installment and other debts outstanding	☐ 23–1	☐ –2	☐ –3	☐ –4	☐ –5	☐ –6	☐ –7	☐ –8	☐ –9

3. During the past 12 months, have you

	Yes	No	If yes, approximate cost	
Purchased a home	☐ 24–1	☐ –2	$..................	25–29
Purchased a car	☐ 30–1	☐ –2	$..................	31–35
Purchased major durables, appliances, or furniture	☐ 36–1	☐ –2	$..................	37–41
Made major alterations or repairs on your home	☐ 42–1	☐ –2	$..................	43–47

Thank you very much for your cooperation in filling out this questionnaire. If you would like to receive a summary of the results when the study is completed, indicate by X.

☐ Would like summary

Supplemental Questionnaire: Twenty-Five Year Follow-Up Survey

1971, 3000 persons

We would like you to answer the following few questions, which represent items of information that will be helpful to us in interpreting some of the data from the original questionnaire. Please use the return envelope provided for your convenience. Thank you.

Identification

Please mark □ in the appropriate box: The numbers at the right are for tabulation purposes.

Q1: Are you working at the same job as last year?
- □ 6–1 Yes – same job
- □ 6–2 No – have changed job

Q2: Have you ever owned and operated a full-time business (do not include medical or law practice, etc.)?
- □ 7–1 Yes – own and operate business at present (please write in type of business________________________
____
- □ 7–2 Yes – have owned and operated business in past, but no longer doing so

If answer is Yes please go to 2A:
- □ 7–3 No – have never owned or operated business

Q2A: Did you receive any help from a Veterans Administration loan when you got started in this business?
- □ 8–1 Yes
- □ 8–2 No

Q3: How would you describe the town in which you grew up?
- □ 9–1 Rural area
- □ 9–2 Small town (under 10000)
- □ 9–3 Moderate sized city (between 10000 and 50000)
- □ 9–4 Large city (between 50000 and 500000)
- □ 9–5 Metropolitan center (over 500000)

Q4: How would you describe your high school record?
- □ 10–1 Very high grades
- □ 10–2 High grades
- □ 10–3 Average grades
- □ 10–4 Poor grades

Q5: Was your high school work mainly concentrated on:
- □ 11–1 Academic-type courses (college preparation)
- □ 11–2 Vocational-type courses (work preparation)

Q6: In the high school that you attended, were most of the other students:
- □ 12–1 Financially better off than you
- □ 12–2 Financially about the same as you
- □ 12–3 Financially worse off than you

Q7: Please indicate below how many brothers and sisters you have (including those no longer living)

Older brothers and sisters		Younger brothers and sisters	
☐ 13–1	None	☐ 14–1	None
☐ 13–2	1	☐ 14–2	1
☐ 13–3	2	☐ 14–3	2
☐ 13–4	3	☐ 14–4	3
☐ 13–5	4 or more	☐ 14–5	4 or more

Q8: [For those who attended college.]
Do you think you would have gone to college if there had not been a 'G.I. Bill' which took care of most expenses?

☐ 15–1 Yes – would have gone anyway
☐ 15–2 Probably would have gone anyway
☐ 15–3 No – couldn't have gone without G.I. Bill
☐ 15–4 Don't know

A Supplement to the Twenty-Five Year Follow-Up Survey

Sponsored by the National Bureau of Economic Research, New York, New York

1972, 4400 People

We plan to begin tabulations in 10 DAYS, and would appreciate your returning the questionnaire as soon as possible.

Identification

Disregard the small numbers to the right of the boxes; they are for tabulation purposes.

FAMILY BACKGROUND AND EARLY CHILDHOOD INFORMATION

1. While you were growing up and going to school, what type of house did you and your family live in?

   Single-family house that we owned .... ☐ 6–1
   Single-family house that we rented .... ☐ –2
   Apartment .... ☐ –3
   Other .... ☐ –4

2. Did you share a room with other children or have a room to yourself while you were growing up?

   Shared room .... ☐ 7–1
   Had own room .... ☐ –2
   Both, at different times .... ☐ –3

3. Up to graduation from high school, about how many times did you and your family move?

   Never moved – stayed in same house .... ☐ 8–1
   Moved once or twice .... ☐ –2
   Moved three or four times .... ☐ –3
   Moved five times or more .... ☐ –4

4. (For those who moved at least once.) Were all of these moves within the same neighborhood or town?

   Yes – within same neighborhood .... ☐ 9–1
   Yes – within same city or town .... ☐ –2
   No – moved to different city or town .... ☐ –3
   No – moved from farm to city or town .... ☐ –4

5. At what age did you start going to school?

Under five years old (nursery school or kindergarten)	☐ 10–1
Five years old (kindergarten or first grade)	☐ 10–2
Six years old	☐ 10–3
Seven years old	☐ 10–4
Eight or older	☐ 10–5

6. What kind of elementary (grammer) school and high school did you attend? (If more than one, check all schools attended and circle the one from which you graduated.)

Type of school	Elementary school	High school
Public school	☐ 11–1	☐ 12–1
Parochial (religious) school	☐ –2	☐ –2
Private (tuition-paying) school	☐ –3	☐ –3

7. Before you started school and while you were in elementary school, did your mother have a regular job of any kind?

	Your age and school status	
Mother's work status	Age 0–5 (Pre-school)	Age 6–14 (Elementary school)
Worked full time each year	☐ 13–1	☐ 14–1
Worked full time some years	☐ –2	☐ –2
Worked part time each year	☐ –3	☐ –3
Worked part time some years	☐ –4	☐ –4
Did not work	☐ –5	☐ –5
Don't recall	☐ –6	☐ –6

8. How many years of formal schooling did your mother receive?

0–4 years	☐ 15–1
5–6 years	☐ –2
7–8 years	☐ –3
9–10 years	☐ –4
10–11 years	☐ –5
12 years (finished high school)	☐ –6
13–15 years (some college training)	☐ –7
16 or more years (college graduate)	☐ –8
Don't know	☐ –9

9. Aside from your regular school, did you also attend religious instruction or other church-related schools or classes?

Yes – several times a week	☐ 16–1
Yes – weekly	☐ –2
Yes – occasionally	☐ –3
No	☐ –4

10. Please rank the following activities, indicating how you were most likely to spend free time while you were growing up? Indicate your choice by circling the appropriate number on the scale from 5 (most often) to 1 (hardly ever)

Type of activity	Most often ←				→ Hardly ever	
Sports	5	4	3	2	1	17
Hobbies	5	4	3	2	1	18
Reading	5	4	3	2	1	19
Chores around home	5	4	3	2	1	20
Part-time job	5	4	3	2	1	21
Other (please specify)						
....	5	4	3	2	1	22

11. (Answer only if married.) How many years of formal schooling did your wife's mother receive?

0–4 years	☐ 23–1
5–6 years	☐ –2
7–8 years	☐ –3
9–10 years	☐ –4
10–11 years	☐ –5
12 years (finished high school)	☐ –6
13–15 years (some college training)	☐ –7
16 or more years (college graduate)	☐ –8
Don't know	☐ –9

INFORMATION ON WIFE AND CHILDREN

Please answer Questions 1 through 5 only if married.

1. Approximately how long have you been married?

.... years 24, 25

2. What is the approximate age of your wife at the present time?

.... years 26, 27

3. What type of school did your wife attend when she was growing up?

Type of school	Elementary school	High school
Public school	☐ 28–1	☐ 29–1
Parochial (religious) school	☐ –2	☐ –2
Private (tuition-paying) school	☐ –3	☐ –3

4. Since your marriage, has your wife ever had a regular full- or part-time job?

Yes	☐ 30–1	Please answer Question 5
No	☐ –2	Please skip to Question 6

5. Please check the appropriate boxes to show your wife's employment history from the time of your marriage. Note that many people have different answers depending on number of years after marriage; for example, many wives do not work during their first five years of marriage but work part time later on, etc.

Years after marriage	Wife did not work	Wife worked part time	Wife worked full time	(If worked, type of job)	
1–4	☐ –1	☐ –1	☐ –1	....	31, 32, 33
5–9	☐ –2	☐ –2	☐ –2	....	
10–14	☐ –3	☐ –3	☐ –3	....	
15 or more	☐ –4	☐ –4	☐ –4	....	

Please answer Questions 6 and 7 only if you have one or more children.

6. Indicate the ages and the current school status of your children, including children no longer living with you. In the last column, indicate how many years of schooling you eventually expect each child to complete.

School status of each child: N = Nursery school; K = Kindergarten; 1 = First grade; 16 = College graduate

Children	Age	Sex (M or F)	Type of school now attending: Public	Parochial	Private	Not in school	Present grade	Grade expected to complete (or completed)
Oldest	....	....	☐ 34–1	☐ –2	☐ –3	☐ –4	....	....
....	....	....	☐ 35–1	☐ –2	☐ –3	☐ –4	....	....
....	....	....	☐ 36–1	☐ –2	☐ –3	☐ –4	....	....
....	....	....	☐ 37–1	☐ –2	☐ –3	☐ –4	....	....
....	....	....	☐ 38–1	☐ –2	☐ –3	☐ –4	....	....
....	....	....	☐ 39–1	☐ –2	☐ –3	☐ –4	....	....
....	....	....	☐ 40–1	☐ –2	☐ –3	☐ –4	....	....
Youngest	....	....	☐ 41–1	☐ –2	☐ –3	☐ –4	....	....

7. Have any of your children attended nursery school or other pre-kindergarten school?

All attended	☐	42–1
Some attended	☐	–2
None attended	☐	–3

HEALTH HISTORY

1. What is the state of your general health at present?

Excellent	☐	43–1
Good	☐	–2
Fair	☐	–3
Poor	☐	–4

2. During the years you were attending high school what was the state of your health?

Excellent	☐	44–1
Good	☐	–2
Fair	☐	–3
Poor	☐	–4
Don't recall	☐	–5

3. During the time you were attending high school, how many weeks, per year did you lose from school, on the average, due to your own illness or injury? (Exclude injuries from athletics.)

None	☐	45–1
Less than a week	☐	–2
1–2 weeks	☐	–3
More than two weeks	☐	–4
Don't recall	☐	–5

4. Since you began working, have you ever lost any time from work because of your own illness?

Yes	☐	46–1
No	☐	–2

5. (If yes on 4.) Approximately how much total time (in terms of weeks) have you lost through illness during your working lifetime?

.... weeks 47, 48

6. Since you left military service after World War II, have you ever been unemployed?

Yes	☐	49–1
No	☐	–2

(If no, skip to General Information.)

7. (If yes on 6.) Approximately how much total time have you lost because of unemployment since you left the service?

.... weeks 50, 51

8. On how many different occasions have you been unemployed?

Once	☐
Twice	☐
Three or more times	☐

GENERAL INFORMATION

1. What was your rank when you left active military service after the Second World War?

   ....

2. At what age do you expect to retire?

   At age 52, 53

3. Between now and the time you plan to retire, do you expect your earnings to:

Increase substantially	☐ 54–1
Increase somewhat	☐ –2
Stay about the same	☐ –3
Decrease somewhat	☐ –4
Decrease substantially	☐ –5

4. Over the last several years, have the average number of hours you work each week:

Increased substantially	☐ 55–1
Increased moderately	☐ –2
Stayed about the same	☐ –3
Decreased moderately	☐ –4
Decreased substantially	☐ –5

5. What are the major reasons for any change in the number of hours you have worked in recent years? (Please write in.)

   ....

   ....

6. What is the approximate size of the town or city where you now live?

Rural area (under 2500 people)	☐ 56–1
Small town (2500–10 000)	☐ –2
Town (10 000–50 000)	☐ –3
Moderately sized city (50 000–250 000)	☐ –4
Large city (250 000–1 million)	☐ –5
Major metropolitan area (over 1 million)	☐ –6

OCCUPATIONAL HISTORY

1. What is your occupation at the present time?

   ....

2. We are interested in the kind of jobs people take when they first begin working, especially for those who leave school before finishing in order to begin work. Please indicate, by checking Yes or No, whether any of the following circumstances were present when you began working full time.

When you began work:	Yes	No
Were you married?	☐ 57–1	☐ –2
Did you have children?	☐ 58–1	☐ –2
Did you receive an exceptional job offer?	☐ 59–1	☐ –2
Were you self-employed?	☐ 60–1	☐ –2
Was there financial pressure to work?	☐ 61–1	☐ –2
Did you spend much time looking for a job?	☐ 62–1	☐ –2
Did you regret having to leave school?	☐ 63–1	☐ –2
Did you have any specific vocational training for the job?	☐ 64–1	☐ –2

3. As best you can remember, what factors influenced your decision to enter the occupational field you are in at the present time? Check yes or no to each of the following and indicate factors that were of special importance.

Factors that influenced decision to enter present occupation:	Yes	No	Of special importance
Type of training in school	☐ 6–1	☐ –2	☐ 7–1
Type of training in military	☐ 8–1	☐ –2	☐ 9–1
Personal contacts (friends or relatives)	☐ 10–1	☐ –2	☐ 11–1
Salary or pay offered	☐ 12–1	☐ –2	☐ 13–1
Prospects of eventual financial success	☐ 14–1	☐ –2	☐ 15–1
Chance to do interesting work	☐ 16–1	☐ –2	☐ 17–1
Chance for independent work	☐ 18–1	☐ –2	☐ 19–1
Chance for a lot of person-to-person contact	☐ 20–1	☐ –2	☐ 21–1
Chance to help others	☐ 22–1	☐ –2	☐ 23–1
Represented a challenge	☐ 24–1	☐ –2	☐ 25–1
Job security	☐ 26–1	☐ –2	☐ 27–1
Provided a lot of free time	☐ 28–1	☐ –2	☐ 29–1
Always liked that kind of work	☐ 30–1	☐ –2	☐ 31–1

Please check below if you wish to receive a summary of the results from this questionnaire.

I would like to receive the summary of results ...... ☐

Use this space for additional explanation where needed.

The following description of the test scores and factor analysis is taken from Taubman–Wales, pp. 203–209.

We have scores on 17 different tests in the sample. A brief description of the tests, taken from Thorndike and Hagen (1959, pp. 9–12), indicates the types of material and abilities covered in each test[1].

Reading Comprehension A test of comprehension of rather technical passages. Primarily a measure of verbal comprehension, it also depended somewhat on mechanical experience and on general reasoning ability.

General Information–Navigator An information or vocabulary test dealing with the terminology of such fields as astronomy, trigonometry, and science. The common factor measured was one of verbal ability, though the content suggests that the test also reflects technical and quantitative academic leanings.

Mathematics A test of knowledge of advanced arithmetic, algebra in large amount, and trigonometry to some extent. Performance appeared to depend upon a complex of factors, including numerical fluency, verbal comprehension, background in school mathematics, and general reasoning ability. [This is referred to in the text as Mathematics A.]

Arithmetic Reasoning A test composed of arithmetic word-problems of the sort that are common in the subtests of both scholastic aptitude and school achievement batteries, but cast in terms of planes and aviation. Numerical fluency, general reasoning, and verbal comprehension were the main factors identified in this test. [This is referred to in the text as Mathematics B.]

Numerical Operations I and II These were two scores, obtained separately for scoring convenience, representing speed and accuracy in simple numerical computations. Test 1 included addition and multiplication, Test II subtraction and division. These were nearly pure tests of numerical fluency.

Dial and Table Reading The first part of this test required the subject to determine the numerical value represented by the reading on one of a set

[1]For the convenience of the reader, we also include the description of the information in the biographical items. The pilot and navigator biography keys are *not* included in the factor analysis.

of airplane instrument dials, whereas the second part required him to locate entries in rather complex numerical tables. The test involved a number of ability factors, primarily numerical fluency, spatial relations, and perceptual speed.

Speed of Identification This was a speeded test requiring the matching of visual forms. It was a rather pure measure of speed of visual perception.

Spatial Orientation I This was also a perceptual matching test. In this case, small excerpts from aerial photographs had to be matched against locations in the complete photographs. Perceptual speed was again the chief factor involved.

Spatial Orientation II This test required the matching of sections of aerial photographs with the locations on aerial maps corresponding to the photographs. Perceptual speed was again a major factor, together with some dependence upon spatial visualizing and on social studies background.

Mechanical Principles This test was patterned closely after Benett's Mechanical Principles Test, except that the items were cast in an aviation setting. Pictorial situations presented problems involving mechanical concepts and principles. Performance on this test depended primarily on factors of mechanical experience and of visualizing ability, but also to a slight degree on verbal comprehension and general reasoning.

Two-Hand Coordination This was an individual apparatus test in which the examinee, by manipulating lathe-type controls, had to keep a pointer in contact with an irregularly moving target button. Performance on the test appeared to depend in part upon mechanical experience, in part upon spatial factors, and in part upon psychomotor coordination.

Biographical Data Blank–Pilot Key The Biographical Data Blank was an assembly of questions about home and family background, school activities and successes, out-of-school activities and hobbies, work experience, and certain other items. The pilot key was an empirical keying of those items that were found to predict success in pilot training. The main factor represented in the pilot key was mechanical experience.

Complex Coordination This test was an individual apparatus one in which the examinee manipulated stick and rudder controls similar to those encountered in a light airplane. By moving the controls appropriately, he could match patterns of stimulus lights presented to him. His task was to match as many of the stimulus patterns as he could in a limited test period. The test appeared to measure primarily factors of spatial relations and psychomotor coordination.

Rotary Pursuit with Divided Attention The subject's basic task was to keep a metal stylus resting on a target button that rotated on a 78 rpm phonograph turntable. At the same time, with the other hand, he had to depress the response button corresponding to one of two signal lights. The test appeared to measure psychomotor coordination as well as some type of spatial factor.

Finger Dexterity This was a peg-turning test in which the subject was required to remove each of a series of square pegs from its hole, rotate it through 180°, and reinsert it. He was scored in terms of the number of pegs turned in a series of brief trials. Common factors measured by the test included psychomotor coordination and precision, visualizing, and possibly a little perceptual speed.

Aiming Stress Basically, this was a test of hand steadiness, in which the subject had to keep a stylus pointed in a target hole without touching the edges of the hole. Verbal heckling was introduced in some trials to try to add an element of emotional stress. However, the only common factor appearing in this test was one of psychomotor coordination, so it should be thought of primarily as a motor test.

General Information–Pilot This test was made up of a rather heterogeneous collection of information items selected because they appeared to have validity for predicting success in pilot training. These included items about planes and flying, auto driving, sports, and hobbies. The test appeared quite heterogeneous, and involved factors of pilot interest, verbal comprehension, mechanical experience, and perceptual speed.

Discrimination Reaction Time This test was an individual test of speed of reaction. The reaction was to a pattern of visual stimuli, and the subject was required to choose the correct one of four response switches. Stimulus patterns were presented one after another, at about four second intervals, and the subject had to respond as rapidly as possible to each as it occurred. The test measured a complex of different factors, including spatial relations, psychomotor precision, perceptual speed, and visualizing.

Biographical Data Blank–Navigator Key A second empirical key was established for the Biographical Data Blank, weighting those items that were found to predict success in navigator training. The key seemed to provide primarily a measure of extent of mathematical background.

From the titles and the above descriptions, it is clear that many of the tests measure different facets of the same ability. Rather than use all the tests or any arbitrary subset, we decided to use factor analysis to obtain a measure of a few types of ability[2]. The actual factor analysis was conducted by A. Beaton.

The basic idea in factor analysis is that any test contains information on one or more general abilities and a test-specific content. That is,

$$SC = F + u,$$

where S is the set of scores; F represents the set of general abilities; and u represents the test-specific components. Using the scores on each of the tests, it is possible to estimate C by imposing certain conditions on u. Estimates of F can then be found from SC where C is the factor loadings. Each F is, of course, just a weighted average of the test scores[3]. In some instances, however, the major weights in each average are attached to items that measure one type of attribute; this attribute is then used to describe the factor.

In the NBER–TH data, the factor loadings for each of four factors are

[2]It is, of course, true that the factors are linear combinations of the test scores; thus the same results could be achieved by entering linearly all the scores in our regressions. However, we are interested in studying nonlinear effects of various ability measures and interactions of ability with education, as well as determining which types of ability influence earnings. For these purposes it is appropriate to use the factors.

[3]Because the original test scores are standardized and then manipulated as correlations, all weights have to lie between $+1$ and -1. The importance of each test in a factor is indicated by the absolute size of its loading coefficient.

as in table E-4. Consider the second factor, in which Rotary Pursuit, Two-Hand Coordination, and Complex Coordination all have loadings in excess of .65. In addition, Finger Dexterity, Aiming Stress, Discrimination Reaction Time, and Mechanical Principles have weights in the range .35 to .54. Since the common element in all tests is coordination, we refer to this as the complex-coordination factor. For the fourth factor, the only important tests are Speed of Identification and the two Spatial Orientation tests. Given the description of the Speed of Identification test, it seems clear that the fourth factor measures spatial perception and, perhaps, abstract reasoning.

Both these factors are easy to interpret or identify. The first and third are somewhat more difficult, although the first is clearer. In the first factor, the most important items, with loadings of at least .69, are Numerical Operations, mathematics (Math A), arithmetic reasoning (Math B), and Dial and Table Reading. All these tests are concerned with mathematics and quantitative skills and primarily measure numerical

Ability test	*Factor loadings*			
	1	*2*	*3*	*4*
Reading Comprehension	0.4123	0.0700	0.7186	0.0136
Mechanical Principles	0.0149	0.3522	0.7210	0.0247
Dial and Table Reading	0.6990	0.2566	−0.0129	0.3260
Spatial Orientation II	0.0658	0.1042	0.3117	0.6420
Spatial Orientation I	0.2217	0.1379	0.0311	0.7642
Numerical Operations I and II	0.7822	0.0597	−0.2183	0.1030
Speed of Identification	0.0500	0.1008	0.0643	0.7831
General Information–Navigator	0.4842	−0.1199	0.5605	0.1495
General Information–Pilot	−0.0811	0.0329	0.5874	0.3567
Mathematics B	0.7444	−0.0104	0.3514	−0.0717
Mathematics A	0.7464	−0.0469	0.3060	0.5071
Rotary Pursuit	−0.0304	0.6772	0.0453	0.0396
Two-Hand Coordination	−0.0385	0.6870	0.2703	0.0572
Complex Coordination	0.1251	0.7026	0.1877	0.2028
Aiming Stress	−0.0111	0.4128	0.0009	0.0093
Discrimination Reaction Time	0.3891	0.3800	0.0940	0.2636
Finger Dexterity	0.1974	0.5438	−0.1664	0.1253

fluency or speed and accuracy, but not necessarily problem-solving techniques. Secondary but still important weights (.48 to .39) are accorded to General Information–Navigator, Reading Comprehension, and Discrimination Reaction Time. The navigator test does emphasize mathematical material, but the other two items do not. Nevertheless, we treat this as a mathematical-ability test.

In the third factor, Reading Comprehension and Mechanical Principles have loadings in excess of .7. General Information–Pilot and General Information–Navigator have loadings of about .5, while Math B and A have loadings of .35 and .30, and Spatial Orientation II has a loading of .31. In general, these tests encompass verbal ability, mathematical skills, reasoning, *and mechanical principles.* The first three items would be found in standard verbal-I.Q. tests, but mechanical principles would not. We have chosen to call this third factor I.Q.[4]. It is important to note, however, that Thorndike has written us to say he believes that the first factor would correlate much more closely with an I.Q. measure and should be named as such, while the third factor tends toward mechanical principles. The reader should keep this caveat in mind when examining our remarks about the importance of the different types of ability and when comparing the NBER–TH results with those of Wolfle–Smith.

The tests were administered in 1943, whereas the primary earnings data are for 1955 and 1969. If tested in 1955 or 1969, a person would not score the same on each test (or achieve the same standing on a particular factor) because of post-1943 education, general maturation effects, and sampling error from any test. The test-retest validity on the tests used was fairly high, so we can ignore the last possibility. The effect of post-1943 education on particular cognitive skills can be captured by, or impounded in, the overall effect of education on earnings. The available evidence in, for example, Bloom (1964) would indicate that, on the average, maturation effects are small between the ages of 20 to 50, though this may not be true for soldiers in a war. However, in our analysis we only use a dummy variable indicating to which fifth of the distribution a person belonged. Thus, we merely need to assume that a person's relative ability position did not change enough over time to move him to a different fifth.

[4]Of course, we have constructed the factors to be orthogonal (for the 9700 people). Although I.Q. and mathematical tests in general are correlated, it would be possible to factor-analyze such tests to extract several factors.

Finally, it might be asked if the differences in pretest education affect the test scores and, thus, the ability measure. In ch. 5, we demonstrated that the differences in the quantity and regional quality of pretest education had little or no effect on the scores.

It is of some interest to study the response bias in terms of ability and biography measures[5]. If the 3743 respondents in 1969 whom we study were a random drawing, there would be about 748 people in each fifth[6]. The number of 1969 respondents in each fifth for the various factors, which are presented in Table E-5, clearly indicate a tendency for respondents to be in the higher ability ranges. This is very pronounced for the mathematical and I.Q. factors, but it is also true for the other two.

[5]As discussed below, the biography variable represents a mixture of ability, education, and socioeconomic background factors.

[6]Some of the initial 4443 observations were eliminated because of missing data. The quintile points were calculated from the distribution of the 9710 individuals in the 1955 sample.

APPENDIX B

The tables in this appendix are reproduced from Wolfe, B., 'A Socioeconomic Analysis of Family Building Behavior', unpublished Ph.D. dissertation, University of Pennsylvania, 1973.

Table 1.
Comparison of income percent distribution.

		U.S. population		
			Age of head[b]	
	NBER–TH 1969 salary	White college[a] graduates	35–44	45–54
Under $3000	.22	2.9	5.4	6.8
3000–4999	.80	3.6	6.9	7.7
5000–6999	4.6	5.6	9.9	9.9
7000–8999	10.4*	15.8*	12.8	11.2
9000–11999	21.9		21.1	17.7
12000–14999	17.7	31.7	16.9	14.9
15000–24999	28.4		21.7	24.4
25000–49999	12.2	40.5	4.8	6.5
50000+	3.4		0.5	0.8

*Includes $7000–9999, next category for white college graduates includes $10000–14999.

[a]U.S. Department of Commerce, Bureau of the Census, *Current Population Reports*, Series P-60 as presented in *Statistical Abstract of The United States*, 1971.

[b]U.S. Department of Commerce, Bureau of the Census, *Current Population Reports*, Series P-60, No. 78, May 20, 1971.

Table 2.
Level of education of fathers.

	NBER–TH		U.S. population[a], March 1969
	Father	Father-in-law	White males 65–74[b]
0–4 years	7.5	3.4	13.3
5 years	2.6	1.7	3.6
6 and 7 years	10.9	8.1	14.4
8 years	28.8	27.3	25.9
9 years	2.8	2.3	6.1
10 years	5.5	5.2	5.3
11 years	1.2	1.3	2.9
12 years = H.S.	23	31.3	15.6
13 years	2.3	1.4	1.5
14 years	4.6	3.8	3.1
15 years	.6	.5	0.9
16 years = B.A.	8.2	9.3	4.1
17+	2	2.8	3.2
Median	9	11	8.7
Number	4787	4450	5252*

*In thousands of persons.

[a]U.S. Department of Commerce, Bureau of the Census, *Current Population Reports*, Series P-20, No. 194.

[b]If average age of parents was approximately 26–28 at the birth of respondents and respondents' average age is 46 in 1969, father's average age would be 72–74. In No. 195 of the same series of *Current Population Reports*, median age at first marriage in 1947 showed a 3.2 year difference between husband and wife. Other references would put the age difference closer to 2 for men currently 46 years of age. Subtracting 2 or 3 from 72–74 gives an average age of 69–72 for the wife's father.

Note: Vital Statistics Rates in the U.S. 1900–1940, table 46, gives 28.1 as the mean age of the mother in 1921–25. The age shows a declining trend from 1918 to the 1940s. In the 1940s it is 26^{+}.

Table 3.
Marital status.

	NBER–TH	U.S. population[a], Males 35–44	U.S. population[a], Males 45–54
Single	2.3	7.2	7.6
Married	94.8	89.3	87.2
Widowed	0.53	0.6	1.6
Divorced	2.16	2.9	3.6
Total	99.8	100	100
Number	5083	11239	11236

*In thousands of persons.

[a]U.S. Department of Commerce, Bureau of the Census, *Current Population Reports*, Series P-20.

Table 4.
Comparison of NBER–Thorndike sample's occupational distribution and that of subgroups of the U.S. population.

Occupations	NBER–TH, 1969	U.S. population, white males, college graduates[1], 1960 (30–34)	U.S. population, white males, college graduates[1], 1960 (35–44)
Professional, technical, kindred	29.0	46.1	42.8
Manager, official, and proprietor except farm	49.8	21.7	27.6
Sales	6.7	15.2	12.6
Farm proprietor	2.5	1.2	1.6
Office	1.5	7.1	6.3
Service	2.5	0.8	1.0
Blue collar*, skilled	4.6	7.0	7.8
Blue collar†, unskilled	3.5	0.5	0.4

*For U.S. population, this figure combines craftsmen, foremen and kindred with operatives and kindred.

†For U.S. population, this figure combines laborers except farm and mine with farm laborers and foremen.

[a]1960 Census, Educational Attainment PC(2) 5B.

Table 5.
Education levels.

	NBER–TH		U.S. population[a], March 1969			
	Males	Females (wives)	White males 35–44	White males 45–54	White females 35–44	White females 45–54
Less than high school		5	35.2	42.5	32.8	39.1
High school	24.5	47.3	34.5	34.1	47.3	44.2
Some college	25.3	22.8	11.9	11.0	10.3	9.8
B.A.	28.5	19.2	10.0	6.6	6.7	4.8
Some graduate work	5.2	2.0				
M.A.	8.8	2.1	8.4	5.8	2.9	2.1
Ph.D.	7.5	.3				
Number	5089	4944	23021*	23298*	10493	10684
Median	15	12	12.4	12.2	12.5	12.4

*In thousands of persons.
[a]U.S. Department of Commerce, Bureau of the Census, *Current Population Reports*, Series P-20, No. 194.

Table 6.
Characteristics of the NBER–Thorndike data sample. Percentage distribution of occupations.

Occupations	Respondent	Father	Wife's father
Business proprietor	19.32	29.32	45.99
Manager	30.65	8.27	13.38
Self-employed professional	6.68	4.30	9.04
Salaried professional	15.48	3.67	6.16
Technical	5.93	1.85	3.94
Office worker	1.71	2.53	4.30
Salesman	6.46	4.60	7.99
Services worker	2.89	4.26	8.75
Other (blue collar)	10.81	41.13	.36
Number	4551	3008	2742
Farm proprietor	120	405	376

APPENDIX C

In this Appendix, we will discuss several different technical issues related to the equations presented in Appendix A and discussed in ch. 3. First, we will consider the extent of the bias on the education coefficients that would have arisen if we had not held certain variables constant. We will then examine the usefulness of equations for the log of earnings rather than earnings. We will examine the effect of internal migration on earnings. Finally, we include a list of all variables tried in our analysis whether significant or not.

1. Bias

Unfortunately, it is true that economists often have to choose between using representative samples such as the Census which do not contain crucial information or using nonrepresentative samples such as NBER–TH or that used by Griliches and Mason. In making their choice economists must balance several factors. A piece of information, for example, can be crucial in the sense that it explains much of the variance or allows a hypothesis to be tested. Alternatively, even if the information is not important to the study, such data can still be crucial if its omission results in biased estimates of other parameters of interest. Formally, if our true equation is

$$Y = XB + Z\alpha + u, \tag{A.1}$$

but we estimate the equation omitting Z, the expected value of b, (the least squares estimate of B), is equal to $B + \alpha d$ where d is equal to $(X'X)^{-1}X'Z$ or the least squares of Z on X. Thus, a bias arises if either d or α is nonzero[1].

In recent years, most discussion of bias has focused on the education

[1]It is important to note that since α and d are slope coefficients, our use of a stratified random sample still yields results that can generalize to the population over the sample space covered.

coefficients. The bias can be expressed as the percentage difference between the coefficients of the same variables in the final and incomplete equation, with the denominator coming from the latter equation[2]. We have many nonfinal or incomplete equations, but we have chosen to use eqn (1) as the basis of our comparison since (with the exception of the biography variable) all the other information would be available in Census data. Thus, we are calculating the additional bias arising from the special information in this sample. Comparisons of eqns (1) and (2) indicate that in 1969 the bias at the some college level is $\frac{1}{2}$ and is $\frac{1}{3}$ at the bachelor's and some graduate level. (Eqn (2) is evaluated at an average Gourman rating of the some college group, which requires adding about 2.0 to all the education coefficients.) The masters and Ph.D. biases are much smaller, largely because the inclusion of the nonpecuniary preference variables causes these education coefficients to increase. In 1955, the bias at the lower education levels is about 30 to 40% (after adding about 0.6 for the Gourman quality index). At the upper education levels, the bias is generally around 10%. It is important to reemphasize that this is the bias arising from including nonstandard variables. As compared with the differences in average earnings by education levels, the biases indicated by eqn (2) are approximately twice as large in both years at the some college and bachelor's level.

2. Logarithmic equations

The analysis, thus far, has concentrated on the linear equation. We have also estimated the same equations using the log of earnings. These equations permit interactions among independent variables, provide a partial but incomplete correction for heteroskedasticity, and as explained below, permit estimation of certain parameters (under certain assumptions). Since nearly all our independent variables are dummy variables, the five point improvement in R^2 primarily represents the lesser weight given to large earnings, which are not explained very well and the

[2]As noted earlier, part of the effect of education can be included in some variable which is partly determined by education. A change in the education coefficient from such a source should not be classified as indicating bias. Earlier we argued that such a capturing of the education effect was not important in this study.

interaction effects. Since only a few variables are significant in the linear and not in the log equation and vice versa, and only private high school changes sign, there would seem to be little to gain in analyzing these equations. But Becker and Mincer have demonstrated that under certain rather stringent conditions, the coefficient, a, on years of school in an equation of the form $\ln Y_t = \ln Y_0 + a$ years schooling $+ b$ (age–years of schooling) is an estimate of the rate of return to education. (Among the conditions necessary for this interpretation are that there be no non-monetary or consumption returns to education.) In our equations, given in table 1 of this appendix, we rescale the years of schooling by discrete dummy variables. But using two years for some college and four years for a bachelor's degree, we can estimate the rates of return as less than 6% for all education levels in both years, ignoring G.I. bill benefits[3,4].

3. Regional wage structures and internal migration

In ch. 3, we indicated that both the size of the community in which the person lived in 1969 and interregional mobility after 1955 are significant and important determinants of earnings in 1955 and 1969. Now we will explore further the consequences of geographic location and mobility by examining the following questions. Are the effects of all variables the same in different regions of the country or do they differ by more than (a proportionate) amount equal to differentials in cost of living? Do earnings vary by area in which the person attended high school? Has internal migration altered the earnings of nonmigrants?

4. Regional wage equations

The first question we examine will be the difference in wage equations by region. The four regions used are New England and Mid-Atlantic, East

[3]There is a minor problem in using these equations since most people have zero business assets. In the equations, we convert zero assets to $1. This transformation can affect coefficients, but we did not want to delete more than half the sample.

[4]Work by others with this sample suggests that allowance for the G.I. bill benefits would perhaps double the rate of return to education estimates implied by Mincer's work.

Table 1.
1955 LN earnings equations.

Independent variables	(1) LN *Y*55 Coef.	*t* value	(2) LN *Y*55 Coef.	*t* value
Education:				
Some college	.05	3.3		
Bachelor's	.11	6.7	.03	1.9
Some grad.	.10	4.1	.03	1.3
Master's	.06	2.7	−.04	−2.1
Ph.D. + L.L.B. + M.D.	.10	2.7	−.04	−1.3
L.L.B.	−.00	−.10	−.02	−.52
M.D.	.32	5.0	.21	3.8
Ability:				
2nd fifth	.04	2.2	.07	1.1
3rd fifth	.05	3.0	.03	1.7
4th fifth	.08	4.6	.04	2.5
(top) 5th fifth	.12	7.2	.06	4.0
Biography:				
2nd fifth, 3rd fifth	.05	3.4	.03	1.9
4th fifth, 5th fifth	.06	4.2	.05	3.6
Father high school				
Father college				
Religion:				
Jewish	.20	7.6	.10	4.5
Protestant	−.02	−1.4	.00	.12
Attended religious school often	−.04	−1.7	−.02	−1.1
Attended religious school never	−.01	−0.6	−.00	−.02
Father-in-law high school +	.01	4.2	.00	2.6
Mother-in-law high school +	.02	1.4	−.00	−0.4
Time spent on sports	.01	1.8	.00	0.5
Time spent on chores	−.00	−1.1	.00	0.5
Time spent on hobbies	.00	0.7	.01	1.8
Time spent on part-time job	.01	3.3	.00	1.3
Never moved before high school	−.01	−1.3	−.01	−.9
Attended private high school	.11	3.0	.06	2.0
Attended private elementary school	.06	.78	−.00	−.00
Factors influenced entering occupation:				
Future financial prospects, no = 1	−.08	−6.2	−.00	−2.2
Independence, no = 1	.01	1.1	−.00	−.00
Challenging work, no = 1	−.02	−2.0	−.00	−.2

Table 1 (*contd*).

Independent variables	(1) LN *Y*69 Coef.	*t* value	(2) LN *Y*69 Coef.	*t* value
Help others, no = 1	.05	3.9	.02	1.9
Job security, no = 1	.07	−6.4	.04	4.2
Prefers to be salaried	−.05	−3.8	−.02	−1.5
LN other assets (own business, real estate), 1969[a]	.01	5.5	.00	1.6
Self-employed businessman, 1969	.10	6.3	.04	2.8
Self-employed professional, 1969	.05	2.1	−.01	−.3
Teacher, pre-college	−.10	−3.8	−.05	−2.1
Hours on main job, 1969	−.00	−.9	−.00	−3.9
Hours on second job, 1969	−.00	−4.6	−.00	−1.7
Weeks lost from illness, 1969	.00	−2.1	.00	.59
Mobility 1955 to 1969	.01	3.9	.00	.71
Age	.01	3.6	.01	4.7
Year of first job	−.01	−6.1	−.01	−5.3
Current residence in town of 50, to 1000000	.07	5.5	.03	3.0
Current resident in excess of 1000000	.12	6.6	.04	2.8
College quality (Gourman rating)	−.06	−2.1	.04	−1.5
Weight, 1969	.83	3.3	.23	1.1
Weight squared, 1969	−.21	−3.1	−.05	−.9
Town grew up in:				
Small				
Medium				
Major metropolitan area				
Dummy for nonresponse in 1972	.17	5.2	.11	3.9
College quality (Gourman scale)				
LN *Y*69			.40	36.16
Constant	.96	3.4	.56	2.3
R^2	.20	.3	.38	
Stand error	.34		.30	
Degrees of freedom	4547		4546	
Education:				
Some college	.08	4.6		
Bachelor's	.20	10.6	.14	8.4
Some grad.	.19	6.2	.13	4.9
Master's	.27	9.7	.24	9.6
Ph.D. + L.L.B. + M.D.	.37	8.2	.31	7.9
L.L.B.	.04	.76	.05	.92

Table 1 (*contd*).

Independent variables	(1) LN $Y69$ Coef.	(1) LN $Y69$ t value	(2) LN $Y69$ Coef.	(2) LN $Y69$ t value
M.D.	.26	3.4	.09	1.3
Ability:				
2nd fifth	.05	2.6	.03	1.8
3rd fifth	.07	3.3	.04	2.1
4th fifth	.10	5.2	.06	3.5
(top) 5th fifth	.16	7.7	.09	4.9
Biography:				
2nd fifth, 3rd fifth	.07	3.7	.04	2.3
4th fifth, 5th fifth	.04	2.2	.01	.33
Father high school				
Father college				
Religion:				
Jewish	.24	7.7	.13	4.6
Protestant	−.04	−3.3	−.04	−3.0
Attended religious school often	−.05	−1.5	−.02	−.8
Attended religious school never	−.02	−1.2	−.01	−1.1
Father-in-law high school	.01	3.83	.00	2.1
Mother-in-law high school	.05	3.7	.04	3.5
Time spent on sports	.01	2.7	.01	2.1
Time spent on chores	−.02	−3.2	−.01	−3.1
Time spent on hobbies	−.01	−1.9	−.01	−2.5
Time spent on part-time job	.02	4.3	.01	3.2
Never moved before high school	−.01	−1.0	−.00	−.4
Attended private high school	.12	2.7	.06	1.4
Attended private elementary school	.16	1.7	.13	1.5
Factors influenced entering occupation:				
Future financial prospects, no = 1	−.14	−9.0	−.09	−6.8
Independence, no = 1	.04	2.4	.03	2.2
Challenging work, no = 1	−.06	−3.8	−.04	−3.2
Help others, no = 1	.07	4.6	.04	3.1
Job security, no = 1	.08	5.7	.04	3.0
Prefers to be salaried	−.08	−5.2	−.05	−3.9
LN other assets (own business, real estate), 1969[a]	.01	8.7	.01	6.9
Self-employed businessman, 1969	.15	8.2	.10	5.8
Self-employed professional, 1969	.16	4.9	.13	4.5
Teacher, pre-college	−.13	−4.1	−.07	−2.6

Table 1 (*contd*).

Independent variables	(1) LN *Y*69 Coef.	*t* value	(2) LN *Y*69 Coef.	*t* value
Hours on main job, 1969	.00	5.3	.00	1.5
Hours on second job, 1969	−.01	−6.5	−.01	−4.9
Weeks lost from illness, 1969	−.01	−5.6	−.01	−5.2
Mobility 1955 to 1969	.02	7.0	.02	5.8
Age	−.00	−1.1	−.01	−3.2
Year of first job	−.01	−3.2	−.00	−.03
Current residence in town of 50, to 1000000	.09	6.0	.05	3.9
Current resident in excess of 1000000	.19	8.6	.12	6.3
College quality (Gourman rating)	−.06	−1.7	−.02	−.8
Weight, 1969	1.5	5.1	1.04	4.0
Weight squared, 1969	−.39	−4.8	−.27	−3.8
Town grew up in:				
Small				
Medium				
Major metropolitan area				
Dummy for nonresponse in 1972	.15	3.9	.05	1.6
College quality (Gourman scale)				
LN *Y*/55			.56	36.2
Constant	.99	2.93	.46	1.5
R^2	.33		.48	
Stand error	.41		.36	
Degrees of freedom	4547		4546	

[a]If assets are zero, they are changed to $1.

North Central and West North Central, South Atlantic and East plus West South Central, Mountain and Pacific – all as defined by the Census. In table 2, we present equations for 1969 estimated separately for each of the four regions, as well as one for the whole country[5]. The equations are similar to the 'final' one in ch. 4; but to assist in the migration analysis as well as certain other questions, we included dummy variables on high

[5]The overall equation includes some 35 observations for people who reside outside the four regions. No adjustments were made for price level differences, which might explain proportional differences in coefficients. See, for example, Coelho and Ghali.

Table 2.
1969 earnings equations for migrants and nonmigrants.

	All		H.S. state = 69 state		H.S. state ≠ 69 state	
	Coef.	*t* value	Coef.	*t* value	Coef.	*t* value
Education:						
Some college	.96	2.8	1.11	2.2	.81	1.8*
Bachelor's	2.67	7.4	3.36	6.4	1.86	3.8
Some grad.	2.47	4.2	3.22	4.0	1.52	1.7*
Master's	3.51	6.5	3.59	4.6	3.69	4.9
Ph.D. + L.L.B. + M.D.	5.38	6.2	5.24	4.6	5.50	4.0
L.L.B.	.84	0.8*	.43	0.3*	1.09	0.7*
M.D.	3.12	2.1	3.67	1.9*	1.97	0.8*
Ability:						
2nd fifth, 3rd fifth	.70	1.9*	.72	1.3*	0.73	1.4*
4th fifth, (top) 5th fifth	1.4	3.7	1.70	3.1	1.12	2.1
Biography:						
2nd fifth, 3rd fifth	1.03	3.0	1.19	2.4	.89	1.9*
4th fifth, 5th fifth	.93	2.8	1.12	2.3*	.80	1.7*
Religion:						
Jewish	4.33	7.3	2.92	3.4	5.61	6.8
Protestant	−.80	3.0	−.70	1.9*	−.93	2.5
Attended Religious school often	−1.09	1.9*	1.44	1.8*	−.65	0.8*
Father-in-law education	.13	3.7	.19	3.7	.08	1.5*
Mother-in-law high school	.70	2.6	.60	1.5*	.73	1.9*

Time spent on sports	.23	2.6	.27	2.1	.18	1.4*
Time spent on chores	−.25	−2.7	−.38	2.8	−.09	0.7*
Time spent on part-time job.	.31	4.0	.26	2.3	.37	3.4*
Attended private high school	−.08	3.7	−.07	2.4	−.09	2.5
Attended private elementary school	4.86	2.8	1.9	0.8*	8.18	3.1
Factors influenced entering occupation:						
Future financial prospects, no = 1	−1.72	5.9	−1.57	3.8	−1.91	4.6
Independence, no = 1	.91	3.1	0.61	1.5*	1.26	3.1
Challengong work, no = 1	−1.07	3.7	−1.11	2.7	−1.03	2.6
Help others, no = 1	.96	3.4	.79	2.0	1.08	2.7
Prefers to be salaried	−1.27	4.3	−1.09	2.5	−1.31	3.2
Other assets (own business, real estate), 1969	.19	9.1	.18	6.8	.20	5.7
Self-employed businessman, 1969	1.01	2.7	1.04	1.9*	1.26	2.4
Self-employed professional, 1969	3.15	5.2	3.01	3.3	3.53	4.3
Teacher, pre-college	−2.15	3.5	−2.68	3.2	−1.76	2.0
Hours on main job, 1969	.08	5.6	.09	4.6	.06	3.0
Hours on second job, 1969	−.12	5.3	−.12	3.3	−.13	4.0
Weeks lost from illness, 1969	−.15	3.3	−.11	2.0	−.24	3.0
Age	−.12	2.1	−.12	1.5*	−.11	1.5*
Year of first job	−.13	2.6	−.21	3.0	−.04	0.6*
Current residence in town of 50, to 1000000	1.44	4.8	1.40	3.1	1.38	3.4
Current resident in excess of 1000000	3.50	8.4	3.04	5.1	3.92	6.6
Weight, 1969	24.28	4.2	22.71	2.9	23.49	2.7
Weight squared, 1969	−6.30	4.1	−6.0	2.9	−5.89	2.5
69 region 1	.68	1.7*	.90	1.6*	1.01	1.7*
69 region 2	−.59	1.3*	−.46	0.8*	−.41	0.6*
69 region 3	.36	.05*	.37	0.4*	.80	0.8*
69 region 4	−.20	−0.4*	−.52	0.7*	.52	0.6*
69 region 5	.06	0.2*	.29	0.6*	−.37	0.7*

Table 2 (*contd*).

	All		H.S. state = 69 state		H.S. state ≠ 69 state	
	Coef.	t value	Coef.	t value	Coef.	t value
69 region 6	.03	0.05*	−.03	0.1*	−.32	0.4*
Dummy nonresponse in 1972	3.17	4.7	2.47	2.5	3.71	4.0
Constant	−9.40	1.4	−3.91	0.4*	−13.24	1.4*
R^2	.30		.29		.32	
Standard error	7.87		8.0		7.68	
Degrees of freedom	4547		2293		2205	

* = Not significant at the 5% Level.
Region 1 = mid-Atlantic and East North Central.
Region 2 = West North Central and South Atlantic.
Region 3 = East South Central.
Region 4 = West South Central.
Region 5 = Mountain.
Region 6 = Pacific.

school location[6]. To accommodate these dummies within our 50 variable limit, we dropped a few variables from the final equation. As with the question of the interaction of ability and education, we use covariance analysis to determine if we explain more of the variance by breaking the sample into regions. The computed F statistic for the null hypothesis that the equations in the four regions are the same is 5.8, which is different from zero at any reasonable level of significance[7]. Thus, we reject the hypothesis that there are no regional differences in the earnings function or in the earnings received for each of the various characteristics.

An examination of the coefficients in the various regions indicates some interesting differences. For example, the education coefficients are larger and always significant in the Northeast and North Central areas, while the ability coefficients are larger and more often significant in the South and West. The Jewish dummy is always positive and significant but smallest in the South. The Protestant dummy is only significant in the North Central area.

In these equations, mobility is represented both by the high school region dummies and the post-1955 mobility dummy. If mobility determines earnings, the null hypothesis that these variables do not reduce the variance in our equations should be rejected. The null hypothesis that these variables have no significant effect on the residual variance yields an F test in excess of 30. Thus we reject the hypothesis that mobility does not determine earnings. When we examine the separate influences of post-1955 mobility and high school region, we find each set is significant. No particular pattern on the high school region dummies is evident.

5. Migration and regional wage differences

The previous sections indicate that the earnings equations differ by region. Of course, we could obtain this result because we are using nominal wages which have adjusted to regional price (or income tax) differences. But if this were the only source of regional variation, we

[6]Below we will explain how we assigned high school location to some for whom the datum was missing.

[7]If we wish to argue that 35 Alaskans, etc. constitute a fifth group whose variance was zero, the F statistic would only fall to 3.3.

would expect all coefficients to differ proportionately over regions rather than the observed pattern. Since we and others have found that the wage structure varies by region at young, middle, and old age, a natural question is why people do not migrate to take advantage of this difference.

Some studies, such as Bowles, have found that migration is related to regional wage differences; thus, the answer to the above question may be either that migration has not been large enough to completely offset pre-existing regional differences or that new and unexpected shocks to the system always occur and disturb equilibrium[8].

6. *Definition of mobility*

Mobility, of course, implies a move from one address to another during some time interval. Since the migration hypotheses are generally related to disequilibrium in wages, the appropriate area over which to measure mobility would be the local job market[9]. We do not have such detailed job market information and will use as a proxy either the state or Census region in which the person was living in 1969 as compared with the same area at time of high school graduation, which occurred between 1933 and 1943. We also can determine if the migration occurred before 1955. Within such large areas, people who migrated for economic reasons from New York City to Buffalo or rural to urban residence in the same state will be counted as nonmigrants. Thus, it should be more difficult to find significant differences between our migrant and nonmigrant groups. Using the Census Bureau's ten region breakdown, in 1969 when the men were about 47 years old, $\frac{1}{3}$ of the people were not living in the same *region*[10]. Similarly, 40% of the people were not living in the same *state* from which they

[8] An alternative explanation is that the observed wage regional differentials are offset by differential nonmonetary costs and benefits from moving, but it is far from clear why such nonmonetary benefits vary by ability, religion, etc.

[9] Hanushek recently has examined the wage structure in local areas, but his study only covered males near the beginning of their careers.

[10] The ten regions are New England, Mid-Atlantic, East North Central, West North Central, South Atlantic, East South Central, West South Central, Mountain, Pacific and Alaska, Hawaii and Rest of World.

graduated high school. Data from the 1960 Census indicates that 35% of men aged 45 to 54 were not living in the state in which they were born[11]. Because some people will move between birth and completion of high school and since over ½ of the 4600 nonresponders (9700–5100) were people for whom we did not have an up-to-date address, it seems clear that mobility was higher in our sample, with its special characteristics, than in the population[12].

7. *Effects of migration on earnings*

Suppose we assume that, on average, people's expectations about regional wage differentials are borne out during their lifetime[13]. Suppose, further, that because of inertia and lack of knowledge, not all migrants who would find a move profitable, actually move. (This would explain why regional differentials persist.) Next, suppose that the nonmigrants in the sending region who have the same measured characteristics as migrants, are indeed, on average, 'like' the migrants. Finally, let us assume that nonmonetary benefits and costs of migration are zero.

The above assumptions would indicate that migrants from a region would receive higher earnings than like nonmigrants. Within a receiving region, natives and like migrants should receive equal earnings once migrants have accumulated (searched out) local knowledge[14]. Combining nonmigrants from sending and receiving areas, we would expect that nonmigrants would earn less (on a discounted post migration working life basis) if the migrants' expectations about wages and if our nonmonetary assumptions are correct. To help distinguish between sending and receiving areas, we have also included the current region as a set of dummy

[11]The 1970 Census data are not yet available in this question.

[12]Since we were able to obtain 1000 new addresses by checking in phone books of the last known community, the noncontacts must be mostly longer distance moves.

[13]This assumption, while stringent, is very similar to the one made by human capital economists such as Becker and Mincer when they estimate earnings equations from cross section data. Mincer, for example, assumes that the observed earnings in one cohort indicate the returns from investment in on-the-job training of a younger cohort.

[14]Some of these natives may have had profitable moves too, but then we are saying that, on average, the migrants were more able than natives in recipient regions and should have higher wages.

Table 3.

Variable	1969 residence							
	Region 1		Region 2		Region 3		Region 4	
	Y_{69} (000)	t values	Y_{69} (000)	t values	Y_{69} (000)	t values	Y_{69} (000)	t values
Some college	1.51	2.4	.66	1.2*	.19	.2*	.71	.8*
Bachelor's	3.43	5.1	2.92	4.7	1.10	1.4*	2.10	2.2
Some graduate	1.74	1.6	3.47	3.1	0.60	0.5*	3.34	2.4
Master's	4.07	4.2	5.02	5.2	1.77	1.4*	1.67	1.3
Ph.D.	5.45	3.4	7.20	4.3	3.24	1.9*	5.30	2.5
M.D.	−3.35	1.2*	4.00	1.5*	7.16	2.3	6.48	1.9*
L.L.B.	−1.83	0.9*	1.46	0.7*	.87	0.4*	2.18	0.7*
Ability Q2	.04	.06*	.70	1.0*	1.29	1.7*	0.51	0.5*
Ability Q3								
Ability Q4	.97	1.3*	1.24	1.7*	1.74	2.4	2.11	2.1
Ability Q5	2.01	2.8	1.54	2.2	3.00	3.7	2.65	2.7
Biog. Q2	1.01	1.6*	0.83	1.4*	0.56	0.8*	0.93	1.0*
Biog. Q3								
Biog. Q4	.66	1.1*	1.79	3.1	−.02	0.1*	0.80	0.9*
Biog. Q5								
Teacher	−1.94	1.7*	−3.38	3.1	−1.71	1.3*	−0.96	0.6*
Year of first job	−.05	0.6*	−.23	2.5	−.14	1.3*	−.08	0.7*
Weeks ill	−.16	1.9*	−.20	1.9*	.07	.5*	−.19	2.3
Age	−.10	1.0*	.01	0.1*	−.24	2.0	−.05	0.4*
Protestant	−.65	1.3*	−.80	1.8*	−.36	0.5*	−1.46	2.2
Jewish	4.31	5.1	7.06	4.9	2.62	1.6*	4.36	2.4
Attended religious school often	−1.13	1.2*	−.53	0.5*	0.71	0.5*	−2.49	1.7*
Factors influencing entering occupation, no = 1:								
Future financial prospects	−2.09	3.9	−1.22	2.3	−1.79	2.9	−1.70	2.4

Independence	.41	0.8*	0.73	1.4*	1.93	3.1	0.87	1.2*
Help others	1.23	2.3	0.40	0.8*	1.08	1.8*	0.93	2.6
Challenging work	−.66	1.2*	−1.06	2.1	0.73	−1.2*	−1.98	2.6
Weight, 1969	36.46	3.4	21.98	2.1	19.1	1.5*	6.15	0.5*
Weight squared, 1969	−9.22	3.2	−5.96	2.2	−4.7	1.3*	−1.91	0.5*
Prefers to be salaried	−1.65	3.1	−1.22	2.4	−1.13	1.8	−0.60	0.7*
Father-in-law Education	0.15	2.2	0.11	1.7*	.19	2.7	.08	0.8*
Mother-in-law high school	1.05	2.0	1.02	2.1	.69	1.2*	−.74	1.1*
Private high school	−.14	4.5	−.08	1.2*	−.11	2.4	.09	1.7*
Private elementary school	11.36	4.4	1.58	0.2*	4.2	0.9*	0.88	0.2*
Other assets, 1969	.25	8.2	0.20	2.9	.22	5.0	.01	0.1*
Self-employed professional	1.58	1.4*	2.52	2.3	.63	5.1	1.50	1.0*
Self-employed businessman	−1.03	1.4*	1.15	1.7	1.45	1.9*	4.03	4.1
No response in '72	3.45	2.7	4.17	3.6	4.03	2.9	0.30	0.1*
Size of current residence								
500000 to 1 million	1.10	2.1	1.91	3.7	2.16	3.2	.08	0.1*
In excess of 1 million	3.33	4.0	4.08	5.8	3.26	3.6	3.38	3.0
Time spent on sports	.31	1.8*	.23	1.4*	0.08	0.5*	.25	1.1*
Time spent on chores	.17	0.9*	−.07	0.4*	−.35	1.8*	−.38	1.6*
Time spent on part-time job	.28	1.8*	.14	1.1*	.56	3.5	.42	2.1
H.S. Mid-Atlantic	.40	.9*	1.18	1.2*	1.34	1.5*	2.90	2.4
H.S. East North Central	3.18	2.4	−.98	1.8*	1.95	2.1	0.94	1.0*
H.S. West-North Central	0.11	0.1*	−2.00	3.2	−.87	0.7*	−.22	0.2*
H.S. South Atlantic	.13	0.1*	−1.86	1.1*	−.34	0.5*	4.99	1.9*
H.S. East South Central	.32	0.4*	−.64	1.0*	.55	0.8*	0.98	1.0*
H.S. West South Central	1.39	0.5*	−2.20	−1.0*	.18	0.2*	−.33	0.2*
Hours	0.13	4.4	.08	3.5	.06	2.2	.03	1.0*
Hours on second job	−.08	1.61*	−.11	2.6	−.16	3.5	−.12	2.1
Constant	−28.18	2.3	−6.86	−.6*	.13	0.1	7.91	0.5
R^2	.33		.33		.31		.26	
Standard error	7.81		7.61		7.81		8.01	
Degrees of freedom	1272		1375		1011		711	

* = Not significant at 5% level.

variables. For migrants, these dummies are the receiving areas, while for natives, the dummies are the home areas.

As a partial test of this conclusion, we have examined separately the 1969 earnings equations for migrants and nonmigrants (high school state versus 1969 state).

Table 3 contains separate 1969 earnings equations for migrants, nonmigrants and the whole sample. The equations shown are the final ones used in ch. 3 except that to provide space for dummy variables for region of current residence, we have dropped some of the chapter's insignificant variables. In examining the equations, the reader might note that the coefficients in either the migrant or nonmigrant equations are very similar and that most of the current region dummy variables are not significant in any of the equations presented.

To test whether the effects of *all* the variables are the same for migrants and nonmigrants, we computed the identical equations for both groups combined and applied Chow's covariance test. The F statistic so obtained was 1.4, which is not significant at the 5% level[15]. Hence, we can conclude that the effects of all the variables in table 2 do not vary significantly by migrant status. In other words, migrants in 1969 do not earn more than 'like' natives[16].

To conclude this section, we find there are regional differences in wages. If we assume these differences were known or anticipated by some individuals, then we would expect migrants to earn more than nonmigrants who did not take advantage of the wage differentials. But we do not find differences in the earnings function of migrants and nonmigrants. We do, however, find that post-1955 migrants earn more. Thus, it is only early migration that does not have a significant effect on 1969 earnings.

[15]Suppose we were to compute another equation in which every variable had one coefficient for migrants and another for nonmigrants. Since the two tests are equivalent, we would find that the second equation did not reduce the standard error significantly.

[16]Hanushek has reported a similar result for recent veterans who left after no more than 2 years service.

Variables insignificant in 1969 and 1955 earnings equations.

Mother's education
Father's education
Single, marital status
Father owner-manager
Father professional
Mother's work status
Had own room as child
High school health
Rank in military
Raised by grandparents
Raised on farm
Number of moves within neighborhood when growing up
Type of house grew up in
Time spent reading
Why entered present job:
  Salary or pay offered
  Personal contacts
  Provided a lot of free time
Retirement information
Military service after World War II
Length of service in military
Being the youngest and oldest child
Present health condition
Voting habits: frequency of participation in local, state and national elections
Political self concept: degree of conservativeness or liberalness
Opinion on extent of freedom of youth
Opinion on people's concern with financial security
Opinion on rate of racial integration in last 10 years
For the items listed below, how does your total work experience to date compare with what you expected when you first started?
  Requirement for independent judgement
  Responsibility
  Prospects for advancement
To what degree does success in your work depend on
  Your own performance
  Having the right connections
  Being able to get along with people
  Being lucky or unlucky
  Having a college diploma
  Working hard
Do you enjoy your work?

Based on your own personal experience, what do you think high schools colleges should concentrate on?

Basic skills
General knowledge
Career preparation
Activities
Social awareness

APPENDIX D

Comparison with Census data

While this is, to our knowledge, the first study to examine the profile in earnings inequality for a group of people as they age, cross sections of people of different ages have been used for the same purposes. How do our 'time series' results compare with these cross section studies?

Mincer provides an extensive and thoughtful analysis of the pattern of inequality in the 1960 Census by education and years of work experience or age. In table 1, we present some of his results for people who were 30, 35, and 45 to 49 then[1].

In comparing the results, it is necessary to keep in mind certain noncomparabilities in the sample. Most importantly, the Census sample is designed to be a random drawing of the population (although there are response biases), while the NBER–TH has a truncated distribution of ability, probably has less average risk averseness, has more self-employed persons and may differ in other dimensions from the U.S. population. When we adjusted our variables for the x's, the results still are not comparable since our adjusted inequality measures have netted out the influence of ability, SES, etc. while these earnings determinants have not been held constant in the Census results. Another difference arises because the Census has an open-ended class. While Mincer estimates the mean of this class, he does not adjust the standard error, etc. for any within (open-ended) class dispersion[2].

As shown in table 1, in the 1960 Census the standard deviation, the

[1]Mincer provides estimates for each 5 year interval; his age profiles are seldom linear between these two age groups.

[2]There are several differences that are probably less important. First, Mincer uses only white, nonfarm males, while the NBER–TH sample has a few farmers and may have a few nonwhites. Second, in the NBER–TH sample, the respondents ranged in age from 31 to 38 in 1955 with an average of 33 and with less than 25% of the people older than 34 which is Mincer's upper limit then. In 1969, the age range was 45 to 52 with an average of 47 and a few people older than 49.

Table 1.
Earnings inequality: 1960 Census and NBER–TH.

	Standard deviation				Variance of logs				Skewness[a]			
	H.S.	Some college	Bachelor's	Graduate	H.S.	Some college	Bachelor's	Graduate	H.S.	Some college	Bachelor's	Graduate
1960 Census, white nonfarm												
1960 Census, white nonfarm												
Age 30–34	\$2590	N.A.	4530	N.A.	.23	N.A.	.25	N.A.	.15	N.A.	.28	N.A.
Age 45–49	\$4070	N.A.	8590	N.A.	.34	N.A.	.55	N.A.	.22	N.A.	.36	N.A.
NBER–TH adjusted for all variables												
1955 – age 31–38	\$2510	4000	4160	2840					2.34	5.19	6.49	1.64
1969 – age 45–52	\$6080	8740	8710	8380					2.89	2.94	2.52	2.71
NBER–TH unadjusted												
1955 – age 31–38	\$2790	4270	4380	3190	.13	.16	.14	.14	2.77	5.41	6.17	2.53
1969 – age 45–52	\$7130	9790	9640	10030	.21	.26	.22	.23	3.59	3.29	2.81	2.96

Sources: Census from Mincer, tables 11, 12, NBER–TH tables.

[a]Mincer uses Bowley's measures = $[(P_{90} - Md) - (Md - P_{10})]/(P_{96} - P_{10})$ where P is the earnings at a given percentile and Md is earnings at median. We use the third moment divided by σ^3.

variance of the log, and the positive skewness of (1959) earnings are all greater for college graduates than high school graduates in the two age groups shown. Also for a given education level, each aspect of inequality is greater for the older age group[3]. In the NBER–TH sample, as education increases, the unadjusted series shows a large increase in the standard error in the two years, only tiny increases in the variance of the logs, and a larger increase in relative skewness in 1955 but a smaller decline in 1969 (using a different measure than Mincer). Within an education level, the standard deviation and the variance of the logs increases with age, while skewness increases for high school graduates but decreases for college graduates. The adjusted series yields essentially the same results.

A more detailed examination reveals that the standard deviation for high school graduates has a much greater increase in the NBER–TH sample over time. Because of this, the range in the standard error in 1969 is considerably smaller than in the corresponding Census group, while earlier the range in the two samples was about the same. The variance in the logs, which is scale-free, always has a much lower value in the NBER–TH sample than in the corresponding Census groups; and there is much less of a growth with age among college graduates. The reversal in ranking of skewness between the high school and college graduates in the NBER–TH and its decrease in skewness among college graduates is certainly a striking difference from Mincer's results.

Since in all three measures of inequality, there is at least one major difference between the Census and the NBER–TH results, it seems fair to conclude that the cross section and longitudinal results differ. This, of course, raises the two interrelated questions of why they differ and what insights they provide into the earnings distribution's formative factors?

There are several possible reasons for the difference. First, the assumption that all variables which have distributions different from the population have been included in our equations may be wrong. It is difficult to assess this argument directly, but some indirect evidence is provided by the change over time in inequality. That is, either some variables or their coefficients must be changing; and these changes have to cause skewness to increase with age among college graduates in the Census but decrease

[3]Mincer's findings do *not* indicate that inequality uniformly increases with education or age.

in NBER–TH. According to Mincer, the standard error and skewness change over time because of investment in on-the-job training and the correlation between on-the-job training and other determinants of earnings. Thus, Mincer could argue that the on-the-job training investment pattern is different in the two samples[4]. Since the standard error of high school graduates in the NBER–TH increases much more rapidly, Mincer's theory implies that our respondents have a much greater distribution of investment paths than in the Census. yet the AGCT and other criteria for entering the Air Cadet program were such that it seems likely that our high school group spans a narrower portion of the population than our bachelor's degree holders and might be thought to have a narrower range of investment paths[5].

Another explanation of the difference is that the implicit assumption made by Mincer and many others – that the distribution of ability and other variables is the same in the 30–34 and 45–49 year old groups within the Census or any cross section – is invalid. Taubman and Wales, for example, have shown that the average level and distribution in mental ability of college entrants has varied over time. Such possible intercohort differences is one major reason why longitudinal studies are desirable.

Finally, the NBER–TH sample may yield different results because, in the 14 years involved, the economy has changed so that different types of skills, etc. are more or less important.

The second question we posed was whether these differences help us in understanding the earnings distribution's determinants. We will consider this question in ch. 7.

[4]Available evidence suggests maturation effects on skills is limited between the ages of 20 and 50.

[5]This is borne out by comparisons of the ratio of the average earnings in our sample to the corresponding figures by age and education of the population in 1955 and 1969. This ratio is much higher for our high school students then college graduates (with both exceeding 1.0) and with the ratios greater in 1969 than 1955.

APPENDIX E

This appendix contains results on sources of inequality based on earlier and less complete equations for 1969 and 1955.

Table 1.
Sources of inequality in 1969 and 1955.

	Standard error	Skewness	Kurtosis
1969			
Y	9.42	3.05	13.90
$Y - Y_1$	7.96	2.77	14.40
$Y - Y_2$	9.04	3.20	15.17
$Y - Y_3$	9.23	3.10	14.30
$Y - Y_4$	8.55	2.80	13.22
$Y - Y_5$	9.07	3.07	14.41
$Y - Y_6$	9.03	3.08	14.42
1955			
Y	3.81	5.35	61.99
$Y - Y_1$	3.46	5.50	75.80
$Y - Y_2$	3.74	5.46	65.30
$Y - Y_3$	3.77	5.41	73.91
$Y - Y_4$	3.65	5.39	68.70
$Y - Y_5$	3.69	5.46	65.74
$Y - Y_6$	3.75	5.46	65.00

Y_1 = all variables; Y_2 uses only education, age, year first job, hours.

Y_3 = ability, hours, age, year of first job.

Y_4 = S.E., business assets, hours, age year first job, S.E. professional.

Y_5 = Father education, Father occup., father-in-law and biog. age, year of first job.

Y_6 = uses single, health, proferences, teach, hours, age, year of first job.

Table 2.
Effects of various sets of variables on inequality by four levels of education, in 1955 and 1969.

	1955			1969		
	Standard error	Skewness	Kurtosis	Standard error	Skewness	Kurtosis
High school						
Y	2.79	2.77	13.00	7.13	3.59	21.36
$Y-Y_1$	2.48	2.19	10.70	5.95	2.79	17.83
$Y-Y_2$	2.77	2.77	12.95	7.01	3.60	21.80
$Y-Y_3$	2.76	2.79	13.32	7.07	3.60	21.99
$Y-Y_4$	2.58	2.26	9.99	6.26	3.16	19.63
$Y-Y_5$	2.69	2.78	13.58	6.89	3.48	20.74
$Y-Y_6$	2.73	2.77	13.30	6.95	3.60	22.38
Some college						
Y	4.27	5.41	52.02	9.79	3.29	15.20
$Y-Y_1$	3.95	5.21	52.90	8.61	2.91	15.53
$Y-Y_2$	4.26	5.39	51.85	9.29	3.26	14.89
$Y-Y_3$	4.26	5.40	51.63	9.71	3.26	14.97
$Y-Y_4$	4.10	5.35	53.57	8.99	3.04	15.25
$Y-Y_5$	4.13	5.38	52.72	9.46	3.25	15.44
$Y-Y_6$	4.22	5.46	53.10	9.57	3.30	15.39
Bachelor's degree						
Y	4.38	6.17	73.23	9.64	2.81	11.50
$Y-Y_1$	4.10	6.59	89.70	8.56	2.53	10.85
$Y-Y_2$	4.36	6.22	74.60	9.51	2.83	11.66
$Y-Y_3$	4.33	6.24	74.95	9.51	2.86	11.94
$Y-Y_4$	4.23	6.34	82.55	8.90	2.49	9.83
$Y-Y_5$	4.26	6.41	79.19	9.27	2.87	12.29
$Y-Y_6$	4.32	6.35	77.40	9.34	2.87	12.05
Graduate work						
Y	3.19	2.53	10.74	10.03	2.96	12.73
$Y-Y_1$	2.80	1.53	8.00	8.33	2.59	12.75
$Y-Y_2$	2.99	2.21	9.70	9.35	3.16	14.64
$Y-Y_3$	3.13	2.65	11.68	9.73	3.02	13.23
$Y-Y_4$	3.02	2.32	9.90	8.90	2.83	12.97
$Y-Y_5$	3.11	2.52	11.05	9.65	3.02	13.20
$Y-Y_6$	3.10	2.60	11.40	9.43	3.10	14.25

Table 3.
Effects of various sets of variables on inequality by five ability levels.

	1955			1969		
Ability fifth	Standard error	Skewness	Kurtosis	Standard error	Skewness	Kurtosis
Bottom fifth						
Y	2.93	2.97	15.14	7.82	3.41	18.36
$Y - Y_1$	2.74	2.11	10.8	6.86	3.28	22.54
$Y - Y_2$	2.90	2.91	14.75	7.54	3.62	20.70
$Y - Y_3$	2.94	2.89	14.29	7.78	3.41	18.29
$Y - Y_4$	2.85	2.45	12.00	7.23	3.33	20.69
$Y - Y_5$	2.84	2.68	12.56	7.68	3.27	17.72
$Y - Y_6$	2.91	2.94	14.9	7.66	3.42	18.54
2nd fifth						
Y	3.82	5.46	51.68	9.22	3.46	17.26
$Y - Y_1$	3.56	5.53	59.0	7.84	3.09	17.77
$Y - Y_2$	3.77	5.59	59.0	8.86	3.52	17.76
$Y - Y_3$	3.81	5.50	52.40	9.14	3.42	17.03
$Y - Y_4$	3.70	5.47	54.81	8.37	3.11	16.38
$Y - Y_5$	3.71	5.61	55.52	8.97	3.52	18.32
$Y - Y_6$	3.77	5.59	54.1	8.94	3.47	17.64
3rd fifth						
Y	3.37	3.01	13.38	9.03	3.34	16.31
$Y - Y_1$	2.96	2.18	9.91	7.58	2.84	16.15
$Y - Y_2$	3.27	2.86	12.6	8.69	3.48	17.73
$Y - Y_3$	3.37	2.95	13.13	8.94	3.34	16.42
$Y - Y_4$	3.12	2.61	11.55	7.98	3.00	15.32
$Y - Y_5$	3.28	2.95	13.40	8.73	3.45	17.59
$Y - Y_6$	3.31	2.99	13.5	8.73	3.36	16.96
4th fifth						
Y	3.84	3.72	23.03	9.62	2.75	11.40
$Y - Y_1$	3.45	3.61	25.0	8.08	2.60	12.30
$Y - Y_2$	3.74	3.87	24.5	9.24	2.90	12.61
$Y - Y_3$	3.84	3.72	23.11	9.51	2.74	11.55
$Y - Y_4$	3.65	3.56	22.60	8.63	2.61	11.87
$Y - Y_5$	3.73	3.84	24.98	9.17	2.77	11.91
$Y - Y_6$	3.79	3.75	23.6	9.30	2.78	12.14
5th fifth						
Y	4.50	7.39	97.06	10.26	2.80	11.51
$Y - Y_1$	4.21	7.77	114.0	9.01	2.38	9.71
$Y - Y_2$	4.47	7.41	98.12	9.94	2.90	12.22
$Y - Y_3$	4.49	7.63	97.76	10.16	2.78	11.33
$Y - Y_4$	4.35	7.66	107.34	9.48	2.48	9.65
$Y - Y_5$	4.47	7.43	98.8	9.82	2.78	11.39
$Y - Y_6$	4.43	7.64	102.6	9.94	2.84	11.96

APPENDIX F

Investment functional forms and the growth in earnings

In this appendix we shall assume investment functions differ by individuals; and we shall examine the relationship between the amount of investment at the time of overtaking, t, and the change in earnings. For simplicity, we will study only two individuals i and j who are alike in all characteristics that determine earnings except that they have followed different investment paths. We will also simplify the problem a bit by measuring investment in year as a percentage of Y^*, which as a constant can be ignored in the analysis that follows. We will simplify the notation by letting I be current investment and K the stock of investment. Further, we will assume that

$$rK_{it} = I_{it} \text{ but that} \tag{F.1}$$

$$rK_{jt} < I_{jt} \text{ which implies that } Y_{it} < Y_{jt}. \tag{F.2}$$

The change in earnings for any individual can be written as

$$\frac{dY}{dt} = \frac{r\,dK}{dt} - \frac{dI}{dt}. \tag{F.3}$$

Given inequalities (F.1) and (F.2), can we say if I_{it} exceeds I_{jt} and if (F.3) greater for i than j?

Suppose first that the investment function is of the exponential form

$$I_{mt} = A_m\, e^{-a_m t} \qquad m = i, j. \tag{F.4}$$

Therefore

$$K_{mt} = A_m \int_0^t e^{-a_m n}\, dn. \tag{F.5}$$

Note also that I_t/K_t can be written as

$$\frac{I_m}{K_m}t = \frac{-a_m}{1-e^{a_m t}} \geqq 0. \tag{F.6}$$

Differentiating (F.6) with respect to a, we find that

$$\mathrm{d}\left(\frac{I}{K}\right)t/\mathrm{d}a = -\frac{(1-e^{at})+ate^{at}}{(1-e^{at})^2} = -\frac{1+(t-1)\,e^{at}}{(1-e^{at})^2}. \tag{F.7}$$

Except when t equals zero, (F.7) is negative; hence, if eqn (F.1) is true at some t, then for (F.2) to hold, a_i must be greater than a_j.

With this particular investment, eqn (F.3) can be written as

$$\mathrm{d}Y_t/\mathrm{d}t = (r+a)I_t. \tag{F.8}$$

$$\mathrm{d}^2Y_t/\mathrm{d}t\ \mathrm{d}_a = I_t(1+(r+a)(-t)). \tag{F.9}$$

But, since near the overtaking point, $tr = 1$, eqn (F.9) will be negative. Furthermore, $\mathrm{d}I_t/\mathrm{d}a = -tI_t < 0$. Therefore with investment described by 4, if $a_i < a_j$,

$$\begin{aligned} &I_i > I_j && \text{for all time periods, } n \\ &\frac{I_i}{K_i} > \frac{I_j}{K_j} && \text{for all } n \\ &\frac{\mathrm{d}Y_i}{\mathrm{d}t} > \frac{\mathrm{d}Y_j}{\mathrm{d}t} && \text{for all } n \text{ at least greater than } t. \end{aligned} \tag{F.10}$$

Mincer, however, often specifies that a is constant but Am varies. From (F.6), it follows that in this case the overtaking point would be the same for all Am but that $\mathrm{d}Y^2/\mathrm{d}t\ \mathrm{d}A > 0$ or that those who invest more would have a faster growth rate after overtaking.

Next suppose that our investment functions are linear in time.

$$I_{mt} = C_m + b_m N \qquad \begin{matrix} m = i, j \\ C_m > 0 > b_m \end{matrix} \tag{F.11}$$

$$K_{mt} = C_m t + \frac{bm}{2}t \tag{F.12}$$

For time at which eqns (F.1) and (F.2) hold, it is necessary that

$$\frac{C_i + b_i t}{C_i + \frac{b_i t}{2}} < \frac{C_j + b_j t}{C_j + \frac{b_j t}{2}} \tag{F.13}$$

which reduces to

$$C_i b_j < b_i C_j, \tag{F.14}$$

or since the b's are negative

$$\frac{C_i}{C_j} > \frac{b_i}{b_j} \tag{F.15}$$

For I_i to exceed I_j at t, it is necessary that

$$C_i - C_j + (b_i - b_j)t > 0. \tag{F.16}$$

But for any pair of b_i and b_j, it is possible to find values of C_i and C_j such that both (F.15) and (F.16) hold. But if (F.16) is true, then it is also true that

$$[C_i - C_j + (b_i - b_j)(t+1)] - (b_i - b_j) > 0. \tag{F.17}$$

But with the linear investment function in (F.11), we can write the difference in the change in earnings for i and j as:

$$\mathrm{d}Y_i/\mathrm{d}t - \mathrm{d}Y_j/\mathrm{d}t = r[C_i - C_j + (b_i - b_j)(t+1)] - (b_i - b_j). \tag{F.18}$$

Eqn (F.18) differs from (F.17) in that only the first term in (F.17) is multiplied by r. Thus, provided $b_i - b_j$ is positive, there must be some r such that (F.18) is negative and others that it is positive. Suppose, however, that $(b_i - b_j)$ is negative. Then, since the first term in the right hand side of (F.18) is indeterminate, the sign of (F.18) is still indeterminate.

Similarly, it is possible to show that the condition given in (F.15) does not preclude $I_{it} < I_{jt}$ and that the sign of expression comparable to (F.18) is indeterminate. Thus we can conclude that with linear investment functions, both of whose parameters vary over individuals, it is possible for eqns (F.1) and (F.2) to both hold with $Y_{it} < Y_{jt}$. However, such information does not indicate whether $I_{it} \gtreqless I_{jt}$. Moreover, even if we know which investment is larger, we still do not know if $\mathrm{d}Y_i \lesseqgtr \mathrm{d}Y_j$. In other words, with linear investment functions, knowledge of Y_{it} and Y_{jt} does not tell us who is investing more or whose growth rate should be higher. However, suppose (as Mincer generally does) that the linear investment functions have the same b but different C's. Then from (F.16), we require C_i to exceed C_j. But then equation (F.18) will always be positive. Thus the ith person would invest more, have a greater increase in earnings, and a faster growth rate in earnings than the jth individual with the same earnings at the overtaking point.

Time spent and preference equations (estimated by ordinary least squares).

Independent variable	(1) Independent work, no		(2) Help others, no		(3) Challenging work, no		(4) Job security, no	
	Coef.	*t* value	Coef.	*t* value	Coef.	*t* value	Coef.	*t* value
Time spent on:								
Sports	.01	1.2*	−.01	2.1	.003	.5*	.01	1.2*
Hobbies	.001	.4*	−.001	.2*	.005	.9*	.02	3.8
Chores	.001	.3*	−.02	2.9	.03	.5*	−.01	1.2*
Part-time job	−.005	1.3*	.001	.1*	−.01	1.6*	.01	1.5*
Prefer to be salaried	.11	6.2	.01	.5*	.02	.9*	−.12	6.1
When entered occup., did following factors influence you? no = 1;								
Future financial success	.21	13.1	.01	.7*	.10	6.1	.08	4.5
Independent work			.30	20.0	.10	6.3	−.04	2.4
Help others	.30	20.0			.17	10.7	.16	9.5
Challenging work	.09	6.3	.16	10.7			−.13	7.6
Job security	−.04	2.5	.14	9.5	.11	7.6		
Some college	−.03	1.6*	.01	.4*	−.001	.1*	.13	6.0
Bachelor's	.01	.7*	−.05	2.5	−.02	1.0*	.20	9.3
Some graduate	.04	1.2*	−.17	5.1	−.01	.3*	.25	7.0
Master's	.09	3.2	−.33	11.9	−.05	1.7*	.14	4.7
Ph.D., L.L.B., M.D.	−.09	2.8	−.33	10.4	.03	.8*	.26	7.5
Jewish	−.09	2.6	.03	.8*	.05	1.4*	.10	2.8
Protestant	.01	.5*	−.03	1.7*	−.04	2.3	.01	.6
Financial opport. in 1969 compared to expectations when started (1 = low, 3 = about same, 5 = high)								
Biog. 2	.07	1.7*	−.01	.2*	−.03	.7*	−.02	.4*
Biog. 3	.07	1.8*	−.02	.5*	−.06	1.4*	−.02	.6*
Biog. 4	.07	1.8*	−.001	.1*	−.06	1.5*	−.01	.2*
Biog. 5	.07	1.6*	−.03	.6*	−.08	1.8*	.02	.5*
Constant	.04	.7*	.47	9.0	.32	6.0	.25	4.5
R^2	.186		.205		.084		.076	
S.E.	.44		.45		.46		.48	

*Not significant at the 5% level.
There are 4022 observations.

Table 1 (*contd*).

	(5) Prefer to be salaried		(6) Future financial success, no	
Independent variable	Coef.	t value	Coef.	t value
Time spent on:				
Sports	−.005	1.1*	−.01	2.4
Hobbies	.003	.6*	.003	.7*
Chores	.001	.1*	.01	1.1*
Part-time job	−.001	−.4*	.001	.2*
Prefer to be salaried			.06	3.2
When entered occup., did following factors influence you? no = 1;				
Future financial success	.05	3.2	.20	13.2
Independent work	.09	6.2	−.01	.7*
Help others	.01	.5*	.09	6.1
Challenging work	.01	.8*	.06	4.5
Job security	−.08	6.1	−.01	.3*
Some college	−.05	2.9	−.06	3.1
Bachelor's	−.06	3.7	−.11	5.5
Some graduate	−.06	2.1	.05	1.5*
Master's	−.04	1.7*	.14	5.3
Ph.D., L.L.B., M.D.	−.09	3.3	.03	1.0*
Jewish	−.11	3.5	−.09	2.6
Protestant	−.01	1.0*	.01	.4*
Financial opport. in 1969 compared to expectations when started (1 = low, 3 = about same, 5 = high)				
Biog. 2	.01	.3*	−.01	.3*
Biog. 3	.05	1.4*	.01	.3*
Biog. 4	.08	2.1	−.04	1.1*
Biog. 5	.05	1.2*	−.08	1.9*
Constant	.21	4.5	.23	4.5
R^2	.041		.103	
S.E.	.40		.43	

Bibliography

Aitchison, J. and Brown, J. A. C. (1957). The Lognormal Distribution, with Special Reference to its Uses in Economics. Cambridge University Press: Cambridge.

Anderson, T. and Goodman, L. O. (1952). Statistical inference about Markov chains. Annals of Mathematical Statistics.

Antos, J. and Rosen, S. (1974). Discrimination in the market for public school teachers. Mimeograph, University of Rochester.

Arrow, K. and Lind, R. (1970). Uncertainty and evaluation of public investment decisions. American Economic Review.

Astin, A. (1968). Undergraduate achievement and institutional excellence. Science.

Atkinson, A. B. (1970). On the measurement of inequality. Journal of Economic Theory, 2; Vol. 3.

Bartlett, M. (1937). Properties of sufficiency and statistical tests. Proceedings of the Royal Statistical Society (series A).

Becker, G. (1964). Human Capital. Columbia University Press; New York.

Becker, G. (1967). Human capital and the personal distribution of income: an analytical approach. Woytinsky Lecture No. 1, University of Michigan, Ann Arbor.

Blau, P. and Duncan, O. D. (1967). The American Occupational Structure. John Wiley: New York.

Bloom, B. S. (1964). Stability and Change in Human Characteristics. John Wiley: New York.

Bowles, S. (1972). Schooling and inequality from generation to generation. Journal of Political Economy (part II).

Bronfrenbrenner, M. (1971). Income Distribution Theory. Aldine: Chicago.

Burt, C. (1971). Quantitative genetics in psychology. The British Journal of Mathematical and Statistical Psychology, Vol. 24 (part I).

Cavalli-Sforza, L. L. and Bodmer, W. F. (1971). The Genetics of Human Population. Freeman & Co.: San Francisco.

Champernowne, D. G. (1953). A model of income distribution. Economic Journal.

Chiswick, B. (1973). Income inequality: regional analysis within a human capital framework. National Bureau of Economic Research.

Christensen, L. (1970). Tax policy and investment expenditures in a model of general equilibrium. American Economic Review.

Clark, B., Heist, P., and McConnell, T., et al. (1972). Students and colleges: interaction and change. Center for Research and Development in Higher Education, University of California at Berkeley.

Clark, J. B. (1899). The Distribution of Wealth. Macmillan: London.

Cobb, C. and Douglas, P. (1928). A theory of production. American Economic Review.

Coelho, P. and Ghali, M. (1971). The end of the North-South wage differentials. American Economic Review.

Crockett, J. (1960). Technical Note. In: I. Friend and R. Jones (Ed.) Consumption and Savings, Vol. II, University of Pennsylvania Press: Philadelphia.

Darling, D. (1955). The Cramer–Smirnov test in the parametric case. Annals of mathematical Statistics.

Eckland, B. (1965). Academic ability, higher education, and occupational mobility. American Sociological Review.

Featherman, D. (1971). The socioeconomic achievement of white religio-ethnic subgroups: social and psychological explanations. American Sociological Review.

Friedman, M. (1957). A Theory of the Consumption Function. Princeton University Press: Princeton.

Friedman, M. (1953). Choice, chance and the personal distribution of income. Journal of Political Economy.

Goldberger, A. (1972). Maximum likelihood estimation of regressions containing unobservable dependent variables. International Economic Review.

Gourman, J. (1956). The Gourman Report. The Continuing Education Institute: Phoenix.

Griliches, Z. and Mason, W. (1972). Education, income and ability. Journal of Political Economy.

Grossman, G. (1972). The demand for health: a theoretical and empirical investigation. Occasional paper 119, National Bureau of Economic Research.

Hanushek, E. (1973) Regional differences in the structure of earnings. Review of Economics and Statistics.

Haspel, A. (1974). Occupational decision making: a socioeconomic analysis. Unpublished Ph.D. dissertation, University of Pennsylvania.

Havemann, E. and West, P. (1952). They Went to College: The College Graduate in America Today. Harcourt, Brace: New York.

Hill, R. and Stafford, P. (1974). Family background and lifetime earnings. Conference on Income and Wealth, Ann Arbor, Michigan.

Hunt, S. J. (1963). Income determinants for college graduates and the return to educational investment. Unpublished Ph.D. dissertation, Yale University.

Jinks, J. L. and Fulker, D. W. (1970). Comparison of the biometrical, genetical, MAVA and classical approaches to the analyses of human behavior. Psychological Bulletin, Vol. 73, No. 5.

Johnson, T. (1970). Returns from investment in human capital. American Economic Review.

Kagan, J. and Tulkin, S. (1971). Social class differences in child rearing during the first year. In: H. R. Schaffer (Ed.) The Origins of Human Social Relations. Academic Press: New York.

Kalecki, M. (1945). On the Gibrat distribution. Econometrica.

Kendall, M. G. and Stuart, A. (1961). The Advanced Theory of Statistics. Griffin: London.

Kohen, A., Parnes, H., and Shea, J. (1972). Income instability among young and middle-aged men. Center for Human Resources Research, Ohio State University.

Kravis, I. (1959). Relative income shares in fact and theory. American Economic Review, Vol. 49.

Kravis, I. (1962). The Structure of Income: Some Quantitative Essays. University of Pennsylvania Press: Philadelphia.

Lebergett, S. (1959). The shape of the income distribution. American Economic Review.

Leibowitz, A. (1974). Home investments in children. Journal of Political Economy (part II).

Lillard, L. (1974). The distribution of earnings and human wealth in a life cycle context. Conference on Income and Wealth, Ann Arbor, Michigan.

Little, J. (1958). A State-Wide Inquiry into Decisions of Youth about Education Beyond High School. University of Wisconsin: Madison.

Lydall, H. (1968). The Structure of Earnings. Clarendon Press: Oxford.

Mandelbrot, B. (1962). Paretian distributions and income maximization. Quarterly Journal of Economics.

Mayer, T. (1960). The distribution of ability and earnings. Review of Economics and Statistics.

Merton, R. (1949). Social Theory and Social Structure. Free Press: Glencoe, Illinois.

Miller, H. (1966). Income distribution in the United States, 1960. Bureau of the Census Monograph, Washington, D.C.

Miller, H. (1960). Annual and lifetime income in relation to education: 1939 to 1959. American Economic Review.

Mincer, J. (1970). The distribution of labor incomes: a survey with special references to the human capital approach. Journal of Economic Literature, Vol. III, No. 1.

Mincer, J. (1974). Schooling, experience and earnings. Columbia University Press for the National Bureau of Economic Research.

Mittler, P. (1971). The Study of Twins. Penguin Books.

Modigliani, F. and Ando, A. (1963). The life cycle hypothesis of saving. American Economic review.

Morgan, J. (Ed.) (1974). 5000 American families. Survey Research Center, University of Michigan.

Mostellar, F. and Moynehan, P. (1972). On Equality of Educational Opportunity. Vintage Books.

Neudecker, H. and Theil, H. (1957–1958). Substitution, complementarity and its residual variation around Engel curves. Review of Economic Studies.

Parsons, D. (1975). On the Economics of Intergenerational transfers. American Economic Review.

Project Talent. (1964). The American high school student. Cooperative Research Project No. 635, University of Pittsburgh.

Ramsey, J. B. (1969). Tests for specification errors in classical linear least squares regression analysis. Journal of the Royal Statistical Society (Series B).

Reder, M. (1969). A partial survey of the theory of income size distribution. In: L. Soltow (Ed.) Six papers on the Size Distribution of Wealth and Income. National Bureau of Economic Research.

Ricardo, D. (1951). Principles of political economy. In: P. Sraffa (Ed.) Works and Correspondence of David Ricardo. Cambridge University Press: Cambridge.

Rosen, S. (1972). Learning and experience in the labor market. Journal of Human Resources.

Roy, A. D. (1950). The distribution of earnings and of individual output. Economic Journal.

Scheffé, H. (1959). The Analysis of Variance. John Wiley: New York.

Schiller, B. (1974). Relative earnings mobility in the U.S. Mimeograph, University of Maryland.

Schultz, T. P. (1972). Long term changes in personal income distribution. American Economic Review.

Sewell, W. H. and Shah, V. P. Socioeconomic status, intelligence, and the attainment of higher education. Sociology of Education, 40, Winter.

Sewell, W. H. and Hauser, R. Education, Occupation and Earnings Achievement in the Early Career. Academic Press: New York. (forthcoming)

Simon, B. and Ellison, A. (1973). Does college make a person healthy and wise? In: L. Solmon and P. Taubman (Ed.) Does College Matter? Academic Press: New York.

Solmon, L. (1973). The definition and impact of college quality. National Bureau of Economic Research, Inc. Working Paper No. 7.

Solmon, L. and Wachtel, P. The effects on income of type of college attended. In: Sociology of Education (forthcoming).

Solow, R. (1974). Capital Theory and Rates of Return, Rand McNally: Chicago.

Spence, M. (1972). Market signalling. Mimeograph, Harvard University.

Summers, R. (1956). An econometric investigation of the size distribution of lifetime annual income. Unpublished Ph.D. dissertation, Stanford University.

Taubman, P. and Wales, T. (1974). Higher Education: An Investment and a Screening Device. Carnegie Commission on Higher Education and The National Bureau of Economic Research, Inc: New York.

Taubman, P. and Wilkinson, M. (1970). User cost, capital utilization and investment theory. International Economic Review.

Terman, L. and Odin, M. (1959). The Gifted Group at Mid-Life: Genetic Studies of Genius, Vol. V. Stanford University Press: Stanford.

Thaler, R. and Rosen, S. (1973). Estimating the value of a life. Income and Wealth Conference, Washington, D.C. (forthcoming).

Thorndike, R. and Hagen, E. (1959). Ten Thousand Careers. John Wiley: New York.

Tinbergen, J. (1959). On the theory of income distribution. In: Selected Papers. North-Holland Publishing Co.: Amsterdam.

Wales, T. (1972). The effects of school and district size on education costs in British Columbia. Discussion Paper No. 83, University of British Columbia.

Wales, T. (1973). The effect of college quality earnings: results from the NBER–Thorndike data. Journal of Human Resources.

Weiss, Y. (1974). The risk element and occupational choice. Journal of Political Economy.

Welch, F. (1973). Education and racial discrimination. In: O. Ashenfelter and A. Rees (Ed.) Discrimination in Labor Markets. Princeton University Press: Princeton.

Wise, D. Academic achievement and job performance: earnings and promotions. Ph.D. dissertation, University of California at Berkeley.

Wolfe, B. (1973). A socioeconomic analysis of family building behavior. Unpublished Ph.D. dissertation, University of Pennsylvania.

Wolfle, D. and Smith, J. (1956). The occupational value of education for superior high school graduates. Journal of Higher Education.

Author index

Subject index